# THE NEW
# GAME

# Also by Steve Paikin

The Life:
The Seductive Call of Politics

The Dark Side:
The Personal Price of a Political Life

Public Triumph, Private Tragedy:
The Double Life of John P. Robarts

# THE NEW GAME

### HOW HOCKEY SAVED ITSELF

## STEVE PAIKIN

VIKING
CANADA

VIKING CANADA

Published by the Penguin Group

Penguin Group (Canada), 90 Eglinton Avenue East, Suite 700, Toronto, Ontario, Canada M4P 2Y3
(a division of Pearson Canada Inc.)

Penguin Group (USA) Inc., 375 Hudson Street, New York, New York 10014, U.S.A.
Penguin Books Ltd, 80 Strand, London WC2R 0RL, England
Penguin Ireland, 25 St Stephen's Green, Dublin 2, Ireland (a division of Penguin Books Ltd)
Penguin Group (Australia), 250 Camberwell Road, Camberwell, Victoria 3124, Australia
(a division of Pearson Australia Group Pty Ltd)
Penguin Books India Pvt Ltd, 11 Community Centre, Panchsheel Park, New Delhi – 110 017, India
Penguin Group (NZ), 67 Apollo Drive, Rosedale, North Shore 0745, Auckland, New Zealand
(a division of Pearson New Zealand Ltd)
Penguin Books (South Africa) (Pty) Ltd, 24 Sturdee Avenue, Rosebank, Johannesburg 2196,
South Africa

Penguin Books Ltd, Registered Offices: 80 Strand, London WC2R 0RL, England

First published 2007

1 2 3 4 5 6 7 8 9 10 (RRD)

Copyright © Steve Paikin, 2007
Interior photographs: Steve Paikin

Manufactured in the U.S.A.

Library and Archives Canada Cataloguing in Publication data available upon request.

ISBN-13: 978-0-670-06560-8
ISBN-10: 0-670-06560-9

Visit the Penguin Group (Canada) website at **www.penguin.ca**

Special and corporate bulk purchase rates available; please see
**www.penguin.ca/corporatesales** or call 1-800-810-3104, ext. 477 or 474

*To My Parents*
*Marnie and Larry Paikin*
*who instilled in me*
*a love for our great game*

# CONTENTS

# THE NEW
# GAME

# *PREFACE*

The first National Hockey League game I ever saw was in the autumn of 1966. The Toronto Maple Leafs were hosting the Boston Bruins on a Saturday night at Maple Leaf Gardens. It was a huge deal. Our family lived in Hamilton, which meant my parents had to make the one-hour drive along the Queen Elizabeth Way with two little hyperactive kids—my brother and me—in the back seat. And these were in the days before mini-vans with built-in DVD players to tranquilize the kids. My father drove and my mother entertained us. In those days, game time was 8:00 P.M. (games start an hour earlier today to accommodate Saturday night doubleheaders). We always left Hamilton at 6:30, after a quick dinner, and managed to arrive at the Gardens in time to catch the players' warm-up.

On that wonderful night, I fell in love with hockey. The Leafs were victorious, 3–0. Johnny Bower earned the shutout and was the game's first star. Even though my younger brother slept through the entire third period (he was only 4), he decided that night that Bower was his hero and he would henceforth become a goalie himself.

Thousands of dollars in netminding equipment and hockey schools later, my brother gave up playing goal. For my part, although my affection for the game grew stronger, I never played much hockey growing up—at least, not on ice. I attended a couple of different summer hockey schools. Former Hamilton Red Wing Nick Libett, who went on to play 12 years and ultimately become captain of the Detroit Red Wings, ran one. Dave Keon and the late Billy Harris, both Maple Leafs, ran another.

Road hockey was a different matter. I was fortunate enough to live in a neighbourhood in Hamilton where there were several Catholic families and, therefore, never a shortage of players. Across the road, the Scimes alone had seven kids (were there really seven? It seemed so) and could always be relied upon to supply players for both teams. I got pretty good at road hockey, but those skills never translated onto the ice, where I was consistently mediocre. I never made my school team. I never played house league. Once, I made the second line of a team playing another intramural team within our same school. That game is seared into my memory because the first line never got off the ice. My brother and I, both second-line players, had the best view of the game in the arena, but that was it. My brother was furious. I, frankly, sympathized with our coach, who wanted our side to have a chance at winning and knew, as I did, that putting Jeff and Steve Paikin into the game would not have achieved that result.

I was truly blessed to grow up in a household where one of my parents was as mad about hockey as my brother and I were— and that parent was my mother. Marnie Paikin came to her love of sports honestly. Her father, Jack Sibulash, played for the Toronto Argonaut juniors in 1933, and Marnie would end up going to a ton of Argo games with her family at Varsity Stadium.

Her husband, Larry Paikin, took her to a Maple Leafs game at the Gardens in the early 1960s. After the couple had two children, their interest in hockey went in different directions. My father allowed himself to be dragged to innumerable sporting events, but never without his trusty transistor radio and earphones, so he could listen to the opera or some classical music during the game. However, my mother became a rabid fan, read the sports section aloud to my brother and me at breakfast, and still cares far too much about the Maple Leafs, Blue Jays, and Canadian Football League Hamilton Tiger-Cats. In fact, my mother has never missed a Blue Jays opening day baseball game. That's 31 consecutive opening days if you're doing the math.

I took after my mother in her passion for professional sports. My first professional summer job in media was as a sports reporter for CJJD Radio in Hamilton. I was up at four o'clock every morning to do the morning-drive sportscasts, and then I went to Ivor Wynne Stadium to report on the Tiger-Cats' practice. In the evening, I often covered either Ticats football or Hamilton Cardinals baseball before I dragged my butt into bed at around midnight. And I could not wait to do it all again the next day. I think I was 18.

While an undergraduate student at the University of Toronto, I attended classes occasionally and went to the campus radio station and one of the student newspapers frequently. My co-religionist at U of T Radio was a Toronto native named Michael Landsberg, with whom I did twice-weekly sportscasts and play-by-play of every hockey and football game we could attend. I was the broadcast voice of the Varsity Blues. Landsberg was the colour commentator. We were truly appalling but, fortunately, few people were listening, and these games allowed us to get some useful experience. Michael now hosts one of the country's best sports shows, *Off the Record* on TSN. He is incredibly self-assured on the air, dresses smartly, and knows his stuff. I have known him for almost 30 years, and back then he was incredibly self-assured, dressed smartly, and knew his stuff. True, he was also chubby and his voice was high-pitched, but those things seem to have changed.

Without question, the greatest achievement of my university years in Toronto was convincing the media relations director for the Maple Leaf hockey club, Stan Obodiac, to give me a season pass to all the games at the Gardens. Somehow, I actually made the case that university students never read any of the Toronto dailies, and if Obodiac wanted to ensure interest in the Leafs among the U of T's tens of thousands of students—many of whom would be his future customers—then he needed coverage of the Leafs in my newspaper. To my delight and astonishment, Obodiac bought that argument and as a result, I attended darned near every Leaf home game during my U of T years in the late 1970s and early '80s. For a guy who gets stopped on the street almost every day of the week to talk about the machinations of Parliament Hill, I actually know hockey better than the sport of politics. At least, *I* think I do.

In the early 1980s, I also returned to playing the game. During my first year at U of T, I actually had the gumption to try out for the Victoria College intramural hockey team. I was the skinniest, the smallest, and the worst player on the ice. Not surprisingly, I was the first to be cut from the squad. But after finishing my post-secondary education, one of my brothers-in-law invited me to join his regular Tuesday night game at a midtown Toronto arena. I resisted, he insisted, and I relented, assuming I could repeat my experience at Victoria College and leave it at that.

To my delight, I actually fit in. These were not players who still thought an NHL career lay before them, but rather a group of guys who went to high school together, were now teachers, lawyers, and accountants, and just wanted a night of (mostly) friendly competition.

A quarter-century later, most of those originals have left the game, including my brother-in-law (who, come to think of it, isn't my brother-in-law any more). But Tuesday Night hockey is still one of the highlights of my week and, frankly, my life. Those of us who continue to play on a regular basis have not improved much, but we are not a lot worse either. And every now and then, the game provides a moment that nothing else in life could possibly replicate.

I play defence. One night last year, I picked up the puck at my own blue line and began to stickhandle up the ice. As I was streaking down the right wing (it's my story, and if I say I was streaking, then I was streaking) the thought occurred to me that I just might have a step on the other team's blueliner and perhaps I should try to make a move around him and attempt to score. This was a truly novel thought because I have absolutely no offensive imagination, typically score perhaps three or four goals all year, and am perfectly satisfied to be a stay-at-home defenceman. But I did have a step on the D-man and thought, "What the hell, why not see what happens here."

To the shock and dismay of both of us, I did manage to go around the defender. Shock, because in 25 years of playing with these guys, I had never done that before. Dismay, because now I was in alone on the goalie and would have to think of something clever to do. I have no idea how I did it or where the inspiration came from, but at that moment, I felt my skill level go through the roof. I faked a move to my backhand, brought the puck seamlessly back to my forehand, skated across the goalie's crease, and gingerly tucked the puck through the "five-hole." If that were not enough, the goaltender accidentally (I think) tripped me as I was coming across his crease, so I flew through the air as the puck was going in, landing hard on my front. I was in the air for at least 10 seconds (I'm positive of this). The play happened in slow motion.

Instantly, I recognized two things. First, this was the most beautiful goal I had ever scored in my life and would ever score in my life. What a joy to learn that at age 45, that kind of new experience was still possible. Second, I was sure I had just replicated the most famous goal in National Hockey League history. Anyone who has seen the footage of Bobby Orr scoring the overtime Stanley Cup–winning goal in Game 4 of the 1970 Final against the St. Louis Blues will never forget it, because no one had ever scored a goal like that before, and no one has since ("Number 4rrrrrrrrrr! Bobby Orrrrrrrrrrr!" marvelled play-by-play man Dan Kelly). We all knew that Orr was Superman, but he confirmed it when he went flying through the air after potting the winner and giving his Boston Bruins their fourth Stanley Cup championship.

Immediately, the goaltender skated over and congratulated me. I barely heard what he said. What I was thinking to myself was "I just scored the Bobby Orr goal." I kept repeating this to myself, but silently, not out loud because, no doubt, I was the only person in the building who saw the goal that way. So I skated to the bench for a well-deserved break when the incredible happened. My teammate Larry Teitel said this to me:

"You know, Paikin, that goal looked just like Bobby Orr's goal."

Euphoria. This is why we still play the game.

I give you all of this background partly to establish my bona fides. I have now watched and played a lot of hockey over the years. I am a very forgiving fan (all Maple Leaf fans really should be, to keep their sanity) because I know how hard it is to take an accurate shot, to put a pass right on the tape of a teammate's stick when he, or she, is in flight, or to break up an opposing rush. It is for this reason that I have never ever booed the players who toil for my favourite NHL team. Because, even when they are playing badly, getting shellacked, or disgracing their blue-and-white sweaters, there is a large part of me willing to recognize that even the worst player on the ice is still one of the very best in the entire world at what he does, and he does it ten thousand times better than I do.

One thing that has fascinated me throughout the more than four decades I've spent watching hockey is how much the game continues to change. Yes, the rink is the same size. There are still five skaters and one goaltender per team. The lines are still changed when players get tired. Miscreants are still sent to the penalty box for an assortment of infractions including roughing, tripping, hooking, and slashing.

At the same time, the game has changed drastically in the past couple of years. Rule changes have been introduced—and more surprisingly, have been consistently enforced—to speed the flow of the game. The evolution of the sport has been so dramatic that I decided to take a break from writing books about politicians and do one about the game I love more than any other.

Incidentally, we've made every effort to ensure this manuscript is as up to date as possible. But one feature of the new NHL is significant player and management change, happening on an almost daily basis. No doubt, some of the people described in these pages will have changed teams over the summer of 2007, traditionally the NHL's busiest shopping season.

With the on- and off-ice changes the National Hockey League has brought in since 2005, the best players are now more able to demonstrate their talent, the cleverest coaches can implement their superior strategies, and the wisest general managers can showcase their ability to evaluate talent without the option of burying their mistakes by overspending.

It is a great time to be a hockey fan, as we shall see in *The New Game: How Hockey Saved Itself*.

# THE NEW GAME

*Hockey is its own game. It's completely different than all the other games, although it's getting way too close to soccer.*
—BRETT HULL

It was one of the most dramatic and heartwarming hockey stories of recent memory. The two most exciting words in team sports—Game 7—featured a ragtag bunch of blue-collar players who had somehow found their stride at exactly the right time in the 2003–04 season. It was an improbable place for the Calgary Flames to find themselves. After all, they had missed the playoffs in each of the previous seven years. Now, they had become not only southern Alberta's team, but also all of Canada was cheering for them. Even Edmontonians joined the chorus, and that's saying something.

The Flames had only one star forward that the rest of the league coveted. Jarome Iginla had scored 41 goals during the regular season. The next highest scorer on the team had just 18 tallies. Iginla added 13 more goals in the playoffs and dazzled everyone with his deft scoring touch and bruising style of play. The Flames also had an emerging superstar in Miikka Kiprusoff, whom the team had acquired from the San Jose Sharks midway through the season. While with the Sharks, Kiprusoff was in goal for 5 wins and 14 losses. As the old joke goes, the back of his neck was getting sunburned from the glare of the goal light. But the Flames' brain trust saw something there and brought him to Calgary whereupon "Kipper" led the club to 24 wins and only 10 losses the rest of the way, compiling a spectacular 1.69 goals-against average. And now he was backstopping his team of upstarts to the seventh and deciding game of the Stanley Cup Final.

Canada's surprising adopted team was up against the Tampa Bay Lightning—a side not without its Canadian supporters. Tampa's three best players were Canadian, two of them from small towns whose residents were conspicuously absent from the Flames' bandwagon: Vincent Lecavalier, the first overall draft pick in 1998, was from Ile Bizard, Quebec; Brad Richards, who would win the Conn Smythe Trophy as the most valuable player in the 2004 playoffs, put Murray Harbour, Prince Edward Island, on the map; and Martin St. Louis, the diminutive but spectacular forward, hailed from Laval, Quebec.

But Tampa's most delightful story focused on Dave Andreychuk, a greying 40-year-old player from Hamilton, who was desperately trying to buck a trend that had, to this point, dogged his entire career. Tampa Bay was his seventh stop in the NHL. The Buffalo Sabres had drafted him way back in 1982, and he quickly established himself as a dependable 30- to 40-goal scorer. But, since then, his career had been a roller-coaster ride, with stops in Toronto (where he twice scored more than 50 goals in a season), New Jersey, Boston, Colorado, and Buffalo again, before he found his way to what was then the worst team in the National Hockey League.

The Tampa Bay Lightning had been an embarrassment to professional sports even before the team had played a single game. In 1991, the NHL was preparing to add two additional franchises. The Ottawa Senators would be one. And, despite some concerns about how securely financed the team was, Tampa won the second franchise, mostly on the strength of the blue-chip talent in the front office whom the league governors knew well. Phil Esposito, the former scoring sensation for the Boston Bruins, was president, general manager, and the public face of the Lightning; his brother Tony, one of the game's best-ever goalies, served as chief scout; and behind the bench was Terry Crisp, who twice won the Stanley Cup as a player with the Philadelphia Flyers in the mid-1970s, and another as coach of the Calgary Flames in 1989.

In selecting Tampa (and Ottawa, almost as financially shaky as the Tampa bid), the NHL bypassed Hamilton, which had put together its umpteenth bid for a team and clearly demonstrated its superior fan and financial base. It did not matter. The league governors were charmed by Esposito's bravado, and the notion of expanding the NHL into the U.S. Sunbelt. Sadly, those same governors quickly learned there was not much to back up Espo's braggadocio routine.

Almost instantly, Esposito's Lightning ownership group fell apart. While the league tried to put a brave face on the impending disaster, the choice of Tampa over Hamilton was looking even stupider, particularly since the Steel City bid was backed by Ron Joyce, who owned the Tim Hortons doughnuts empire. Money wasn't going to be a problem there.

Somehow, Esposito found new backers (led by a mysterious group that owned golf courses in Japan) and the Lightning survived. Their inaugural season was actually not too bad. But before long, the franchise found new ways to define the word *embarrassing*. By the end of the 2000–01 season, Tampa had registered four straight 50-loss records, the first franchise in NHL history to do so.

And that was not the worst of it. Off the ice, the US Internal Revenue Service investigated the club's finances, which looked suspect. Speculation suggested the Japanese ownership was trying to use the club to launder money from illegal activities in the Far East. Some wondered whether the Japanese owners even existed. The club was often behind in paying its creditors. Players wondered whether they could count on their next paycheque. Losing $100 million in six years did not exactly enhance the franchise's cachet. In 1997, both *Forbes* magazine and *Sports Illustrated*—respectively, the leading business and sports magazines in the United States— had called the Lightning the worst-run franchise in all of professional sports.

This was the hockey club that Dave Andreychuk was now going to play for. But as often happens in sports when people least expect it, something wonderful was taking place. New ownership stabilized the franchise. So many last-place finishes meant high draft choices and the new management selected wisely. By 2003, the Lightning had a stable of young, up-and-coming talent, and the savvy veteran Andreychuk, who, despite pushing 40, put together back-to-back-to-back seasons of 20-plus goals.

Here he was, in Game 7 of the Stanley Cup final, trying to erase the all-time record for championship futility by an individual player. Dave Andreychuk had played 22 years in the NHL— that's 1597 regular season games, plus another 162 playoff games—without winning the Stanley Cup. No one in league history had ever put together such an unenviable streak.

When Craig Conroy scored for the Flames with 10:39 left in the third period to narrow the Lightning lead to 2–1, it set up a magnificent finish to a thrilling series. All the storylines were in play.

The Flames bombarded the Lightning net, but they just could not penetrate what Tampa fans called The Bulin Wall—Russian goaltender Nikolai Khabibulin. In the end, Calgary came up a goal short, losing by that 2–1 count.

"One shot, one shot," muttered Jarome Iginla in the Flames' dressing room after the game.

While many in Canada sighed a little bit after the Flames' defeat, it was hard not to feel good for Andreychuk. As captain of the Lightning, it was the grizzled veteran's honour to receive the Stanley Cup at centre ice. The Hamilton native did so, hoisting it with remarkable force, as if to shuck off two decades of playoff frustration.

It was such a great series. Seven games. A one-goal difference in the last game. The league's one-time worst franchise moving from the outhouse to the penthouse. Passion. Emotion. Skill. It was fabulous.

And then it all ended. Not just the season. Everything.

INSTEAD OF PROPELLING the NHL and its players into the following season on a terrific high, and allowing fans to watch the progress of these and other exciting young teams, professional hockey at its highest level came to a screeching halt when the owners locked out the players in September 2004. Incredibly, the owners and players couldn't agree on how to divide up $2 billion in revenues. Two billion dollars. Fans were disgusted. How greedy could they all be?

From the league's standpoint, this was a showdown that had been years in the making. The players, they insisted, were being unreasonable. Too many teams were losing money. Salaries were going through the roof as overly ambitious owners refused to keep their own spending in check. All it took was one out-of-control owner to establish the new benchmark for inflated salaries across the entire 30-team league. Maybe the New York Yankees could afford to pay a player $10 million a year, but the legendary Bronx Bombers were worth a billion dollars. How could hockey sustain those kinds of salaries for franchises worth a tenth as much, or even less? The owners required cost certainty, and said they needed a limit on what each club was allowed to spend—a salary cap. And this time they were serious about getting one.

For their part, the players and their union (the National Hockey League Players' Association, or NHLPA) failed to understand why it was suddenly their responsibility to make the owners spend more wisely. Was there ever a player in any sport who forced an owner at gunpoint to offer what many perceived as increasingly unjustifiable salaries? Of course not. If the owners were willing to pay the game's best players salaries in the high seven figures, then who were the players to tell them not to do it? And besides, the players thought, the owners were lying about the state of their finances. The days when one person owned a professional sports team—and that team was his or her only business—were ending. Now, multinational, multi-layered corporations were scooping up NHL teams using increasingly complicated ownership models. If a cable television multinational owned a hockey team, then bought the rights to televise that team's games—in effect, moving money from one corporate pocket to another—who really knew whether a fair market price was being charged? Who really knew who was making money and who was not? Furthermore, the players thought, what owner offers to pay these kinds of salaries if he or she can't afford to?

There were two significant historical precedents for what was about to transpire. One was U.S. football. National Football League owners wanted cost certainty, and many of them thought it unfair that the New York Giants should be able to outspend the Green Bay Packers tenfold because of the disparity in the size of their respective markets. How could the Packers compete under those circumstances? So, with considerable foresight and delicious irony, the richest, most aggressive capitalists in the United States who ran the NFL opted for a business model based on socialism. They would equally share all national television revenues and impose a salary cap—in effect, establishing a salary threshold above which no team was permitted to spend no matter how rich it was. It would level (and has levelled) the playing field. You cannot "buy" a championship in the NFL. Now that every team's budget is essentially the same, each one simply has to spend more wisely and play better than its competitors to win.

Conversely, baseball players, who make up professional sport's most militant union, have always successfully fought against salary caps. They went on strike near the end of the 1994 season to reinforce their opposition to the measure, in the process depriving fans of a World Series for the first time since the latter's inception at the turn of the twentieth century.

Which way would hockey go? As it turned out, the head honchos of hockey took one significant lesson from baseball—

do not start a season you may not be able to finish. And so, on September 14, 2004, just three months after staging a highly entertaining Stanley Cup final series, the league locked out its 600-plus players and told the NHLPA there would be no more hockey until a new, more equitable economic system was in place.

The NHL owners and players had faced these kinds of labour disputes before. In 1994–95, a work stoppage forced cancellation of nearly half the season. The owners tried to achieve the cost certainty they said they needed in that dispute. But in the end, they settled for something much less and gave the NHLPA the sense that when push came to shove, the owners would not let their buildings sit empty for a full season. When the 2004–05 season arrived, the players may have made the same assumption: if they just waited the owners out, eventually the CEOs would cave.

But the players miscalculated. The owners did not cave. The 2004–05 season came and went without NHL hockey. That had not happened since 1919, when the league suspended play because of the threat posed by Spanish influenza.

Strangely enough, Canadians professed not to miss their national sport. As former Montreal Canadiens goaltender and current Liberal MP Ken Dryden observed, watching NHL hockey seems to have become more of a habit than a passion for many people. As the lockout dragged on, we continued to play the game ourselves. We attended more games at the junior and minor-pro level where the motives were purer. No players on the Ontario Hockey League's Sudbury Wolves or the American Hockey League's Hamilton Bulldogs were making multi-million-dollar annual salaries.

Perhaps most importantly, we started debating not just about hockey's off-ice woes, but also about the merits of the game on the ice—a long-overdue conversation that had been postponed because the 2004 finals were so exciting. Now that we had time to think about it, weren't there far too many dull games played during the regular season? And wasn't there way too much hooking, grabbing, and tackling that deprived fans of seeing the truly skilled players do their thing? And weren't some of the existing rules badly out of date, exacerbating the sense that the game was being played in molasses? Maybe Brett Hull, one of the most gifted goal scorers ever, had it right when he warned that the game was "too depressing, too boring." Hull's concluding thought sent shock waves through the NHL's head office in New York: "This game sucks to watch," he said. And a lot of people agreed with him.

BRENDAN SHANAHAN was born on January 29, 1969, in what was then called Mimico and now has been absorbed into the southwest corner of the Toronto megacity. Great things were anticipated for young Shanahan right from the start, as evidenced by the fact that the New Jersey Devils made him their first draft pick, second overall, in the 1987 entry draft.

Shanahan started slowly, scoring only 7 goals in his first season, but he bumped that up to 22 in his sophomore year, and 30 in his third. After four solid seasons in New Jersey, Shanahan was traded to the St. Louis Blues, where he became a superstar. In his second season in the Midwest, he scored 51 goals in just 71 games, then followed that up with 52 goals and 102 points in 1993–94.

Every player's career experienced a hiccup the next year, when half the season was wiped away in the lockout. Still, Shanahan managed 20 goals in 45 games. In 1995–96, the trade winds blew through Shanahan's life again, this time taking him to perennial also-ran Hartford, where he returned to form, scoring 44 goals. The following year, yet another trade, but this time, the fit seemed perfect. Shanahan would spend the next nine seasons in "Hockeytown"—Detroit, Michigan—where he helped the Red Wings win three Stanley Cups. His individual statistics dropped somewhat. Before the lost season of 2004–05, he notched a pair of 40-goal seasons and four 30-goal campaigns—completely respectable numbers. But the year before the lockout, Shanahan had his worst goal-scoring season since his sophomore year in the NHL, and observers began to wonder whether at age 35 his hockey career was winding down.

Still, Shanahan was widely respected within the league. He was a 7-time all-star and had scored 1161 points over 17 seasons. He was also tough. At 6'3" and 220 pounds, he had over the years demonstrated a willingness to drop the gloves and duke it out with any young punk who threatened to take advantage of his good nature. Unlike most other star players, Shanahan had compiled more than 100 penalty minutes in almost every season he had played. He had also represented Canada at international hockey events and seemed to speak for the entire country after the 1998 Nagano Winter Olympics when he offered a heartfelt apology for the failure of the men's team to win a medal of any colour.

Shanahan was also a thoughtful fellow who took the game of hockey seriously. And he was the kind of player—a natural leader, really—whom players and management alike listened to. So, when Shanahan got worried about the state of the game, people paid attention.

Brett Hull had already made his feelings known. In November 2004, at the annual Hockey Hall of Fame ceremony, inductee Paul Coffey added his two cents' worth. Coffey, who was the fantastically gifted offensive D-man on those great run-and-gun Edmonton Oiler championship teams of the 1980s, decried the state of the game. His comments represented more than an oldtimer's lament that the game wasn't as good as it had been back in the day. Coffey was right and everyone knew it.

But it took Brendan Shanahan to do something about it.

At his own initiative and expense, Shanahan launched a hockey summit in Toronto that December. It was a gutsy move. The NHL was shut down, the relationship between owners and players was tense, and everyone was focused on the economic issues. But Shanahan made them all look at the game itself. He wanted the best and brightest hockey minds to get together and fix the game, so when the lockout ended there would actually be something worth watching.

Shanahan gathered some of hockey's major stakeholders at the two-day event. In attendance were 26 invitees—coaches, general managers, agents, television executives, and, most important, players. The summit also had the blessing of three of hockey's heaviest hitters: NHL commissioner Gary Bettman; the league's director of hockey operations, Colin Campbell; and the head of the NHLPA (the players' union), Bob Goodenow. Their presence meant that, perhaps for the first time ever, significant progress was actually possible.

"I love his enthusiasm about the game and wanting to repair it in a way where the players will get a say," said Denis Potvin, the Hall of Fame defenceman and anchor of four Stanley Cup–winning teams with the New York Islanders in the 1980s.

"I am glad that he took the bull by the horns and said, 'Hey, you are not doing anything here unless the players start having a say.'"

That was different. In the past, it was usually left to a committee of conservative general managers to decide what was working (almost everything, they thought) and what was not (very little, they thought). On their timid advice, the league would merely tinker with the rules. The result was a game that had needed a radical overhaul for years but never got it. And God forbid should the competitors who actually played the game ever be consulted. If nothing else, Shanahan's summit represented an end to that kind of thinking.

First and foremost, the group wanted to restore skill and talent to its rightful place. The sad truth about hockey was that, increasingly over the years, it had encouraged mediocrity, and let the proper enforcement of the rules lapse so that players of marginal ability could keep up with the truly skilled players.

"They [the old-school managers] thought if they allowed all the best players to play without being restricted, then some of the weaker teams would be nowhere [in terms of] competing," confirmed Rick Dudley, assistant general manager for the Chicago Blackhawks.

Goaltender Sean Burke, another veteran who has logged many miles for Team Canada over the years, was a participant in some of Shanahan's early meetings to discuss rule changes.

"I think he has had a huge influence," Burke said. "I think that it was overdue for somebody to take charge and to start to address some of the issues that everybody has talked about."

Those issues essentially were why scoring was down and why dull, overly defensive-minded systems—such as the neutral zone trap—ruled the day. These tendencies had led Brett Hull to conclude that the game "sucked."

In the past, ideas designed to open up the game and crack down on the clutching and grabbing were ignored. Shanahan's group wanted that situation changed. In hindsight, the concept seems so simple, and yet at the time it was considered controversial. The more progressive people wanted the game, once again, to feature players who could skate better, shoot faster, and stickhandle more creatively. Strangely enough, this view had opponents. But for the first time in decades, they found themselves in the minority. Finally, the skilled players were in the ascendant.

The group emerged from the summit with a wish list, which Shanahan then took to both Bettman and Goodenow in separate meetings. When the lockout was finally over and a new collective bargaining agreement put in place, the league had already agreed, thanks to the Shanahan summit, to the most radical overhaul of the rules in league history. The dimensions of the neutral and attacking zones were altered to open up play. Rules were changed to discourage stoppages and encourage increased "flow." Fighting was to be more severely and consistently punished and officials were instructed to strictly enforce the existing rules against stickwork and harassment. It all represented an astonishingly comprehensive rethinking of the way the game should be played.

PROFESSIONAL HOCKEY in North America has instituted more significant changes in the past 2 years than it had in the previous 50. The metamorphosis has been breathtaking. The new economic system led, in the very first post-lockout year, to a Stanley Cup final matchup that otherwise would have been unimaginable: the Carolina Hurricanes versus the Edmonton Oilers, two small-market teams with among the lowest budgets for player salaries in the old NHL. The new rules have improved the product on the ice so much, even people who completely gave up on hockey have come back for a second look. Attendance at the NHL's 30 arenas reached an all-time high the year after the lockout.

Scoring is up. Fan interest is up. Clutching and grabbing are down. Goonery is down. The great Jean Béliveau observed that the game is finally once again being played the way it was meant to be played.

In 1983, Ken Dryden gave us a glimpse into the soul of hockey with *The Game,* perhaps the best book ever written about the fastest sport on ice. Almost a quarter of a century later, it seems a good time to revisit the subject, and explore *The New Game.*

In the old game, teams such as the Rangers, Red Wings, and Maple Leafs could attempt to bury their mistakes by simply outspending everyone else. Not in the new game.

In the old game, the financial deck was badly stacked against the small-market, lower-revenue teams such as in Edmonton, Ottawa, or Buffalo. Not in the new game, as both Edmonton's 2005–06 playoff success and Ottawa's run to the 2007 Stanley Cup Final demonstrated.

In the old game, the old-school coaches and general managers inexplicably favoured the clutching and grabbing, the constant hooking, slashing, and spearing that happened under the radar and rarely resulted in a penalty. Somehow, they found religion, and pushed through major rule changes to spice up the new game and allow hockey's most talented and creative players to show their stuff.

In the old game, there was always a place for a player who couldn't score goals but knew how to drop the gloves and beat his opponent's brains in. Not in the new game. Those one-trick ponies now have an almost permanent seat in the press box or are losing their jobs altogether.

The old game, 30 years ago, featured players overwhelmingly from Canada, some from the United States, and almost none from Europe. Journalists covering today's NHL can improve their access to stories immeasurably by knowing a little Russian, Czech, Slovakian, Swedish, Finnish, Ukrainian, not to mention the obvious: French. That is also part of the new game.

And it is not just the plethora of different languages. Hockey is welcoming more players and coaches of colour, more women both reporting on the teams and in their front offices, even the odd Muslim player.

Not everything about the new game is great. But most of it is. Perhaps the 310-day lockout was worth it after all.

# THE NEW RULES

*Rules are made for people we don't like.*
*New rules are made for people we REALLY don't like.*
*Brand new rules are for you.*
—LAWYER GREGORY HOSKINS

---

The new rules require officials to strictly enforce regulations that in previous years were more often honoured in the breach than in the application. Now there is zero tolerance on interference, hooking, and holding. Any player who shoots the puck directly over the glass from the defensive zone is penalized for delay of game.

---

Gary Roberts, a 19-year veteran forward, has seen this issue from both sides. A decade and a half ago, he was a 53-goal scorer with the Calgary Flames. He has also had two 40-goal seasons, and four 30-goal campaigns. But age and multiple body ailments have taken their toll to the point where a couple of seasons ago, Roberts scrapped, clutched, and grabbed his way to 14 goals with the Florida Panthers in an injury-shortened season.

"I really believe that it is great for the skilled guys in the league to be able to show their stuff and display the moves that they have without getting punched and grabbed," he says.

Roberts has had the pleasure of playing left wing with some elite centremen. There was Mats Sundin in Toronto, and Joe Nieuwendyk early on in Calgary and later in Florida until Nieuwendyk's December 2006 retirement. After that, it was the Finnish star Olli Jokinen, also with the Panthers. Ironically, at age 41—when he should have been getting less ice time and seeing his influence on the team diminish—Roberts found himself on occasion playing 20 minutes a night in Florida.

"Even in the new NHL, that is too much for me," Roberts laughs. "I am usually between 15 and 18 [minutes], which is good. If you're playing really physical and taking the body, 20 minutes is a tough thing to play."

He likes what the new rules have done for his teammates (who are no longer Panthers, but Penguins, as Florida traded Roberts to Pittsburgh on deadline day in February 2007), and by extension for him as well.

"I still need to forecheck hard and take the body and create some loose pucks for my centreman," he says. "But, for sure, I think the rule changes have given me an opportunity to prolong my career a few more years." Not a bad thing for a guy approaching 20 years in the pro game.

"It's a much better game," adds Roberts's former Maple Leaf teammate Darcy Tucker, another competitor who can play the clutch-and-grab style but still has managed to pot 20 goals four times. His best season ever—28 goals and 68 points—came in 2005–06 with the new rules in place. "It's a more free-flowing game." Tucker was on pace for a terrific season in 2006–07, until a stubborn foot injury caused him to miss 26 games. He still managed to score 24 goals.

Even players who scored few goals and earned their salaries the old-fashioned way—mucking it up in the corners and pestering their opponents—seem favourably disposed to the new regime. I asked Martin Gelinas, who has played with 6 different NHL teams over a 20-year career, whether he missed the grind.

"You know what? It was my game," he admits. "I do appreciate the game more now. But it took some adjustment."

Adjustment is an understatement. As Fox TV's Ken Daniels puts it, "You're trying to get the players out of a mindset of what they've been trained all their lives to do." Even Brendan Shanahan, back when he was contemplating reforming the game, figured it would take several seasons for players to adjust. He has been pleasantly surprised.

"I thought this is something that would take three to four years before the games were really appreciated and the level of speed was really evident," he says. "Both sides aren't perfect every night but it came on a lot faster than I thought.

"The new rules point hockey in the right direction but it doesn't mean there won't be growing pains," he says.

Some of Shanahan's Detroit teammates were less than thrilled by the changes. Chris Chelios, the ageless Red Wing defenceman (in professional sports, 45 is ageless), complained that the game wasn't where it should be. Even the Wings' legendary captain Steve Yzerman expressed his displeasure from time to time that the officials were calling too many penalties and interrupting the flow of the game. Watching players adjust to the new rules has been an interesting journey. Watching the game change as the players figure out new ways to play it has been more surprising.

But perhaps the most unanticipated development is the notion of who is now allowed to play this game.

---

The blue lines have been moved 2' closer to the centre red line to make the offensive zones deeper and the neutral zone smaller.

---

For decades, it has been one of the most obvious truisms in pro hockey that size matters, particularly on defence. If a player is not at least 6'2" and 220 pounds, it has likely been almost impossible to get scouts or general managers to take a look at him. The constant battles in front of the net demanded defencemen of a certain size. Forwards who liked to park themselves in front of the goal and disturb the goaltender's concentration had to be dealt with firmly, if not with extreme prejudice. It had got to the point where every management team was looking for the next Zdeno Chara, the 30-year-old Slovakian, who scores roughly 40 points a year (not bad) but who stands 6'9" and weighs 260 pounds (absolutely fabulous by management standards).

Somewhere along the way, the game had forgotten that Bobby Orr was barely 6' tall and less than 200 pounds. Same for Paul Coffey. And Denis Potvin. And Doug Harvey. Scouts had wholly bought into the notion that defencemen should come in one size only: big. Think of the concussion-inducing Scott Stevens (6'2", 215 pounds), or Larry Robinson (6'3", 220 pounds), or Derian Hatcher (6'5", 235 pounds). Not to mention Chara.

But a funny thing happened on the way to the Bell Centre. The new rules prohibited gratuitous tackling and interference by defencemen and, by opening up the offensive zone, encouraged more skilful alternatives, in particular, superior puck-carrying, skating, and passing skills. Suddenly, a world of possibilities opened up for compact blueliners.

"Smaller but very good skating, puck-handling, and passing defencemen now are much more desirable than they used to be," says Harry Neale, the *Hockey Night in Canada* colour commentator and former coach and general manager of the Vancouver Canucks and Detroit Red Wings. "The big, tough guy that didn't handle the puck very well but played physically and was a grabber, those guys are finding that things are tough."

Enter Ian White.

The official website for the NHL generously lists Ian White at 5'10" tall and 185 pounds. In the old game, the odds against White ever seeing the inside of an NHL dressing room were as long as his sometime defensive partner, Hal Gill. Gill is 6'7" tall.

Toward the end of the 2005–06 season, the Toronto Maple Leafs encountered a slew of injuries, particularly on defence. So, more due to necessity than anything else, the club brought White up from its American Hockey League affiliate, the Toronto Marlies. He was 21 years old at the time.

Talk about a dream come true.

Ian White grew up in Steinbach, Manitoba, population 12,000, where he was the town's biggest Mario Lemieux fan. He had started skating as a 3-year-old. Every Wednesday, little Ian, his mother, and some other friends would strap on the blades, doubtless having no clue that those weekly skating excursions would someday help White along to the National Hockey League. When he eventually started playing hockey, White did not gravitate to centre ice where Lemieux made so much history, for reasons he cannot explain to this day. He played defence. It felt comfortable. And he did not seem to have any difficulty getting his name on the scoresheet, so defence was fine.

White played four years of junior hockey for the Swift Current Broncos where his diminutive stature did not pose a problem. There are numerous "undersized" junior hockey players, the vast majority of whom will never get a cup of coffee in the NHL. In the 2001–02 season, his best in junior hockey, White scored 79 points in 70 games and, despite his size, got people taking notice of his game. The Maple Leafs liked what they saw, selected him in the sixth round of the 2002 entry draft, and soon after sent him to the St. John's Maple Leafs, their AHL affiliate at the time.

White continued to impress. Before long, he was quarter-backing the power play for the Baby Leafs and getting a chance to show some offensive punch. When the parent club called him up for a 12-game stint in 2006, White scored 6 points and impressed observers with how the smaller man could play the big man's game.

"A lot of the small men don't make it," said Pat Quinn, White's coach in Toronto at the time and a guy who should know. When he played defence in the NHL from 1968–1977, he stood 6'3", weighed 215 pounds, and felt like a ton of bricks when he hit you. (Just ask Bobby Orr, whom Quinn rendered unconscious once after a massive on-ice collision.)

"But I think the rules today certainly allow the smaller guy a much better chance of playing, if he has some skills, like skating especially, and some discipline—you need all those other ingredients, too, to become a good player."

During his first dozen games with the Leafs, White was paired with another defenceman who could only be described as the antithesis of the Manitoba kid. With 18 years under his belt in the NHL and at 6'4" and 215 pounds, Luke Richardson became the other half of the Leafs' odd couple. Richardson was approaching his 1300th NHL game. He had scored only 33 goals in all those games but spent almost 2000 minutes in the penalty box.

"He's a great kid. I enjoyed playing with him," Richardson said at the end of the 2005–06 season. (Shortly thereafter, Richardson would leave Toronto and sign a contract with the Tampa Bay Lightning.)

Near the conclusion of the 2005–06 campaign, there were moments on the ice when White's size worked against him. On one occasion, an opposing player flipped the puck high in the air toward the Leaf defenceman. White tried to swat the puck down onto the ice with his glove but whiffed on the attempt. The puck went directly to an opposing player who blew past him and scored. The knock on White was that he panicked because two larger players were closing in on him as the puck arrived.

"When you see two guys in the NHL at full steam coming at you, sometimes things don't work out," Richardson said sympathetically.

The NHL has not been completely devoid of smaller defencemen. Both Dan Boyle of Tampa Bay and Brian Rafalski with New Jersey are under 6' tall. Both have won the Stanley Cup. Both are exceptions to the big-man rule. Ian White is trying to join their ranks.

"White's a pretty good example of a player who ought to benefit by the new NHL rules and looks like he can play in this league," says Harry Neale. "And maybe in the past, that wasn't as possible."

Like most young Canadian boys who play hockey, it had always been a dream of White's to play in the NHL. The dream took on an added veneer of possibility after the Leafs chose him in the 2002 draft. Having said that, White was the 191st pick overall—hardly an indication that he was a blue-chip prospect.

And in fact, once White was called up he was given one of those numbers that suggests you may not be with the big club for a long time. He wore number 7 in junior hockey. In hockey numerology, number 7 (along with 9) suggests you are an elite member of your team. Phil Esposito wore number 7. So did Paul Coffey. So did Gary Unger, the NHL's all-time iron man who played 914 consecutive games in a 16-year career. Talk about permanent.

The Leafs gave Ian White number 37. Do you remember all those great NHLers who wore 37? Of course you don't. Because there aren't any. And make no mistake: White knew it. As we chatted toward the end of the 2005–06 season, the young blue-liner admitted that someday he wanted to wear a smaller number, and have everything that suggests.

"If I was a little more established player, and had a year or two under my belt, then that shouldn't be a problem. But, for now, I am happy with number 37."

White would not have to wait long to feel a little more permanent. At the beginning of the 2006–07 season, he asked the team's equipment manager Brian Papineau for his favourite, number 7.

"I figured no one had it so I'd better take it," he now says.

White now proudly wears a number previously worn by the likes of Joe Primeau, Gary Roberts, Max Bentley, Lanny McDonald, and one of the greatest defencemen in Leaf history, Tim Horton.

"I guess it feels a bit better, yeah," he says.

Toward the end of the 2006–07 season, White found himself a seemingly more permanent member of the Leafs' blue line corps. Once again, he was paired with the biggest D-man on the team in Hal Gill.

"It's my job to find a way to get him the puck and let him do what he does," says Gill, a Massachusetts native who played eight seasons in Boston before coming to Toronto in 2006 as a free agent. "You're quick or you're dead in this league and he's quick. A lot of times I'm dead because I'm too big."

While the new rules may give smaller defencemen such as Ian White a chance they otherwise would not have had to play, they have also led to more problems for defencemen.

"The forecheckers are right on your back and sometimes you feel like you have no options," says Brian Pothier, a 6', 200-pound defender with the Washington Capitals. "It's definitely more challenging for the defence."

"The defensemen are easier prey," says Sheldon Souray, a nine-year veteran with the Montreal Canadiens who found the new rules a major adjustment. "It's forcing you to think a lot, which is dangerous for players like me," he adds, not entirely with tongue in cheek.

At the end of the day, Pat Quinn sums up best what it takes to play defence in the National Hockey League. "You have to have a head, a pair of legs, and a lot of jam to play in this league, regardless of what the rules are."

---

Passes from behind the defensive blue line to the attacking blue line, which previously drew an offside call, now are legal. For passing purposes, the centre red line no longer exists.

---

The men who ran hockey in the 1940s reckoned that the game was in trouble. Back then, teams were not permitted to head-man the puck out of their defensive zone. They had to stickhandle it out. Defending teams were jammed in their own end for minutes at a time, as attacking teams simply threw all five men into the zone in a kind of full-court press. Future Hall of Famer Frank Boucher proposed adding a red line at centre ice, ironically in light of today's developments, to speed up the game. Another rule was simultaneously changed. Beginning in 1943, players were permitted to pass the puck out of their defensive zone, but only to their own side of the new red line. The changes did, in fact, open up the game.

But only for a while. As happens in all sports, the defensive strategists eventually found an answer to the offensive threat. The struggle to keep offensive innovation ahead of defensive reaction is constant and necessary in professional sports because spectators would rather see goals than shutouts, touch-downs than punts, and home runs than ground-ball outs. Unfortunately, prior to the most recent rule changes, defensive tactics in the NHL had been allowed not only to catch up to offensive ones, but also to surpass them. This dreary, fan-spurning period in the 1990s and 2000s was commonly referred to as the Dead Puck Era.

Some leagues saw this problem earlier than others. The Alberta Junior Hockey League was Canada's first Junior A circuit to remove the red line for offside passes. They did so as far back as the 1994–95 season. The American Hockey League did likewise a decade later. The NHL followed suit in the first season after the lockout, 2005–06, on the recommendation of Brendan Shanahan's committee.

The motion was far from unanimous. Some thought the change was too radical. Others, such as Martin Havlat, then with the Ottawa Senators, opposed the move saying it was counter-productive. Havlat noted that in his native Czech Republic pro hockey took the red line out, but ended up restoring it after five years. He predicted the breakaway would disappear from NHL hockey as teams would stop forechecking and simply line up along their own blue line to stop the rush.

Still, in spite of opposition from a few players, most support the change.

"I like the no red line," says Jacques Martin, Havlat's former coach in Ottawa, now coach and general manager of the Florida Panthers. "I think you still have a good flow of the game and I think it favours the more skilled players."

"I think for the NHL to incorporate the no red line has been really dynamic for the league," adds Mike Pelino, assistant coach for the New York Rangers.

If the new NHL is all about unleashing the skill players to do their thing, taking out the red line has been an immediate bonanza.

"The more elite players are great at finding the opening and finding the seam and if you have defencemen that see the ice well, they can make those [outlet] passes," Jacques Martin adds.

When I put that notion to Detroit Red Wings' head coach Mike Babcock after one of his team's practices at the Joe Louis Arena, I could practically see the steam coming out of his ears.

"What's wrong with taking out the red line?" I asked.

"You want to know what's wrong with it?" We were in the Wings' dressing room and Babcock was getting more and more revved up by the second. "Let's get this board working." The coach wanted the giant screen depicting the ice surface activated so he could diagram what he despised about the loss of the centre ice red line.

"I'm serious, I'll show you," he said.

When, finally, the board was illuminated, Professor Babcock began the lesson. He explained that in the first year of the new NHL, penalties were up dramatically as the referees called infractions by the book. But the league also changed the dimensions of the teams' ends to create more space for creative, offensive plays to develop. Theoretically, this gives attacking teams 4 feet more depth to score goals. As a result, teams had to adjust their tactics for short-handed play. There were significantly more penalties to kill, and the area they were patrolling was bigger.

Forechecking has also changed, he says, because teams no longer line up along the centre red line. They have to retreat to their own blue line to guard against the breakaway pass (or "stretch" pass) from the attacking team's blue line to the defending team's blue line.

Babcock admits that when it works, it's magic.

"Every once in a while on TV they show you this," he says referring to the new, longer "stretch" passes. "They show you one a month and everyone in the studio raves about it." But Professor B believes, in exchange for allowing those beautiful but rare passing plays, the law of unintended consequences has forced teams into a more defensive shell on their own blue lines.

"One play a month for jamming this up totally," he says disgustedly, while slashing his Magic Marker left to right along the diagram's blue line.

While a successfully executed stretch pass is a marvel to behold, Babcock insists its days are numbered.

"Coaches are smart. Players are smart," he says. "They learn to adjust." In fact, while scoring was up in the first post-lockout season under the new rules, it declined in the second season, suggesting a defensive response to every offensive innovation is inevitable.

"The fans really liked it at the start of [2005–06]," Babcock says, "because we didn't know how to defend yet, didn't know how to kill penalties yet." Then he continues: "I believe all of the changes we've made are really good with the exception of the red line. I think that adds to defence. Makes it harder [to score]."

---

A number of the new rules directly affect goaltenders. Limits have been placed on the width of leg pads, the blocking glove, and the chest protector. Goalies can handle the puck behind the net in a trapezoid-shaped area marked by diagonal lines from the back of the net to the boards; they can no longer retrieve the puck from the corners. Netminders are penalized if, in the referee's judgment, they "freeze" the puck unnecessarily.

---

Given that the changes to hockey are designed to speed up the game and increase scoring, it is ironic that the players most affected by the new rules are the ones who skate the least. In the old NHL, goaltenders rather than goal scorers had become the new superstars. Goals-against averages were plummeting; save percentages were going through the roof; average goaltenders were looking like legends. Witness Brian Boucher of the Phoenix Coyotes, who racked up five consecutive shutouts in the year leading up to the lockout—an astonishing achievement for a guy who rarely reminded anyone of the late, great Terry Sawchuk.

Two things in particular were helping goaltenders put up those heady numbers. First, defensive systems and coaching had taken over the game. With teams having so few offensive stars—and an approach to the game that prevented skilled players from doing their thing—coaches were able to successfully develop systems designed to neutralize opposing goal scorers. It was a great way for average teams to stay competitive. But it did not do much for the aesthetic of the game. In addition, rapid expansion over a relatively short period of time saw the NHL jump from a 21- to a 30-team league, without the concomitant offensive talent to stock so many new squads.

The other huge advantage goaltenders had was the size of their equipment. Theoretically, there were rules, but it became a running joke across the league to see how goalies could mess with them. Catching gloves expanded, pads seemed to cover the goaltender's entire lower body, and their shoulder pads made some of them look like the Michelin Man. At some level, fans could sympathize. After all, it is a special breed of athlete that permits opponents to fire a piece of vulcanized rubber at his head at a speed of 160 kilometres per hour. The late Lorne "Gump" Worsley said it best when asked whether you had to be crazy to play goal. "No," the Gumper offered, "but it helps."

As much as the goaltenders liked the old system, even they had to acknowledge that the lack of offensive punch was damaging fan interest in the game. Most acknowledge that the changes were inevitable. Now, at the very least, shooters have a bit more net to shoot at. Of course, goalies now have more to be afraid of, since the speed at which their opponents' shots come at them has not declined with the size of their pads. Many goalies have complained about the "stingers" they are feeling all over their bodies because of the smaller equipment they're wearing.

Detroit's Mike Babcock thinks the league should go even further. He'd like to see the size of the net increased.

"How big were the goalies in the '80s?" he asks rhetorically. "How big are they now? As the goalies get bigger, there's less room to shoot for. I just want more offence."

Babcock is right. The greatest puckstoppers of yesteryear were significantly smaller than today's netminders. Terry Sawchuk, one of the biggest, was 5'11" tall, and 190 pounds; Jacques Plante was 6'0" tall, 175 pounds; and Johnny Bower was 5'9" high, and 170 pounds. Glen Hall, known as Mr. Goalie, played as light as 160 pounds. Today, with the exception of the Red Wings' Dominik Hasek (who at 170 pounds is unusually undersized for today's goaltenders), most of the game's best netminders are much bigger. New Jersey's Martin Brodeur is 6'2" and weighs 215 pounds. Vancouver's Roberto Luongo is 6'3" and 205 pounds; and Jean-Sébastien Giguere of the Anaheim Ducks is 6'1" and 200 pounds. Bigger athletes playing with bigger equipment unquestionably leave less net to shoot at.

In some respects, goaltenders have had handcuffs—or leg irons—put on them. In the old NHL, when attacking teams fired the puck into the opposing team's end, the goaltender often got to it first, "teed it up" for his defenceman, who almost instantly fired the puck out again. As a result, there were few scoring chances.

In the new NHL, if the goaltender touches the puck behind the goal line outside the trapezoid, he is assessed a minor penalty for his troubles. This rule, as much as any other, has caused goalies fits. Adjusting to where you can and cannot touch the puck has resulted in some hilarious flubs. Ed Belfour, one of the game's best ever, made himself look silly one night for the Maple Leafs. He skated out of his net to play the puck, thought better of it because the puck was outside the trapezoid, then tripped over himself on the way back to the crease. An opposing player calmly took the puck from him and popped it home for a goal.

Hasek, another of the game's all-time greats, has had similarly inelegant experiences.

"I still have to think a little bit," he told me midway through the 2005–06 season. "I've already been penalized four times."

The most difficult adjustment has been for goaltenders who were particularly skilled at handling the puck. "That [trapezoid] rule really penalized the great puckhandlers like Martin Brodeur, who was as good as any defenceman in the league fielding shoot-ins," observes Harry Neale of *Hockey Night in Canada*.

"It is something that we have worked on our entire careers to get good at," says the New York Islanders' Rick DiPietro. "To limit that is unfair to us, and unfair to anyone else who has that ability."

DiPietro is the only goalie in NHL history to be drafted first overall. No doubt, part of what made him such a hot commodity was his superior puck-handling ability, a skill that to some degree has now been taken away from him.

"If on one hand, you're Martin Brodeur and you've taken 10 years to learn how to do that, and then on the other hand, you're a rookie, you're suddenly on an equal basis with one of the greats," adds Calgary Flames head coach Mike Keenan. "I think it's had an effect on all goaltenders."

Part of the thinking behind this rule change was the notion that goaltenders had got to a point where they could roam around scot-free. Most times when an attacking forward touched a goalie outside the crease, the referee called a penalty. The league appears to have decided that goaltenders cannot have it both ways. They can no longer play the puck at their leisure, and with impunity.

Having said all that, the goaltender's ability to shoot the puck is not a completely lost art. In Game 1 of the 2006 Western Conference final against Anaheim, Edmonton Oilers goaltender Dwayne Roloson secured the puck in front of his net and lofted a beautiful, arcing backhand pass toward the Anaheim blue line. Oiler teammate Michael Peca, who had sneaked in behind the Ducks' defence, corralled the pass from his goaltender, then skated in unmolested and tucked a backhander under Anaheim goalie Ilya Bryzgalov. Roloson joked that his "fast-break lob" was something he used to do when he played for the University of Massachusetts. To think it would work this deep into the Stanley Cup playoffs was a surprise to say the least.

New rules almost always have unintended consequences. With referees calling a closer game, defencemen are no longer able to get away with much of the tackling, clutching, and grabbing that went on in front of the goal crease. As a result, goaltenders are more vulnerable.

"I think it's putting more pressure on the goalies, definitely," says Rick DiPietro. "I have seen a lot more traffic, a lot more goalies getting run into."

With defencemen having fewer tools to move their opponents from in front of the net, DiPietro is seeing both more pucks deflecting in off those forwards, and more havoc in general in his line of vision.

"I think that's definitely been a big reason why there's been a lot more goals scored, especially on the power play," he says. "I've been bumped into quite a bit this year. I realize it is part of the game but at some point it's going to be something that needs to be looked at."

"There is more freedom in front of the net," echoes Sudarshan Maharaj, who runs a scouting service to monitor up-and-coming goaltenders. "Guys aren't getting their spines rearranged in front of the net like they used to. So there are more loose sticks, and more loose pucks in front of the net."

Mike Keenan saw the same thing when he was general manager in Florida.

"The goalies are more vulnerable," he says. "The [opposing] forwards will go with reckless abandon toward the net. I'm waiting for the first superstar goalie to be taken out, and no one responds because they're afraid of getting a penalty."

Perhaps Keenan is reliving his own dark past on this issue. When Keenan was running the St. Louis team, his 1996 edition of the Blues were a strong threat to make a long playoff run until, depending on whom you talk to, Toronto's Nick Kypreos either charged into, or was pushed into, Blues goalie Grant Fuhr. Fuhr's knee was badly damaged by the hit, and so, coincidentally, were the Blues' Stanley Cup chances.

However, that reservation aside, even some goaltenders realize their particular concerns are less significant than the overall health of the game.

"I like the new way," offers Dominik Hasek. "The goals-against [average] is higher. But this isn't about goalies. It's about the game. Teams can come from two to three goals behind now. That didn't happen before."

In fact, all empirical evidence suggests the new rules have been successful in punching up the offence. In the 2003–04 season—

the last one under which the old rules were in effect—teams scored a combined average of 5.1 goals per game. In the 2005–06 season—the first one after the lockout and under the new rules— the average goals per game shot up to 6.1. The league says that is the largest percentage increase in goal-scoring since 1929–30. And that figure does not include goals scored during shootouts.

And there is more. In the 1995–96 season, the league featured no fewer than eight 50-goal scorers. By 1998–99, the smothering defensive style of play had reduced that number to zero. With the new post-lockout rules in place, 5 players scored 50 goals. In 1995–96, the league boasted twelve 100-point scorers. By 2003–04, that number had dropped to zero. With the new rules in 2005–06 allowing the better players to strut their stuff, there were seven 100-point men in the first post-lockout year.

Admittedly, scoring came down in the second post-lockout year to 5.8 goals per game as defences predictably adjusted to the offensive gains. But that's still up considerably from where the old NHL left off in 2004.

---

No regular season game now ends in a tie. If the 5-minute sudden-death overtime period does not result in a goal, then the outcome is determined by a shootout. In the shootout, three players from each side take a penalty shot. If the score remains tied after three rounds of penalty shots, then the shootout continues in a sudden-death format.

---

The other aspect of life that has put the spotlight on the goal-tenders is the NHL's new way of breaking ties. A generation ago, if a game ended in a tie, that was that. Over time, the league began to believe that too many games were ending in what some called "sister-kisses." The term nicely summed up the notion that a team might settle for the single point awarded for a tie, rather than press for the two points granted for a win, at the risk of gaining no points at all for a loss.

In 1983, the NHL changed the rules relating to games that ended in a tie. At first, the league simply added an extra 5-minute overtime period to try to resolve matters. If a team scored, that squad took the two points that came with victory, and the other side went home with nothing. Again, as with all attempts to inject more offence into the game, the defensive gurus eventually triumphed, to the detriment of the fans. Teams playing on the road (particularly inferior teams) are often more than happy to go home with a tie. And so before long, coaches were simply urging their charges to blanket the other team to ensure no further scoring. Sister kissing was alive and well.

So in 1999, the league went one step beyond. Teams would secure one point for tying after 60 minutes of regulation time. Then both clubs would play the 5-minute overtime period with only 4 skaters aside, instead of the regular complement of 5. If a team scored, it was awarded a second point for the victory. But the losing team still went home reasonably happy, inasmuch as they did not lose the point earned during regulation time. The 5-minute overtime was a huge hit with fans. Given how short the period was, coaches tended to send out their best offensive threats. Since at least a single point was guaranteed, teams did not need to play it safe. They took chances on offence and the result was marvellous end-to-end action. (So much so that some really adventurous observers of the game wondered whether hockey should permanently become a four-on-four sport. Those forces did not carry the day.)

While that was a dramatic departure for the league, some radicals agitated for more. And in the new NHL, there is more. If overtime fails to resolve matters, the game now provides for a series of penalty shots to ensure someone wins.

The penalty shot has always been the most exciting play in hockey. It is the closest thing to mano-a-mano action that hockey has to offer. One skater against one goalie. Everyone else observes from the bench. The closest comparison in sports would be baseball's pitcher–batter duel. It is the quintessential individual competition—one player's desire to score versus another's desire to prevent a goal. (Strangely enough, a comparison to soccer does not work as well, since the rules are so heavily stacked in the shooter's favour. Soccer keepers almost never stop penalty kicks.) In hockey, the offensive player carries the puck in from centre ice. The goaltender cannot move until the player crosses the blue line. After that, it is anyone's guess what will happen. Will the player shoot or deke? Will he go high or low? Will the goalie stay back or try for a poke check? Will he use the butterfly technique, falling to his knees and thrusting his legs out to cover the bottom two corners, or flop on his side, stacking the pads to prevent a shot from going in "upstairs"? The possibilities are endless, which makes this aspect of the game so entertaining.

Before the new shootout rules, penalty shots were rarely called. Technically, if a player was tripped on a breakaway in the act of shooting, or if a defenceman closed his hand on the puck in the goalie's crease in order to prevent a goal, a penalty shot was required. But the call was infrequently made.

Now, fans witness the drama and excitement of the penalty shot on a fairly regular basis. And it hasn't lost any of its lustre. When the home team wins in a shootout, the building explodes with joy and the goaltender's teammates mob him for a job well done. And one cannot help but notice that the hundreds, if not thousands, of fans that used to head for the exits with a few minutes to play, even in a close game, are now staying put. The shootout keeps them in their seats.

The rules make things interesting. If both teams are tied after three shots, the shootout continues until a victor is crowned. No player may shoot twice until every member of the team has shot at least once. You might think the odds against that happening are extremely long and you would be right. However, in November 2005 in Manhattan, both the New York Rangers and Washington Capitals had gone through 14 shooters and still the game was tied. In perhaps the most unusual penalty shot goal ever scored, the Rangers' Marek Malik, a 30-year-old defence-man from the Czech Republic, moved in on Capitals' goaltender Olaf Kolzig. Shooting left, Malik calmly pulled the puck through his legs, behind his left skate, and then, with his stick between his legs and behind his left skate, fired a shot to the top-left corner with such ease, one would have thought he had scored 50 that way. Over the course of 74 games that year, Malik would score a grand total of 2 goals.

The NHL's first shootout took place on October 5, 2005, at the Air Canada Centre and it happened under unlikely circum-stances. With just 1:30 to play in the third period, the Maple Leafs' Eric Lindros scored what 19,452 onlookers assumed was the winning goal, giving the home side a 2–1 lead. But 29 seconds later, the Senators' Daniel Alfredsson popped in the equalizer.

Five minutes of overtime resolved nothing, and as a result, the two teams embarked on a shootout.

Alfredsson shot first and beat Leaf goaltender Ed Belfour with a low shot to the glove side. Jason Allison went next for the Leafs and had the puck poke-checked off his stick by Sens goalie Dominik Hasek. Martin Havlat shot second for Ottawa—his shot glanced off Belfour's stick. Eric Lindros was Toronto's second shooter. His attempt went high, just over the net. This left Dany Heatley in position to end the game with a goal for Ottawa, which was precisely what he did, hitting almost exactly the same spot Alfredsson did. Game over. The Senators were credited with a 3–2 win, and fans went home having seen something new, interesting, and exciting, but were also deflated by the shootout loss.

Rather quickly, coaches around the league began to realize that the shootout was going to be a frequent occurrence. And so, they began to practise penalty shots more and more. But that did not mean players necessarily got better at them.

"You can never recreate the atmosphere of a penalty shot or shootout shot in a game," observes Harry Neale. "For the good of the game, it's great entertainment. Nobody leaves. They stay there to the bitter end."

New York Rangers coach Tom Renney says his team keeps solid scouting reports on most NHL goaltenders for two reasons.

"Number one, in a game, we want to know what are their tendencies," he says. "And, obviously, in the shootout we want to know if they come out and challenge, if they stay back, those types of things. I think we are pretty clear on that."

Renney has one player on his bench most coaches would give their eye teeth for when it comes to participating in a shootout. Jaromir Jagr is one of the most breathtaking goal-scoring talents in the world. Any time the Rangers are in a shootout, Jagr—and everyone else in the arena—knows he will be shooting.

Apart from the obvious superstars such as Jagr, is it hard for coaches to know whom to pick? Apparently it is. Does one go with a lesser player who may have a hot hand or the consistent high scorer? If teams have lost several shootouts in a row, do coaches simply mix it up and send some unlikely faces out there?

"It's a little bit of a crapshoot," acknowledges Florida Panthers coach Jacques Martin.

Remember, the greatest scoring machine in NHL history, Wayne Gretzky, was admittedly very ordinary at penalty shots. Team Canada fans will remember the Great One sitting on the bench at the 1998 Nagano Olympics, having been passed over by the coaching staff when it came time to break a tie against the Czech Republic. Canada lost the shootout, but—remarkably— not many observers second-guessed the coaches because of Gretzky's lack of success on the penalty shot.

The Maple Leafs' Darcy Tucker participated in three shootouts during the tiebreaker's inaugural season. He was stymied twice, but scored the winning goal against Bruins goaltender Tim Thomas on March 15, 2006.

"It's nerve-racking," Tucker admits. "I think you have to control yourself and do your homework. You've got to look over videotape and watch things and know tendencies. It's a different aspect of hockey."

With the game on the line, do players actually want to be selected to take the one shot that could mean the difference between victory and defeat?

"I don't mind it," Tucker says. "It's part of the game and you have to embrace and enjoy it when you're out there. It was a thrill to score the game-winning goal in the shootout this year and, given the opportunity, I enjoy going out there to try to accomplish that."

On October 9, 2006, the Maple Leafs were facing the Florida Panthers at the Air Canada Centre. Regulation time and overtime produced a 1–1 tie. The Panthers' netminder Alex Auld was sensational, stopping 47 shots to get his team to the shootout round. With a potential victory on the end of his stick, Tucker put a move on Auld and from 16' out, buried a backhander behind him to give the Leafs the win.

Players are always in a better mood after they win, so I figured this would be a good time to talk to Tucker about some of his shootout tendencies. I figured wrong.

"Did you have a move in mind before actually doing it?" I asked him.

"I'm not going to tell you what I was thinking," Tucker responded with a smile. But he wasn't joking. Still, I really wanted to understand the strategy of a shootout. Does a player have a move in mind before he even touches the puck? Or does he watch what the goaltender does? Is he looking for a weakness? Or is it just instinct, literally doing what seems appropriate at the very last millisecond? Tucker wasn't biting.

"I'm not going to give that up because that's part of the shootout," he said. "That's part of the surprise. People talk throughout the league so I'm not going to give my side away." And, although I asked more questions, he didn't divulge anything.

This called for a different approach.

"Did you talk to anyone on the bench beforehand for advice?" I asked.

For once, Tucker declined to plead the fifth.

"Yeah, and they told me three different things to do," he laughed. "I went with the exact opposite of what they told me. I did none of the above."

By this point, our conversation had drawn a bit of a crowd, and other players were laughing along with Tucker. He finally cut off my line of inquiry.

"You're asking me too many questions now and you're not going to get any more answers," he said firmly but still smiling. "It's just instinct. You go down, and do what you think. Now we're not going to talk about this any more!"

And we didn't.

For his part, Alex Auld loves shootouts. Like most goaltenders, he wants to be the guy in the spotlight. On this night, he faced Mats Sundin. He had scouted Sundin's tendencies, consulted the Swede's former teammate Ed Belfour (who was now Auld's goal-tending partner on the Panthers), knew exactly what Sundin was going to do, and yet still he gave up a goal to the Leafs' captain.

"The most frustrating thing," Auld told me after the game, "is knowing exactly what Mats is doing and yet he still puts it by you."

Kevin Weekes of the New York Rangers says he decides how he is going to play his opponent as soon as he knows who the opponent is.

"You just try to play his tendencies as best you can," Weekes says. In one game on March 24, 2006, Weekes found himself facing the Florida Panthers in a shootout to break a 2–2 tie. He noted that the Panthers' Slovakian-born centreman Jozef Stumpel generally likes to shoot to the glove side. Sure enough, Stumpel did and Weekes was there to make the save. However, the Rangers lost the game because the two other shooters scored, fouling up Weekes's expectations in the process. Nathan

Horton, who normally shoots to the glove side, tucked a shot through the five-hole instead. And when Panthers leading scorer Olli Jokinen took the final shot, Weekes expected him to shoot to the glove side as in past attempts.

"But he did that five-hole across-body move this time," Weekes says. "So I guessed on the wrong side of their tendencies today."

As for Jokinen, his part in this mini-drama was unusual to say the least. Ordinarily, the coach will notify all three players at the beginning of the shootout that they are the ones to participate. In other words, get ready. Except in this case, Jokinen says he did not find out until after Stumpel missed the second shot that he would in fact be taking the third. No pressure there.

"I wasn't listening," Jokinen confessed, after which I did not do a very good job of stifling a laugh.

Before even touching the puck, Jokinen had mapped out what the ensuing five to seven seconds were going to look like.

"Of course, you have to decide what you are going to try to do and sometimes it works and sometimes not," he says.

So, Jokinen had decided to put a deke on Weekes from the get-go. Did he feel it was going to work?

"I didn't feel anything," he says, trying to convey that we are overanalyzing this thing. "I just went there and shot it."

He shot. He scored. The Panthers won.

At the other end of the rink, the Panthers' goaltender, Roberto Luongo (since traded to Vancouver), was doing his part to give his team a chance to win the shootout. His first test was Michael Nylander, a 79-point man. Luongo remembered that on a previous confrontation Nylander shot high to the glove side, so he guessed that was where Nylander would go again. He was right.

No goal. Next came Czech-born Petr Sykora, who scored, and evened the shootout at a goal apiece. Finally, Luongo drew the unenviable assignment of facing Jaromir Jagr for the Rangers' final shot. Already that night, Jagr had become the NHL's first 50-goal scorer in 3 years. On this occasion, he tried putting a deke on Luongo, but the goaltender spread his pads wide in the butterfly position. Jagr held on to the puck too long, waiting for daylight to appear. But it never did, and he ran out of room, shooting the puck into the side of the net. Luongo's strategy was to be as patient as possible and wait for the other player to make his move. "And then close my eyes and hope the puck hits me," he said, laughing.

Mikael Tellqvist, once the backup goaltender for the Maple Leafs but now with Phoenix, points out that it's not just the goaltenders who feel stress in a shootout. "There's pressure on the shooters too," he says. "They're hand-picked." The Panthers' Martin Gelinas can confirm the pressure the shooters feel. Gelinas has scored some important series-clinching overtime goals in his career. But his reputation is mostly that of a pest whose scoring chances come as a result of skating and hard work rather than natural goal-scoring skill. However, on one occasion, Panthers coach Jacques Martin looked down his bench and picked Gelinas to take his team's fourth shot. Carolina led by one goal. Gelinas had to score to keep the Panthers' hopes of winning the game alive. If he failed, it was game over. What was Gelinas thinking?

"First of all, I didn't think I was going to get picked," he said, laughing. "So when I got picked, I said, 'What is he thinking?' That was my first thought."

What kind of move was Gelinas considering? No move at all. He jokes that he does not have a deke in his "toolbox." So, essentially, he skated in on goaltender Martin Gerber and looked for an opening to shoot at. He did not find one.

"It does put a lot of pressure on you and you don't want to let your teammates down," Gelinas says. "I wasn't thinking too much, except I wanted to score and it was unfortunate that I didn't."

Roberto Luongo says that shootouts are tough on goaltenders. But fans love them so he doesn't complain. Canadian hockey fans will always remember Dominik Hasek as the goaltender that stoned the Canadian men's team's best guns in the shootout that determined the outcome of the semi-finals at the 1998 Nagano Winter Olympics. "I'm not a big fan of [the shootout]," Hasek says. "I could live without it."

And what is Kevin Weekes's opinion of the shootout?

"Pretty way to win, tough way to lose."

For the record, in the first season under the new rules, the NHL's best practitioners of the shootout both offensively and defensively came from the Dallas Stars. Jussi Jokinen, a Finnish-born NHL rookie who ended up the 2005–06 season with a very average 17 goals scored, somehow channelled the ghost of Rocket Richard when it came to shootouts. He scored on 10 of 13 attempts for an astonishing 77 percent success rate. In goal, it was the Stars' Marty Turco who was as spectacular in regular season shootouts as he was disappointing in the team's first-round playoff exit. Turco won 8 of 9 shootouts, saving three-quarters of the shots he faced. The Islanders' DiPietro was tied for second with Martin Brodeur of the New Jersey Devils, both with 8 wins and 3 losses. Dominik Hasek ended up with just 2 wins in 6 shootouts—very un-Hasek-like numbers.

As thrilling as the shootout has now become, only one person I spoke to for this book would even remotely consider using it in the playoffs. The culture of hockey is overwhelmingly against it.

Broadcaster Harry Neale speaks for many when he said, "They can't possibly change that." Only Rick Dudley, assistant general manager of the Chicago Blackhawks, was open to the idea.

"The shootout is just damned exciting. It can't be described any other way," he says. "I would certainly hate to watch it if it was my team. It would be a little tough to do it in the playoffs, and I understand the resistance. But, boy, would it be exciting."

WITH A FEW NOTABLE EXCEPTIONS, reaction across the hockey world to the NHL's rule changes has been surprisingly positive. Hockey has often been criticized for being run by some of the most dinosaur-like owners and managers in all of professional sports. But the leap of faith this group took in overhauling the game was breathtaking, and most fans seem to concur it was worth the risk. Immediately after the conclusion of the first post-lockout season, Decima Research published the results of a public opinion survey conducted during the 2006 Stanley Cup Final between Edmonton and Carolina. Among decided respondents, fully 76 percent approved of the changes to the game. And when asked whether increased enforcement of the rule book by officials had disrupted the flow of the game or made it more exciting, more than two-thirds opted for the latter. Decima concluded that tinkering with hockey's traditional rules was risky, but that "the risk paid off."

Among the few influential voices raised against the changes is that of the second most famous face (assuming that Don Cherry is number one) in the Canadian hockey world. *Hockey Night in Canada* host Ron MacLean, who has refereed hockey games on the side for years, has frequently used his segments on the Saturday night broadcast to criticize the changes

During the second intermission of Game 4 of the 2006 final between Edmonton and Carolina, MacLean put Colin Campbell, the NHL's executive vice-president and director of hockey operations, through his paces. MacLean hammered away at Campbell, expressing his personal distaste for the increase in penalties. Campbell gave as good as he got.

"We're trying to make the game better," he told MacLean. "Previously, there were no lead changes. The players said the game wasn't fun any more. The coaches were getting too smart and just smothering the offence."

"You've gone too far," said MacLean.

"No one says it's perfect," said Campbell. "We'll go at it again in the summer if changes need to be made."

The league did review the rule changes over the summer of 2006. They paid particular attention to rule that MacLean particularly dislikes, which makes it mandatory for referees to call a delay-of-game penalty when a player flips the puck from his own defensive zone directly over the glass, stopping play. It used to be the case that the refs had some discretion. If they judged the puck was flipped over the glass accidentally, they could ignore it. Under the new rules, that discretion is gone.

The rule became controversial in Game 7 of the 2006 Eastern Conference final between the Buffalo Sabres and Carolina Hurricanes. With the score tied 2–2 in the third period, Sabres defenceman Brian Campbell accidentally cleared the puck over the boards and into the seats. The officials had no choice but to call a penalty. On the ensuing power play, the Hurricanes' captain Rod Brind'Amour scored the series-winning goal. Campbell was practically in tears over the incident. But the league reviewed the rule and it remains in place.

"Ron MacLean has had arguably the biggest hockey pulpit in Canada from which to argue a contrary point of view about the effect of the rule changes on the quality of the game," Bruce Anderson, chair and CEO of Decima Research, told the Canadian Press. "He's not winning that argument."

In fact, a great deal of the credit or blame for the new style of play in the NHL should go to the league's director of officiating, Stephen Walkom. In previous seasons, when there was an initial crackdown on interference and stickwork, the referees tended to back off as the season approached the playoffs. This has not been the case since the lockout. Walkom and his officiating crews have stuck to their guns and called it tight since the fall of 2005. And most skilled players appreciated it.

"They seem to be thriving on the fact that the interference and hold-ups and all the things that used to go on in the NHL are penalized now and even the slowest learner among the players is finding out you can't put a stick on a guy," observes Harry Neale.

"There are a lot of penalties called," former Maple Leafs coach Pat Quinn told me one day after a team practice. "But I'm gonna keep my mouth shut. When you criticize the new rules, you get in trouble and I don't want to get in trouble."

"They've taken away some of the aggressiveness and edginess," says Sheldon Souray, the Montreal Canadiens defenseman. "I'm never sure what the referees are going to call. It's an adjustment for players like me." However, Souray must have figured it out, because his average penalty minutes per game for the post-lockout 2005–06 season were actually lower than the final pre-lockout season.

From time to time, of course, the referees would slip. They are only human. And the players would notice.

"You never know from one night to the other as far as what is going to be called," the Panthers' Joe Nieuwendyk complained.

Harry Neale likens the situation to someone suddenly making an announcement that, starting tomorrow, everyone must drive on the other side of the road.

"There would be a few accidents and there'd be a few people who forgot," he says. "So it's not an easy adjustment."

In July 2006 at the Marriott Montreal Chateau Champlain Hotel, 300 hockey types in the broadcasting field gathered to consider the state of the game. The quality of the league's officiating crews was at the top of the agenda. Stephen Walkom made clear he was prepared to "tweak" whatever needed tweaking to improve the consistency and quality of his officials. However, he also added, "I've never met a referee who went to the arena and said, 'Let's see how we can fuck this up tonight.'" The referees get DVDs after every game. They are constantly monitoring their own performances and being evaluated by the teams and league. Walkom consistently instructs his crews not to guess. If they don't see an infraction, they are not to call it. The so-called "phantom calls," where a referee signals an infraction because someone is lying on the ice while another player skates away looking guilty, drive teams crazy, and frankly, still happen too often.

But the officials are definitely calling a tighter game. Power plays are up roughly 40 percent, which no doubt partly explains why scoring is up as much as it is. However, for those detractors who are claiming the new rules somehow have perverted the game, the numbers suggest otherwise. Before the lockout, teams were scoring on 16.6 percent of their power plays. With the new rules in place, that figure jumped to 17.8 percent. A 1.2 percentage point increase does not constitute a revolution.

In one of the great ironies of the first post-lockout season, a casualty of the new on-ice approach was one of the game's all-time greats, whose inflammatory comments forced hockey to see how rotten its product had become. The new game was too fast for Brett Hull. And so, in his 19th season of play, after just 5 games with the Phoenix Coyotes, the 41-year-old Hull retired. He can take immense satisfaction in knowing he once scored 86 goals in a single season, and scored 70 or more on two other occasions. He finished with 741 goals, 3rd on the all-time list behind Wayne Gretzky and Mr. Hockey himself, Gordie Howe.

"You should not be a 41-year-old player in the NHL," opines one of the game's all-time great defencemen, Denis Potvin. "It was never the case and I don't believe it could be the case today."

Two other greats also found the game had passed them by, thanks to the new rules. Mario Lemieux turned 40, played just under one-third of the season, then packed it in, finishing ninth on the all-time scoring list. He surely would have placed much higher had injuries and a bout with cancer not derailed his career and almost his life. And Dave Andreychuk called it quits at age 42, having played half the season, and still relishing his 2004 Stanley Cup championship. Andreychuk has never been considered one of the league's superstars, and yet, there he is, in 11th place on the all-time scoring list after 23 productive seasons.

Finally, in a chapter already replete with statistics, there are a few more numbers worth mentioning. Under the new rules, one player in particular saw a dramatic increase in his production. His goal-scoring abilities, while still eminently respectable, had been tailing off for several years, causing some to wonder whether his time was almost up. He was, after all, 37 years old, in his 18th season in the league, and had made the playoffs in 16 of those seasons. That is a lot of hockey. And yet, this player flourished in the new NHL, scoring 40 goals, his 6th best total ever, and his highest goal total in 6 years. He added 41 assists, putting him in 3rd place in overall scoring on his team. And he did it while still managing to spend 105 minutes in the penalty box. That player's name?

Brendan Shanahan.

After his excellent season with Detroit, Shanahan became a free agent in the summer of 2006. He parlayed his numbers on the ice into a one-year $4-million contract with the New York Rangers. The Rangers were a good team, with legitimate playoff prospects, but some observers wondered if there was another reason he chose Broadway over some of the other cities that might have been interested in his services. The Rangers' home is at Madison Square Garden on Seventh Avenue and 32nd Street. The National Hockey League's head offices are on the Avenue of the Americas, just a block away. Might Shanahan have his eye on the head office some day?

Would he like to be commissioner? When I put the question to him, Shanahan seems tongue-tied. There is a long pause before he responds. Is it really such a far-fetched idea?

"Maybe a little," he says. "It's not something people who spend their careers in rinks are qualified to do."

Others involved in the game don't entirely agree.

"I don't know if a former player can be commissioner because you'd need a legal background," says an NHL observer who knows Shanahan well. "But he could be an assistant. And he'd be good at it. He could be good for the game."

Many would say he already has been.

# THE NEW ECONOMY

*Gary Bettman and Bob Goodenow have completely destroyed the league's reputation in a decade, and even if they both get a deal that appeases both players and owners, neither man is capable of leading the NHL into its golden age.*
—ERIK LEIJON, POPMATTERS

That quote certainly made for provocative reading when it appeared in a self-described "international online magazine of cultural criticism" in April 2005. But it appears to be off the mark just a couple of years after it was posted.

While the former head of the players union, Bob Goodenow, did resign just a week after the end of the lockout in July 2005, NHL commissioner Gary Bettman appears to be more firmly ensconced in his position than ever before. He can boast a healthier league with more teams in the black, more prospects going forward, a better product on the ice, and more people in the seats watching it. Not bad for a guy who two years ago was being castigated for destroying the league that employs him.

It is no exaggeration to say that there has been an economic revolution in the National Hockey League, and Bettman, at one time one of the most polarizing leaders in sports, has led it. Astonishingly, there is virtually no discussion any longer about whether the new system is better than the old one. The debate ended with the lockout. Hockey has a new system and to everyone's amazement, people seem to have bought into the logic of it. That is something few would have predicted during the dramatic, topsy-turvy days when the league unilaterally cancelled 2460 regular season games, plus the Stanley Cup playoffs.

"I think the guys are fed up with talking about it," says Gary Roberts, the veteran forward for the Pittsburgh Penguins. Yes, the players were angry about missing a year of their careers, not to mention a year's salary. Having said that, Roberts feels "we have won because we are back playing and the game is back, hopefully revived and heading in a direction that is going to be good for everybody.

"I didn't want to retire saying, 'Boy, I was part of that group that ruined the game.'"

The philosophy underpinning the new economic system is essentially quite simple. While each of the 30 NHL team owners is in fierce competition with the others to win the Stanley Cup, they are, more significantly, business partners with one another—and now with the players too. It is no surprise that the smaller-market, lower-income teams love the new arrangement. It gives them a fighting chance to be more competitive with the bigger-revenue teams. What is surprising—and why ultimately the owners won the salary-cap issue—is that the rich owners came around to that view as well. They got to a place where they realized that 30 strong and viable franchises, none of which could spend dramatically more on players than the next one, would create a rising tide to lift all boats. The owners were so firm in their belief that hockey needed this new economic system that they were prepared to sustain operating losses of about $250 million, to have their way.* The NHLPA warned its stars that the owners were prepared to forego one season to achieve a salary cap. Bob Goodenow, then the head of the association, told the players they had better be prepared to give up two seasons' worth of their careers and income to stave off a salary-cap system. The players ultimately were prepared to lose one year to achieve their aims, but not two. As a result, the NHLPA caved on its demands and the owners won an unambiguous victory.

What it means is that the days are over when the Detroit Red Wings or New York Rangers were able to spend $80 million a year to acquire the best players, while the Nashville Predators spent just $20 million. The rich teams can no longer use their higher income to their competitive advantage. Yes, they can still spend more than their counterparts on other teams. Not every team has to spend to the top of the cap and not all of them do. Team budgets still take into account local realities. But gone are the days when the smaller-market teams can be outspent by a ratio of four-to-one by the rich outfits.

"I always believed, as a general manager, I could compete with someone who is maybe spending $1.50 for every $1 I was spending," says Blackhawks assistant GM Rick Dudley. "But not when it was $4 to $1. That was a little bit difficult. So from a parity standpoint, it is wonderful."

---

* All dollar figures cited in *The New Game* are in U.S. funds unless stated otherwise.

The immediate effect of a new league-wide salary cap was that all the good free agents did not automatically gravitate to the big-market, big-revenue teams as they had before. Edmonton, the 40th-largest city in North America, managed to sign one of the league's best defencemen in Chris Pronger. Highly touted goaltender Martin Gerber (at least, he was highly touted then) signed with the Senators to replace Dominik Hasek. Ottawa is the 108th-largest city in North America. Forward Anson Carter, who was the overtime hero for Team Canada in the 2003 World Hockey Championship, left Vancouver (66th-biggest North American city) for Columbus (192nd-largest city). And forward Jason Arnott left Dallas (17th-largest city) for Nashville (the 55th-largest) for five years and $22.5 million. If the money is essentially the same wherever you go, then smaller-market teams begin to look more attractive. For teams that have always had to count their pennies, such as the Ottawa Senators, the new system is a godsend.

"The closer we are to the cap the better off it will be for us," says John Muckler, the recently deposed Ottawa general manager. For years, the Senators' front office has had to deal with the frustration of running a very talented club but with only modest means to acquire players. While that hasn't changed, at least Ottawa can take solace in the fact that the richest teams can no longer buy their way past them to the top of the league.

The record shows that for years the teams with the deepest pockets were consistently more likely to make it to the final round of the playoffs. Over the 15 years before the lockout, when salaries really began to explode, the Stanley Cup was won by the Detroit Red Wings (three times), the Colorado Avalanche (twice), and once each by the New York Rangers and the Dallas

Stars, all of whom were among the highest-salaried teams in the league. The New Jersey Devils also won three Stanley Cup titles, proving that an above-average budget could also get the job done, as long as it was combined with superb management and the best goalie in the world. Tampa Bay was the only anomaly, winning the 2004 Stanley Cup series with a below-average budget, but capturing lightning in a bottle in every other department. Money has talked when it comes to winning the Cup.

"The statistics for the last 10 years prove there's a direct correlation between playoff performances and the amount of dollars spent," says Mike Keenan.

While general manager of the Florida Panthers during the lockout, Keenan did the math and concluded the higher-spending teams had a 90 percent chance of making the playoffs. Conversely, the bottom third of the spenders had just a 10 to 15 percent chance of making comparable progress. Even with the new salary cap in place, the richer teams are still outspending the poorer ones by $10 million to $15 million. That represents three or four good solid players that the poorer teams still cannot sign. But at least that's better than being outspent by $60 million, which was a regular feature of the old NHL system.

Perhaps the league's best example of a franchise that has successfully exploited both the new rules and the new salary structure is the Buffalo Sabres. Playing in Buffalo, only the 126th-largest city by population in North America, the Sabres find themselves in a city whose fans are overwhelmingly of modest means. The team's revenues over the years have been a fraction of those of the Toronto Maple Leafs, who play a mere two-hour drive away. However, thanks to the salary cap, the Leafs now outspend the Sabres for players by about $4 million, instead of $40 million, a year. Last year, the highest-paid player on the team was Daniel Brière at $5 million annually. The vast majority of Sabres players earn $1 to $3 million a year. The Sabres have spent wisely.

"We made some assumptions and some guesses and they were correct," says Buffalo head coach Lindy Ruff. "In the end, we were lucky."

But it was more than luck that saw the Sabres put together two excellent post-lockout seasons. The level playing field on salaries certainly helped. But the club's management, better than most, understood the implications of the new rules and designed their team with players that would complement those rules. As a result, Buffalo has iced a team that is remarkably quick on its skates, scores goals by the bucketful, and plays more than adequate defence. And they do it with a lineup of players fully one-third of whom are 6' or less. Brière, their best player, is 5'10" and less than 180 pounds, according to the official Sabres program.

"You make a few mistakes and they're jumping down your throat," says Maple Leafs goaltender Andrew Raycroft. "Their biggest strength is their depth. They have four lines they can roll at you."

With an excellent mix of eight Canadians, five Americans, three Czechs, two Russians, two Finns, one Swede, one German, one Austrian, and no big-name superstars, the Sabres are, in short, the prototypical team for the new NHL.

"I think our management did a very good job at bringing in guys that can skate and take advantage of less clutching and less grabbing," Brière tells me in the Sabres' dressing room after dispatching the Leafs 4–3 at the Air Canada Centre in January 2007.

Where the Sabres did get lucky was in the play of their American Hockey League affiliate, the Rochester Americans. During the lost NHL season of 2004–05, the Amerks (as they're known by their fans) were the best team in the AHL's regular season. Many on the current Sabres roster played on that team. They developed a cohesive style of play while toiling together in the minors. "We have three lines that can be called a number one line on a lot of teams," Brière adds. "We don't care if we're called superstars or stars or whatever we're called. As long as we keep winning."

In fact, during the 2006–07 regular season, no NHL team won more games than the Buffalo Sabres. The significant role Brière played in Buffalo's success enabled him to sign a massive free agent contract before the 2007–08 season. The Philadelphia Flyers inked Brière to an 8-year, $52-million deal.

HERE IS HOW the new system works, and why the owners and players are now genuine partners. Each summer, the National Hockey League estimates what it expects its revenues for the upcoming season will be. The players are guaranteed 54 percent of "hockey-related" revenues. So as league-wide revenues go up, so do both the salary cap for each team and the salaries of individual players. To make sure they guesstimate the split correctly, the league can put a percentage of the players' salaries in escrow. At the end of the year, once the total revenues are known, the escrow account is divided up among the players and owners depending on whether revenue targets were hit or not. This past year, revenues were more buoyant than anticipated and the escrow account was cleaned out.

The league pegged the salary cap in the first post-lockout season at $39 million per team. (It's less frequently mentioned, but the league also put in place a salary floor, below which teams could not spend. The floor is $16 million below the cap.) In the following season revenues went up, so the cap rose to $44 million. The overall pie is growing, and so are the owners' profits and the players' salaries. The first salary cap was based on league-wide revenues of just less than $2 billion. But as NHL revenues increase to $2.2 billion, the players' share will increase to 55 percent. At $2.4 billion in revenues, the players will earn 56 percent, and so on. The players and owners are genuine partners.

The NHL says hockey fans returned in the first post-lockout season in force. Attendance was up 2.4 percent, a remarkable development when you consider how fans responded to the return of Major League Baseball after the 1994 players' strike. In New York, on opening day in 1995, three men jumped onto the field at the Mets' Shea Stadium, each wearing a T-shirt bearing the single word, GREED. They then began throwing dollar bills at the players. In Cincinnati, someone paid a pilot to fly over the Reds' Riverfront Stadium with a sign that said, PLAYERS AND OWNERS—TO HELL WITH YOU. Attendance was down, booing was up, and it took a steroid-aided home run derby in 1998 between Mark McGwire and Sammy Sosa to boost baseball's sagging attendance.

The NHL suffered none of that. Admittedly, hockey does not hold the place in U.S. sports culture that baseball does. In Canada, fans seemed thrilled to have their game back. And, frankly, the players took such a beating on almost every major issue, including the acceptance of a massive pay cut, that it was hard to stay angry with them.

Some observers wondered if the salary cap would put the higher-salaried clubs in deep trouble. It was certainly no problem at all for the Columbus Blue Jackets to adjust to the new system. They had been living on smaller budgets than almost every other team since their inception in 2000. But if you're the Detroit Red Wings, how do you squish an $83-million payroll into a $39-million one? That was a little trickier. Certainly, the basic agreement between the owners and the NHLPA helped, given that the players took a 24 percent pay cut across the board. But the fact was, the general managers for the richer teams had to get a lot smarter and fast.

Most observers thought the New York Rangers would be the first casualty of the new economic reality. The Rangers were stuck with a lot of aging, overpriced, underachieving former stars. The team is rich (it is owned by the Cablevision Systems Corporation with $5.6 billion in annual sales) and it could always afford to chase the biggest names and give them the most money. But not any more. Surprisingly, once the Rangers bought out some of their expensive retreads and adjusted to life on a budget, they spent a lot smarter. The Broadway Blueshirts might have gone deeper into the playoffs in 2006 had some of their best players, including Jaromir Jagr and Martin Rucinsky, not been injured. The Rangers were also the hottest team in the NHL over the second half of the 2006–07 season, finishing behind only the front-running Buffalo Sabres in the Eastern Conference. They dispatched the Atlanta Thrashers in a four-game sweep in the first round of the 2007 playoffs, before bowing out to a superior Sabres squad in six games in the second round.

"What we are finding out this year," said Mike Pelino, one of the Rangers' assistant coaches, "is that the New York Ranger fans are not only great fans because they like the star players, but also because they appreciate hard work and what we are doing."

In fact, Glen Sather, the Rangers' Mr. Everything (president, general manager, and, on occasion, interim head coach), read the writing on the wall, and began to dispose of his under-achievers even before the new NHL came back.

"He made trades and acquired younger players with talent and got rid of some of his high-priced older guys and it has worked very well for them," says Rick Dudley.

But if the high-revenue teams lost the right to outspend their competitors, they also enjoyed one of the great windfalls in sports history. While their payrolls dropped by 50 percent, their buildings were still full, and their ticket, broadcasting, and ancillary revenues either stayed the same or went higher.

"The Toronto Maple Leafs draw as many people as they ever did and their budget will probably be $20 million less than it was," observes Dudley. "So, obviously from a standpoint of making money, it looks good on a team like that."

Meanwhile, life has become infinitely more complicated for the league's 30 general managers. No longer can they sign any player they desire at whatever rate they want. Every contract must be examined to ensure there is adequate space under the salary cap to accommodate it.

"We keep an eye on each other to have an appreciation for what's digestible and assumable by other clubs," says Leafs general manager John Ferguson, Jr., referring to his counterparts and the contracts they have all signed with their players.

The new economic system also has a number of provisions to ensure everyone plays by the same rules. For example, hockey-related revenues are now clearly defined in the new agreement, and any team trying to hide revenue can be fined $1 million, plus the amount misrepresented. Do it a second time, and the offending club faces a $5-million fine, plus double the misreported amount. The NHL has discovered through its own experiences, plus those of other professional leagues, that owners will make nice to each other in public, but behind the backs of their "partners," they will engage in cutthroat practices to gain an advantage. Head office is pulling out all the stops to put an end to that.

And there are other restrictions as well. The league forbids teams from circumventing the cap by paying players in other ways, either through gifts, marketing deals, or reimbursing expenses. No single player can earn more than 20 percent of his team's payroll, in effect, capping the best players in the first post-lockout season at just over $7 million. While no one will cry over athletes trying to "get by" on just $7 million a year, it is worth noting that the great Jaromir Jagr was earning $11 million before the lockout. That's a heck of a pay cut.

If there was any group of players who benefited from the lockout, it was hockey's worst-paid players. Before the lockout, the floor salary was $180,000. After the players returned to action, that minimum was raised to $450,000.

Much of the game's salary inflation was caused by general managers throwing big contracts at rookies who were chosen high in the entry draft. It proved to be impossible to tell veteran players to mitigate their salary demands when rookies were being paid millions. The new agreement dampens that inflationary aspect of the game by capping entry-level players at $850,000 a year. During the previous basic agreement, entry-level salaries could reach almost $1.3 million, and even then, there were ways to work around that ceiling. General managers were permitted to offer signing bonuses of up to 50 percent of a rookie's contract. That's now capped at 10 percent.

General managers have one small consolation. Executives now can say to prospective players—and, most significantly, the fans—that there is only so much they can do to improve their team. In the old days, smaller-revenue clubs had to deal with outraged fans, who saw ticket prices constantly go up, while star players left for greener pastures once their contracts expired.

For all the blows the players have absorbed as a result of the new agreement, they have received at least one significant thing in return. For the past few decades, NHL hockey has seen the least movement by free agents of all the major sports because the rule setting the conditions under which a player could leave his team to go to another one was so restrictive. At one point years ago, when a team wanted to sign a free agent (in other words, a player whose contract had expired), the team losing the player was entitled to ask for a player, or players, from the new team to compensate them for their loss. (For example, in 1991, the St. Louis Blues signed Brendan Shanahan, but for doing so, lost their captain, Scott Stevens, to the New Jersey Devils, the team Shanahan was leaving. In fact, just the year before, the Blues had signed Stevens as a free agent from the Washington Capitals, and were forced to give up *five* first-round draft choices to compensate the Caps. There was nothing free about free agency for the Blues.)

If the general managers couldn't agree on what constituted "just compensation," the teams would go to binding arbitration where an independent arbitrator would make the decision. The purpose of the rule was, frankly, to prevent player movement, rather than facilitate it, and it worked. After a few ambitious general managers had been burned by inappropriate arbitrators' decisions, the free-agent market did not just cool down, it froze up. Consequently, general managers had enormous leverage in their negotiations with unsigned veteran players. Since the demise of the World Hockey Association in 1979, players have had nowhere to go—except, perhaps, Europe—if contract talks bogged down. It's true that over the years, particularly after former NHLPA head Alan Eagleson left the game, the rules around free agency loosened up. More players started getting better contracts on a greater variety of teams. It was nothing like Major League Baseball, which had the most liberal player-movement conditions. But it was better. Teams signing free agents could lose draft choices, but at least they weren't forced to give up stars of equivalent value from their current roster. The new basic agreement now gives the players the most liberal free-agency regulations ever. Before the lockout, players could not become unrestricted free agents—in other words, have the right to sign with any other club without the player's old team receiving compensation—until the player was 31 years old. Last year, players could seek complete free agency at age 29, or with 8 years of service in the NHL. By 2008, a player aged 27 or with 7 years played in the league can become an unrestricted free agent. The nightmare scenario under these new circumstances is being felt in places such as Pittsburgh and Washington. Both teams had recently fallen on hard times and thus have enjoyed high draft choices in the annual entry draft. The Penguins managed to draft and sign the best young Canadian player since Wayne Gretzky: Cole Harbour, Nova Scotia, native Sidney Crosby. The Capitals did the same with Alexander Ovechkin, the top player coming out of Russia. Both the Pens and Caps shudder to think that they could spend millions marketing these two young phenoms, and building their franchises around them, only to have the players skip town as unrestricted free agents by the age of 25, just as they're approaching what are traditionally a hockey player's most productive years.

There are dozens of other regulations designed to level the new NHL's playing field. For example, the top 10 most profitable teams in the league now pay into a fund that can be tapped by the 15 least profitable teams. These payments are meant to address a frequent complaint by the players, who felt frustrated at having to moderate their salary demands to help the lower-income franchises, when the owners themselves did nothing to help their poorer brethren. In the first post-lockout season of 2005–06, 11 of the poorer teams received $90 million in revenue-sharing payments from the richer teams. Clubs such as the Buffalo Sabres and Pittsburgh Penguins should be grateful to the Toronto Maple Leafs and New York Rangers, who kicked in $10 million each. Without that equalization money (what a lovely Canadian concept), Buffalo, Pittsburgh, as well as San Jose and Washington would not have turned a profit. Those equalization payments also allowed the 2006 defending Stanley Cup champion Carolina Hurricanes to turn their first profit ever. Team owner Peter Karmanos says he has sustained nearly $150 million in losses since purchasing the Hartford Whalers in 1995, then moving them to Raleigh-Durham, North Carolina. The new economic system allowed him to pay down some debt last year.

In addition, teams in the largest television markets are ineligible to share in the revenue-sharing booty. That excludes the Rangers, Islanders, and Devils, in the tri-state region; the Kings and Ducks in and around Los Angeles; the Blackhawks in Chicago; and the Flyers in Philadelphia.

As much as his detractors might hate to acknowledge it, NHL commissioner Gary Bettman appears to deserve credit for not only making the players genuine partners with the owners, but also for making the rich owners see that the overall health of the league is as important as their own bottom lines.

"We're all in this together," says the Leafs' GM John Ferguson. "It doesn't at first blush hold true with your natural competitive and business instincts. But it is."

Ferguson admits the Leafs were one of the teams that had to learn how to operate differently, given the new economic restrictions.

"Our competitive advantage in Toronto was not taken for granted," he says. "It was well earned." Their famously deep pockets failed to bring Toronto its first Stanley Cup win since 1967, but the club has been competitive for the better part of the past decade and a half, and four times has made it to the league's semi-finals. A break or two here or there and the Leafs, courtesy of ownership's pockets, almost certainly would have been able to compete in a Stanley Cup final.

However, in the new NHL, Ferguson cannot rely on his owners' superior financial condition to stay competitive. At the time of our conversation, Ferguson said 28 of the league's 30 teams were within $4 million of each other in payroll. That's parity.

"Where I come from, you don't give up any competitive advantages," Ferguson says. "But we did for the health of the league. And sometimes I don't think we get enough credit for it. But that's representative of the leadership our president and board demonstrated."

When the Leafs hired the then 36-year-old Ferguson as their new general manager in August 2003, the club had precisely one player (excluding Tie Domi, who had already been traded away and reacquired) on its NHL roster who had been developed through the franchise's farm system. That was Alexei Ponikarovsky, and he had yet to establish himself in the NHL. Today, Toronto has as many as a dozen players on its roster that come from within the Leaf organization.

"This club had to learn how to operate better," Ferguson says. "Since we have been here, our commitment is to be the best at identifying and managing player assets."

It has been a struggle. In the first post-lockout season the Leafs fell to 18th place overall, missed the playoffs, and fired their coach of 8 seasons, Pat Quinn. It was the first time since 1998 that the Leafs had failed to qualify for post-season play.

But before you start feeling too sorry for their predicament, consider this: *Forbes* magazine, the bible of the business world, last year pegged the Leafs as the most valuable franchise in the entire NHL at $325 million. *Forbes* also estimated that the Leafs enjoyed the biggest increase in franchise value, the highest operating income, and the most valuable team brand. And the Leafs achieved all this while not even cracking the top-10 list of best-managed franchises in the league.

Some might argue that the Leafs are a cult, not a franchise, and hardly typical of other teams around the league. Perhaps, but consider the untraditional hockey market of Anaheim, California. In 2005, Henry and Susan Samueli purchased the hometown Ducks for $70 million—just $20 million more than the value of the team when it was born 13 years earlier. *Forbes* now puts the value of the 2007 Stanley Cup champion Ducks at $157 million. They may have taken the "Mighty" out of the Ducks' nickname, but things are plenty mighty on the balance sheet and on the ice, as the club made abundantly clear in dispatching the Ottawa Senators in a five-game final earlier this year.

Maybe they're just crazy in California? Then try Atlanta, hardly a hockey hotbed. In 2004, when the business of hockey was at its most precarious, an investment partnership ponied up $250 million to buy 85 percent of the NHL's Thrashers, the NBA Hawks, and the operating rights to the local Philips Arena. Today, *Forbes* estimates the value of the Thrashers alone at $128 million.

*Forbes* puts a generous value on other Canadian teams as well. Topping the list: the Edmonton Oilers, whose value the magazine pegs at a whopping 40 percent increase over its pre-lockout value to $146 million. Other Canadian franchises: the Vancouver Canucks, up 30 percent to $192 million; the Ottawa Senators, up 27 percent to $159 million; the Montreal Canadiens, up 18 percent to $230 million; and the Calgary Flames, up 17 percent to $135 million. While some of *Forbes*'s numbers are undoubtedly guesses, the news is encouraging.

Why does hockey appear to be such an improved business opportunity, despite its woeful recent past, anemic television ratings, and dubious penetration of the U.S. sports psyche? It's simple: the new economic system off the ice, combined with a better game on the ice, makes it a more attractive business proposition.

In the old NHL, salaries were skyrocketing beyond what revenues would sustain. NHL deputy commissioner Bill Daly told Tim Wharnsby of *The Globe and Mail* that in the last season before the lockout (2003–04), salaries accounted for 73 percent of the owners' costs—a much higher bite than in any of the other major professional sports. The rich did fine, but the poor were failing. For the 2007–08 season, salaries will be fixed at 55 percent of the league's revenues. With that cost certainty has come added franchise value. The owners estimate they saved more than $600 million in salaries over the first two post-lockout seasons.

Furthermore, while the league has been scrupulous to ensure its 30 teams are on as level a playing field as possible, there are still ways for the richer teams to exploit their situations that do not involve violating the salary cap.

For example, the Maple Leafs have beefed up their scouting department and expanded its coverage. They relocated their American Hockey League affiliate from St. John's, Newfoundland, to 10 minutes away from their arena at Exhibition Place's Ricoh Coliseum. Ferguson believes the ease with which players can now be called up from the Toronto Marlies to the big club, plus the proximity of the Air Canada Centre for those that want to play there some day, is a tangible benefit to the club. The ACC is a tantalizing beacon for those Marlies players toiling close by. "It provides a healthy competition within the organization," he says. "Players on the Leafs have to be looking over their shoulders." Apparently, so do the coaches. When Pat Quinn was fired, the Leafs went no further than their AHL affiliate to find his replacement in Paul Maurice, who had already been hired by Ferguson to coach the Marlies, and well understood the franchise's culture and personnel. Many had already fingered Maurice as the "coach in waiting" during Quinn's final season behind the bench in Toronto.

The Leafs also hired a third assistant coach, a goalie coach, and spent a bucketful of money on state-of-the-art video equipment and a video analyst. The assistant coaches can sit down with a player and review every shift that player took in the previous game. The Leafs also hold a 7-day prospects camp in the summer, run by Paul Dennis, who has spent 17 years with the franchise and has a Ph.D. in sports psychology. Dennis used to be the video analyst for the Leafs, a job now held by his son Christopher. And it doesn't end there. The Leafs also employ a strength and conditioning coach, and have two assistant coaches and a video coach with the Marlies of the AHL. Even in a world of salary caps, all these extras should, in theory, give the Leafs an edge over less prosperous rivals.

Of course, at the end of the day, what the average hockey fan really wants to know is, do these changes make the game better?

"The part that I just don't know yet is, does it drive all teams to mediocrity?" asks Gord Kirke, one of the leading sports lawyers in Canada. "Is there competitiveness, because all teams are relatively equal but at a lower level?" Kirke also wonders whether the phenomenon of the great dynasties such as the Montreal Canadiens of the 1970s, the New York Islanders of the early 1980s, or the Edmonton Oilers of the late 1980s is over.

"It may end up causing this," says Harry Neale. "If you're good and you win a couple of Cups, you're going to get bad because you're not going to be able to afford your lineup."

No more hockey dynasties may be the price we have to pay to get a more competitive league. Most would agree that the price is worth paying.

# THE FIGHTERS

*Michael Landsberg: "Now that you have retired, who is the toughest player in the NHL?"*

*Tie Domi: "There isn't one."*

It was one of the most unexpected conversations about politics I'd ever had.

On January 23, 2006, Canadians had gone to the polls and given the federal Conservatives their first election win since 1988, albeit by a slender margin of victory. Stephen Harper had confounded the experts by running a disciplined campaign that focused on the Tories' five key priorities. Paul Martin's electioneering for the Liberals, in contrast, had been unfocused and ineffective, and, as a result, he found his tenure as prime minister cut short. The Conservatives won a minority government, "out-seating" the Liberals 124 to 103.

One member of the Toronto Maple Leafs found the results completely baffling. Describing himself as "a Liberal, both big and small L," this veteran of 15 NHL seasons was convinced Canadians had made a mistake.

"Canada is a middle-of-the-road country," he told me in the Leafs' dressing room at their alternative training site in Etobicoke after a mid-morning practice. "The mainstream of the country is liberal."

I pointed out that the Conservatives ran a superior campaign, and that the Quebec sponsorship scandal had damaged Liberals' fortunes.

"The scandals hurt," he acknowledged, while taking off his equipment. "We were in Alberta," he added referring to the Leafs, "and Harper was everywhere."

Had this player ever met Paul Martin?

"Yeah, I met him at Larry's house once," he said, referring to the Maple Leafs' owner Larry Tanenbaum, another prominent Toronto sports ownership figure with well-publicized links to the federal Liberals. "It was an intimate gathering. I was very impressed with him. We talked about crime and violence."

Still, he was clearly puzzled about why Canadians would throw the Liberals out of office.

"Our country is in good shape now," he said. "We went from the bottom to the top of the G7." I confess to him that in the hundreds of conversations I have had with hockey players over the years, I have never yet—until this moment—heard any of them refer to the G7. "I read the *Post* and the *Globe*, which educates you well," he says. "I also watched both leaders' debates."

There was more. He volunteers the name of a politician he thinks the Liberals should build their future around.

"Belinda could be a good leader," he says. "She could clean up the whole party. If anybody could be the first elected woman prime minister, it's her."

Within a few months, 11 people will announce their candidacies for the leadership of the Liberal Party of Canada, but Belinda Stronach will not be one of them. The daughter of the founder of the Magna auto parts empire will sit this round out, having lost in her first attempt to lead a federal party—the Conservatives—to Stephen Harper. (In the spring of 2007, Stronach withdrew from politics altogether.)

This Maple Leafs player clearly follows politics avidly. So the inevitable question follows. Would he ever run for Parliament?

"I care about our country and what's going on," he says sincerely. "But it would require me to be in Ottawa a lot and I'm not too well liked in Ottawa."

He smiles. It's true. He is not beloved in Ottawa, or in many other cities around the National Hockey League for that matter. And the reason is that he has been one of the toughest, nastiest, roughest, meanest, and occasionally dirtiest pieces of business this league has ever seen. He is clearly one of the best fighters of all time. Without question he is the best fighter "pound for pound," since he is only 5'10" and 213 pounds (according to team records, which we all know are exaggerated).

As we finish our conversation, I wonder whether he knows—as many are speculating—that his career is almost over, that in a few months' time, the team he gave his heart and soul to will cut him loose, claiming he just does not have what it takes to prosper in the new NHL. These are difficult days for Tie Domi.

ON A COLD FEBRUARY DAY in 2006 at the Lakeshore Lions Arena in Etobicoke, a dozen kids, most of them donning their blue and white jerseys, wait patiently for the Zamboni to finish clearing the ice. The team they worship is about to leave the dressing room and participate in one of the occasional practices that are open to their adoring public. Some of the Leafs are not here today, the most noteworthy of whom is captain Mats Sundin. He is finishing up a two-week tour of duty in Torino, Italy, site of the Winter Olympic Games. The following day, Sundin will win overseas what has always eluded him in Toronto, namely, a championship. His assist on Niklas Lidstrom's third-period goal will give Sweden the Olympic gold medal over archrival Finland.

"Come on, guys, you can come out now," one security guard shouts into the Leafs' dressing room, indicating the ice is now ready.

The doors open. Nothing much happens. Some of the kids start chanting, "We want the Leafs!" And out they come.

"Who was that?" one 10-year-old asks another. (It was Alexei Ponikarovsky.)

Wade Belak comes out and gives a wave. Matt Stajan offers a "What's up, boys?" The players continue to trickle out. Most players simply ignore the kids. A few smile. Eric Lindros says, "Hi guys." Ken Klee nods. The players are all wearing their practice jerseys, which have no numbers on the backs, so whispers of "Who's that?" rustle through the crowd of youngsters.

But the next player to emerge needs no number, no name on his back, and no introduction at all. It is Tie Domi, and his appearance prompts an enormous cheer.

"Hi guys," Domi says, following it up with a big smile. These kids will remember that "hi" and that smile for the rest of their lives. I know this because I still remember waiting outside Maple Leaf Gardens almost 40 years ago, and seeing great players who never felt too important to stop and chat or give an autograph (such as the Blackhawks' Bobby Hull). I also remember players who had no business thinking they were something special and yet snubbed those of us waiting, or, even worse, swore at us (such as the Bruins' John McKenzie).

I can't resist asking one of the kids, who cannot be more than 12 years old, why he apparently loves Tie Domi so much.

"Because he's strong. He's a scrapper," the youngster answers.

"Does he fight too much?" I follow up.

"He doesn't fight enough," the kid responds. "We like the fights."

That exchange reminded me of a conversation I once had with my then 12-year-old son Henry at an AHL game in Hamilton. The Toronto Marlies were visiting the Bulldogs in a fight-filled affair. I looked over at Henry, who was clearly enjoying the spectacle. We had talked about hockey numerous times over the years, but I had never asked him whether he thought fighting should be banned. So I did.

He looked at me as if I were a complete idiot (a look I have seen before—I am his father, after all).

"No," he said definitively.

"Why not?" I asked.

"It gets the crowd going," he said.

Then, his 8-year-old brother Teddy added, "Yeah, it's cool."

These statements, in all their blessed naïveté, say volumes about why Tie Domi has been one of the most beloved Leafs in team history. Domi has scored only 104 goals in more than 1000 NHL games played. He has, however, also spent almost 3800 minutes in the penalty box (regular season and play-offs)—the equivalent of more than 60 full games—and stands 3rd on the all-time penalty minutes list behind Dave "Tiger"

Williams and Dale Hunter. As far as Maple Leafs go, he is the most penalized player in team history, well ahead of Williams, Wendel Clark, and Tim Horton. And it is all about to come to an end, not only for Domi (who retired in September 2006), but also for other players whose most notable skill is the ability to fight. In the new NHL, pugilistic talents alone will prove not to be enough.

I HAVE NEVER BEEN one of those who thought Tie Domi's skills were limited to beating people up. I have always felt that if he had demonstrated just a bit more self-discipline, Tie Domi, the fighter, could have been a much more significant offensive force on the ice. Consider that at age 36, Domi was still one of the fastest-skating Leafs. Consider that in the 2002–03 season, Domi scored 15 goals and added 13 assists, his best season ever for goals and points. And unlike other 15-goal scorers, he did it while spending 171 minutes in the penalty box. Had his playing time not been dramatically reduced in his final 2 seasons in the league, Domi surely would have improved on the 7 and 5 goals respectively that he scored in those final years.

"I think Tie Domi can be a good player," says Chicago's assistant GM Rick Dudley. "Domi can skate, he can get in, and he can force the play. And that is the type of player that is very dangerous now because you can't hold him up."

But the Leaf brass lost faith in Domi. And all those fights eventually caught up with him. Before the 2005–06 season, Domi turned down three other teams, all of whom offered him a three-year contract. Instead, he signed a less remunerative two-year deal with the Maple Leafs, the team he always loved the most, and many observers were surprised Domi even got that deal done.

His time in Toronto looked like it was coming to an end even before the players returned from the lockout. Contract talks were not going well with Leafs' general manager John Ferguson, Jr. But suddenly, the Leafs announced Domi had agreed to a two-year deal. Speculation instantly focused on Domi's special and close relationship with Leafs' owner Larry Tanenbaum. Did the owner nudge (or perhaps urge) his general manager to get Domi signed, given what a fan favourite number 28 was? The talk around town was that Ferguson was less than delighted about Domi eating up precious salary-cap space on his team, and yet next thing you knew, JFJ was proudly welcoming Domi back to the fold.

But after just the first year of that two-year deal in Toronto, the rumour mill cranked itself up again, suggesting that Domi's days as a Leaf were over. This time, the rumours were accurate. On September 19, 2006, Domi went before throngs of cameras and with the logo of his beloved Maple Leafs over his right shoulder, he announced his retirement. In many respects, Domi was the last of his kind—a type of player apparently not needed in the new NHL.

Tahir "Tie" Domi was born in Windsor, Ontario, on November 1, 1969, but grew up in nearby Belle River in Essex County. He played for the Belle River Canadians in the Great Lakes Junior C Hockey League, but his biggest break came with the Ontario Hockey League's Peterborough Petes.

During his second of three seasons in Peterborough, Domi notched 43 points in 60 games, decent scoring numbers made all the more impressive considering he spent 292 minutes in the penalty box during that 1987–88 season.

The Toronto Maple Leafs liked what they saw of his play and drafted Domi in the second round of the 1988 entry draft, the 27th player taken overall. He spent another year in Peterborough, then moved up a notch by playing for the Leafs' American Hockey League affiliate, the Newmarket Saints, in 1989–90. After the AHL season ended, the Leafs called him up to the big leagues where he played in just two games that year (and yet still managed to rack up 42 penalty minutes). But Domi's first stay in Toronto was short. He was traded to the New York Rangers after the 1990 season. Leaving the Leafs might have been heartbreaking except for the fact that Domi ended up playing with one of the all-time greats on Broadway.

Mark Messier won five Stanley Cups in seven years with the Edmonton Oilers and now was being asked to work a miracle with the Rangers, the most snake-bitten playoff team in the NHL at the time. The Rangers had not won the Stanley Cup since 1940 and had gone to the finals only three times since then. In Domi's second year with New York, the Rangers traded for the man widely regarded as one of the most dominant leaders in any sport. Messier would prove to be one of Domi's most influential mentors, both on and off the ice.

Domi was in his early 20s. He was cocky and, despite his diminutive size, quickly developing a reputation as a fearsome fighter in the league. He was undaunted trading punches with players half a foot taller than him—including Bob Probert, perhaps the greatest fighter of them all. One night, Domi had a particularly good game. He scored a goal and an assist, and was named the game's second star. But he could not resist hot-dogging it up after winning one of his fights. He pretended to repeatedly hit a "speed bag," a training technique boxers do to prepare for their fights. After the game in the dressing room, Mark Messier got his teammate's attention.

"Tie, come here," he said. Domi dutifully went over to the Ranger captain. "Listen here, you little shit," Messier blasted him. "You want respect in this league, then cut that shit out." It may have been the single most important piece of advice Domi heard in his entire career. In one brief but sharp exchange, Messier reminded Domi that the NHL was not the World Wrestling Federation, that other tough guys in the league were protecting their star players in the same way Domi was protecting his, and if he wanted the respect of his peers, he had to smarten up.

Domi got the message loud and clear and, as he made his way through the league, passed on the same advice to other up-and-coming tough guys.

After just 82 games in New York over parts of 3 seasons (and most importantly, before the Rangers won their first Stanley Cup in 54 years), Domi found himself on the move again, this time to Winnipeg. The Jets gave up a very good young player named Ed Olczyk to acquire him. (Olczyk was in the midst of a 1000-game career in the NHL, scoring almost 800 points in the process.)

The Jets had a remarkably talented young Finnish player, Teemu Selanne, who in 1992–93—Domi's first season in Winnipeg—scored an astonishing 76 goals and 132 points in his rookie season. To be sure, the Jets needed Domi to be Selanne's bodyguard. No opponent was permitted to take liberties with the Jets' superstar. But some observers noticed that Domi was once again seeking out friendship with the team's star player, this time in Winnipeg, just as he had in New York. The least charitable among them suggested that he was looking for the political cover that comes with being the pal of players who appear to be untouchable. The theory would make more sense if both Messier and Selanne had not left their teams through free agency or trades (albeit both Moose and the Finnish Flash exerted some amount of control over their whereabouts).

Once again, Domi found himself on the trading block. But this time, things could not have worked out better. In April 1995, Domi returned via trade to Toronto, his true love in the hockey world.

Domi would spend the next eleven years in Toronto, becoming one of the most beloved Maple Leafs—and polarizing forces—of all time. Kids and others who loved the fights adored Domi. Others rued the influence he had both in the dressing room and on the ice.

The familiar pattern manifested itself again, in that he befriended not only the biggest star on the team in Mats Sundin, but also the owner, Larry Tanenbaum. Domi also established himself as one of the more community-minded players by participating in numerous charitable events for Variety Village; Santa on Wheels; and Rose Cherry's Home, named after Don Cherry's late wife, which provides pediatric hospice care.

However, the year 2001 proved to be Domi's *annus horribilis*. During a particularly nasty game in Philadelphia in March, Domi got fed up with the Flyers fans who loved jeering him as he made his way to the penalty box. Domi's version of events goes like this: He was sitting in the sin bin and minding his own business when a Flyers fan dumped a beer on him. In retaliation, Domi grabbed his own water bottle and started spraying the alleged offender. The next thing you knew, the Philly fan went nuts and started leaning on the Plexiglas separating the fans from the penalty box. The fan's body language seemed to suggest if only that protective glass were not there, the fan would rip Domi limb from limb. Funnily enough, the spectator, who did not appear to have missed many meals of late, tumbled right over the glass and into the penalty box. Fortunately for him, he escaped with cuts and bruises as Domi refrained from giving him the pummelling he otherwise would have had coming. Still, Domi was fined $1000 for spraying the fan and the neighbouring area with water.

The worst was yet to come. During the second round of the playoffs in May, the Leafs found themselves down two games to one to the New Jersey Devils. Happily for their fans, they came up with an inspired effort. Toronto led 3–1 and was seconds away from celebrating an important series-levelling win, when Tie Domi had the worst brain cramp of his career.

Until that moment, Domi had played a smart, terror-inducing match, completing his checks and skating furiously all over the ice. He was a significant reason that the Leafs were on the verge of tying the series. In less than 10 seconds, in all likelihood, he was going to be named the game's first star. And then, as the puck got dumped into the New Jersey zone and Scott Niedermayer went back to retrieve it, Domi had a flashback to a previous encounter with the Devils' all-star defenceman. As Domi tells the story, a few games earlier, Niedermayer "put his Easton [stick] in my face and cut my face." The Leaf player required several stitches to close the gash. Not only was no penalty called, but Domi also insists Niedermayer laughed at him.

So, with more than 18,000 fans chanting his name in the waning seconds of Game 4, Domi decided to get even. He charged at Niedermayer with his elbow way too high and crushed Niedermayer's cranium into the boards. The Devils' defenceman collapsed in a heap and lay motionless on the ice for several minutes. Suddenly, the building went dead quiet and a wonderful victory turned into a shocking embarrassment for Domi. Niedermayer was unable to play for the reminder of the series. And the entire hockey world heaped opprobrium on the Leafs' tough guy.

The NHL's sheriff in charge of suspensions, Colin Campbell, said Domi had forfeited the privilege of playing any more playoff hockey. He was done for the year. Devils' forward Bobby Holik called the hit "an insult to hockey."

"Disgusting and irresponsible," added John Madden, Holik's Jersey teammate. "A person like that shouldn't be given the right to run around with a hockey stick in his hand and play in the league."

The Devils went on to win the series in seven games. They reached the Stanley Cup final that year, but lost in seven games to the Colorado Avalanche. Who knows what kind of difference a healthy Scott Niedermayer might have made to New Jersey's chances of winning what would have been their third Cup victory in seven years.

Domi would eventually hold a teary-eyed news conference explaining his actions. He tried to apologize to Niedermayer but did it too soon and the Devils' star was in no mood to accept the apology. "Whatever," was Niedermayer's response. Domi would later call the incident "the stupidest thing I've ever done in my life and my biggest regret. I wish I'd stayed in that series. I could have made the difference. Instead, I let my teammates down."

Still, Domi returned to the Leafs the following season. He notched 9 goals and 19 points, then followed it up with his best season ever—15 goals and 29 points in 2002–03. At age 33, he was still rough and tough and effective.

But in 2003–04, Domi's production went down to about half of the previous season's output. He played in every game but two and yet scored only seven goals. And there was another incident. During a game in Toronto against Columbus in which he had already scored a goal, Domi autographed a hockey stick, then tossed it into the Blue Jackets' bench in the third period. The stick appeared to fly in the direction of Jody Shelley, one of Columbus's tough guys. The league fined Domi $1000 and the Maple Leafs $5000 for the stunt.

As the years went on, Domi fought less and less. The injuries hurt that much more, particularly to his right hand. He taught himself to throw punches with his left hand, after his right hand started constantly aching from the pain of knuckles hitting hard plastic helmets. Then came the lockout and a lost season; when Domi came back for the 2005–06 campaign, too much had changed.

Whether it was because management judged his usefulness to be less in the new NHL, because of his advancing age, or because his skills were declining, Domi got reduced ice time toward the end of the 2005–06 season. In fact, rumour had it that Domi was going to be a "healthy scratch"—physically fit but dropped from the lineup—when the Leafs then discovered Domi's next game, March 3 in Buffalo, would be his 1000th in the NHL. The team could not humiliate him on the eve of such an accomplishment and so Domi played. He was also in the spotlight for the team's next home game the following night against the Ottawa Senators, during which an elaborate pre-game ceremony acknowledged his achievement. However, with the theatrics out of the way, Domi was indeed a healthy scratch for the Leafs' next series of games.

He got back into the lineup on March 14 against the Boston Bruins, and at times, Domi seemed like the player he once was. In the first period, he paired off with Bruins' left-winger Dan Lacouture for a good old-fashioned tilt that saw both men go to the penalty box for five-minute fighting majors. Typical of Domi, his combatant was a good five inches taller than he was. (Did Domi ever fight a smaller man? I cannot think of one.)

Then in the second period, through hard work and good forechecking, Domi stole the puck from a Bruins player on Boston's blue line with his team down 3–1. He passed to line-mate Chad Kilger, who promptly sent the disk back to Domi, who followed up with a lovely pass to Jason Allison. Allison one-timed the pass into the net and the Leafs were down by only one. The teams ultimately tied 4–4, and the game showed off the kind of positive impact Domi can have when he plays tough but disciplined hockey.

Domi has always been a proud athlete and no doubt being forced to sit out a handful of games was a blow to his ego. But he made a point of not bitching about it to the media hordes who follow the Leafs during the season. Domi said he wanted to demonstrate to the Leafs' many younger players how a professional deals with disappointment—not by creating headlines, but by keeping his head down, working hard in practice, and just biding his time. But the fact remained that in the new NHL, referees were calling a lot more penalties. That meant more ice time for the highly skilled players, who tended to make up the team's power-play unit, and a bigger workload for the penalty killers, but not so much for non–special teams guys. Before long, because of so many odd-man situations, Domi found himself playing at the most only a few shifts per period. It became increasingly difficult for him to have any impact on the game.

"You're stone cold and people expect you to go out there and do miracles," Domi would explain with evident frustration.

"I think some of the guys that rely on fighting solely really got hurt by that," says St. Louis Blues assistant coach Brad Shaw, referring to the new emphasis on strict officiating. "And, if that is what the league wanted to do, I think they succeeded in leaving some of those guys out."

The Maple Leafs ultimately missed the playoffs in 2006, and by the time the regular season came to a close, journalists were reporting as fact (even though it could only have been speculation) that Domi had played his last game in blue and white.

Reporter Howard Berger from radio station FAN 590 in Toronto led the media scrum with Domi. As he persisted in asking number 28 about his future in Toronto, one could see Domi's mood change from bemusement to irritation.

"I don't speculate on those type of things," he told Berger. "You do your job and everybody has their opinion."

It seemed like an obvious question, so I thought I'd ask it.

"Tie, do you want to come back next year?"

"Yes, I do, I do," he said emphatically. And then, in a voice dripping with sarcasm Domi added, "I'll let the geniuses in the media make their opinions on who should be here and who shouldn't. I don't get caught up in that stuff and nor am I going to start."

"Tie, do you think the team used you in the most effective way this year?" I asked. That seemed neutral enough not to force a rise in him, and yet he could sense that if he told the truth it was going to cause some ripples. Other reporters began leaning in to hear the answer.

"Would I have liked to play more and try to make more of a difference? Yes, for sure," Domi said carefully. "But at the same time, that was out of my control and that's just the way it goes."

That begged a follow-up. I had always been under the impression that Domi and Pat Quinn had a good rapport. Did Domi ever talk to Toronto's head coach and ask for more ice time? Another straight-ahead question, but one that, if he were inclined to do so, might allow Domi to reveal something interesting about his relationship with Quinn.

"Ironically enough," Domi started, "I used to be in his office quite a bit, and I used to barrel down his door a lot. But this year it wasn't the same, and I didn't do that," he added, looking more sad than anything.

Domi went on to explain that he started the year getting a relatively regular shift with Eric Lindros. But at some point "I just disappeared into the fourth line and never got out of there again." Domi speculated that he may have been a victim of the Leafs' youth movement that was forced on the team late in the season thanks to a spate of injuries to veterans. The club had to call up many of its younger players from the American Hockey League, and most of them did reasonably well. Of course, the better they did, the less ice time Domi got.

"I didn't want to be the guy who, selfishly speaking, worried about ice time," he says. "I tried to show these young guys how to be professional in day-to-day work. So you just try and be a leader."

I thanked Domi for his comments, then marched right over to the media lounge where Pat Quinn was about to start his news conference. The first thing I asked him was whether he shared Domi's view that the coach and the player were not as communicative as in years past. Quinn said he did not.

"I've tried to always maintain an open-door policy and be open to discussion, suggestion, criticism, whatever from the players because we are a team," Quinn said. "So it may be that we hadn't had the conversations as much as we might have had in the past. But Tie's an initiator, and that could have happened as well." Quinn seemed to be suggesting that Domi needed to share part of the blame for any communication gap that might have existed between the two old warhorses, since Domi admitted he knocked on Quinn's door less in 2006.

It's hard to think of Tie Domi as one of T.S. Eliot's "hollow men." But the fact was, his 15-year career as one of hockey's most feared enforcers had come to an end, "not with a bang but a whimper." There would be no last-minute glory in the playoffs since the 2005–06 Leafs missed the spring dance. Domi always wanted to be buried, so to speak, in the blue and white, unlike so many other popular Leafs who were denied the privilege (think Darryl Sittler and Borje Salming in Detroit, Dave Keon in Hartford, or Tim Horton in Buffalo). He could not have been more categorical about that at the news conference announcing his retirement. "I'll always be a Maple Leaf fan," he said, "and always want them to win." Despite receiving phone calls from other teams, Domi concluded, "I just couldn't put on another jersey." From some athletes, that would sound like canned propaganda. But it did not from Tie Domi.

"I kiss my lucky charms. I'm one of the few guys who got to play here so long and become a household name in this city," he said perhaps not terribly modestly, but certainly accurately.

Domi's departure from the National Hockey League leaves one wondering whether there remains a place in the new game for the player who is used to spending more than 200 minutes a year in the penalty box and contributing only a handful of goals. A generation ago, no big-league team would play without such an enforcer. Today, officials are calling more penalties, and the players whose skills are chiefly pugilistic are on a much shorter leash.

Is there still a place in the new NHL for Tie Domi?

"I don't think there are as many spots on as many teams," says Harry Neale. "You have to be able to play in addition to being a tough guy."

Goaltender Sean Burke, who played a significant role in Brendan Shanahan's hockey summit, agrees.

"I think that the role of the fighter is a valuable one if the fighter is a good hockey player, somebody that isn't going to hurt your hockey club," he says. "I think if you look back to the days when you just got a couple of guys sitting there waiting to fight, and were a liability for the most part on the ice, I think those days are over."

One month into the 2005–06 season, league commissioner Gary Bettman took great pride in pointing out in a speech in Toronto how life for the fighters had changed.

"The number of fighting majors has been cut by 40 percent as the greater speed and elimination of stickwork has removed many former flashpoints for fighting," he said.

Not everyone agrees with the commissioner that the infrequency of fighting has been good for the game. When I asked Calgary Flames' head coach Mike Keenan who the best fighter in the NHL was today, he replied, "I have no idea. There's not much

fighting any more." And in case I wasn't clear that Keenan regret-
ted the changes, he followed up with this observation: "They've
taken out of the game the ability for players to settle things
themselves," he said. "They've taken some of the passion out of
the game."

WADE BELAK is the prototypical NHL tough guy. At 6'5" and
221 pounds, with flaming orange hair, he might be the last guy
an opponent would want to go into the corner with. In February
2001, the Maple Leafs claimed him off waivers from the Calgary
Flames, but in his five seasons in Toronto since then, Belak still
struggles to be an everyday player. In the last season before the
lockout, he missed 38 games because of injuries, and another
10 games thanks to a suspension in connection with a high-
sticking incident. Belak accumulated 27 penalty minutes in just
1 game that season. He finished the year with 109 minutes,
which doesn't sound that high, until you realize he played only
34 games all year. In 55 games in the first post-lockout season, he
added another 109 minutes to his penalty totals.

Belak is a more useful player than it would seem at first
glance. He can play both right wing and defence. His size clearly
makes him an intimidating presence on the ice. However, only
once in his career has the big man scored more than one goal in
a season—that was in 2002–03 when he netted three. He also
spent 196 minutes in the penalty box during his 55 games played
that year.

Belak grew up in North Battleford, Saskatchewan. His
favourite player was Dave Manson, a product of Prince Albert,
just a one-hour drive away. Belak grew up watching Manson play
for the Blackhawks and loved his take-no-prisoners approach.

"He played back in the day when somebody could beat you wide and you could break your stick over his leg and get only two minutes for slashing," Belak says, laughing. "Everybody was scared of him."

Which is no doubt how Manson got his nickname: Charlie. For a player of limited skill, Manson managed to play 18 years in the NHL, and in a bit of serendipity, was Belak's teammate in Toronto in the early 2000s. In fact, they were roommates on the road, which was a bit of a dream come true for Belak.

Belak is one of those dressing-room guys who keeps his compatriots on their toes with his sense of humour. He loves to needle his teammates and understands what his role is on the club. He turned 30 last summer and no doubt his fists feel older. Does he like to fight?

"I won't say I love to do it every night. But when it needs to be done, I don't mind doing it," he says.

In his playbook, Belak "needs" to fight when one of the Leafs so-called skill players is being picked on. He insists he does not start a fight just for the sake of dropping the gloves. He also acknowledges something most fighters will not.

"When you do win a fight it is definitely a good feeling," he says. "It usually feels good on your face too," he laughs, suggesting that if you won the fight, your face possibly feels less busted up than the other guy's.

Who does he think the best fighter in the league is?

"God, I would still have to say Tie Domi," Belak offers admiringly, looking across the dressing room at his teammate. "He is probably the most feared guy out there. He's a little pit bull—a little ball of muscle. He doesn't fight as much as he used to, just because he doesn't have to.... I wouldn't want to fight him."

The Saskatchewan native stands tall. But he is a big man in another sense: Belak admits to having experienced fear. In his first year in the league in 1996, the young scrapper played just five games with the Colorado Avalanche. One night, he found himself going toe-to-toe with Stu Grimson, a fighter so fierce everyone called him the Grim Reaper. "When he came after me it was a little nerve-racking," Belak recalls. "But once you're in it, there is nothing you can really do about it."

And how did it go?

"It was a draw. I was just trying not to get hit. I was bobbin' and weavin'," he says.

There are fighters in the NHL who seem to think the league is a glorified wrestling arena. They pump their hands in the air after combat and make other foolish gestures. Belak is not one of them.

"There is no glory in gloating," he insists. "You are not going to win every fight. And to go on about it when you do win, it's just going to bite you in the ass someday."

Considering the fact that Belak has spent nearly 1000 minutes in the penalty box over his 330-game career, he actually doesn't look too bad. He says he has had his nose broken a couple of times, once while he toiled in the minor leagues for the Hershey Bears (he does not remember who did it), and another time in the bigs when Colton Orr of the New York Rangers did the honours.

"It doesn't look bad actually," I say to Belak.

"No, it looks good," he says. "Beautiful."

"I wouldn't go that far," I joke, "but it's fine."

Belak disagrees. "I'm a beautiful guy," he says and we both start laughing.

On a later occasion, I ask Colton Orr if he knew he had broken Belak's nose. "I had an idea," he says, and smiles.

There may be no such thing as a "last laugh" in sports. Teams play so many games nowadays that the next rematch is usually never that far down the road. However, on December 19, 2006, the Maple Leafs enjoyed one of the most lopsided victories in the history of the franchise, a 9–2 romp over the New York Rangers. Within six minutes, the Leafs were already up 2–0 and trouble was in the air. Less than two minutes later, in an old-fashioned heavyweight tilt, Orr and Belak were beating each other's brains in.

"He forgot there was a puck out there," Belak said after the game. According to Belak, Orr had been baiting him for their first two shifts of the game, daring him to drop the gloves. Finally, Belak watched his teammates rush the puck toward the Rangers' net but when a scoring chance failed to material-ize, he took Orr up on the offer and grabbed him. Belak clearly scored more punches than Orr during the fight, then pushed Orr to the ice and ended up on top of him. At that moment, Orr was defeated, completely defenceless, and at the mercy of a man whose nose he had broken in a past encounter. I ask Belak why he declined to pummel his prostrate opponent in that instance.

"I could have hit him when he was down, but most guys don't," he said. So there is an honour and code among the game's tough guys. Tie Domi admitted as much when he told The Sports Network's Michael Landsberg that he once said to another tough guy after a bruising brawl, "I love ya, man."

"He's just doing his job," Belak said of Orr. "We got up 2–0 right away and he's trying to turn the momentum around."

In fact, Orr wasn't done. Later in the game, when the outcome was no longer in doubt, Belak says Orr "got in my face," baited him again, and tried to arrange a rematch. Belak declined. "I just told him to look at the scoreboard," he says.

Now that Tie Domi has retired, Wade Belak is unquestionably the best fighter on the Maple Leafs team. Off the ice, he is a laid-back, married father of two very young daughters. He has never met Colton Orr, except on the ice. Does he have any desire to meet him?

"Not really," Belak says. "We have nothing in common. He's years younger. I'm a family man."

Ever since the Philadelphia Flyers won back-to-back Stanley Cup titles in the mid-1970s by combining great goaltending (Bernie Parent), a few skill players (Rick MacLeish, Bill Barber, Reggie Leach, and Bobby Clarke when he wasn't spearing opponents), and a lot of over-the-top hooliganism (Dave "Hammer" Schultz, Bob "Hound Dog" Kelly, Don Saleski, and the list goes on), people who care about hockey have been urging the league to ban fighting. Wade Belak will not second the motion.

"I think the instigator rule should be banned," says Belak, referring to the rule that gives an extra two-minute penalty to the guy that starts the fight.

His rationale is not completely crazy. Belak has been around long enough to know that many NHLers have made their living by being "super-pests." They tend to be smaller than the guys who are fighters. They love to muck it up, and disturb the so-called skill players. In the old days, when a super-pest took liberties with one of the team's stars, the bodyguard could mete out frontier justice by putting the super-pest in his place—in other words, beat him up. Both players would get five minutes for fighting and that was that. Today, when the fighters try to take the law into their own hands, they often find themselves getting additional penalty time for "instigating." Thus, the fighter puts his own team in a manpower disadvantage by taking an extra two-minute minor penalty. He gets the same five minutes for fighting as his opposite number. And he quite possibly earns another ten-minute misconduct for trying do vigilante deterrence on ice. Except when the officials call it that way, deterrence fails and the super-pests win.

"That is how we protect our goal scorers from guys like that who run around and try to hit guys and don't back it up," says Belak.

Hockey has travelled some distance from the days of Philadelphia's Broad Street Bullies, when there was almost nothing spontaneous about the fights, and bench-clearing brawls were commonplace. But if the new rules have de-emphasized the importance of fighting, should the league simply take the next step and do what international hockey has done, namely ban fighting?

If you want to start a good fight, just ask anyone affiliated with the NHL whether fighting should be banned. Or ask the fans. You'll get a resounding no.

"I think there is a place for that type of aggression," says Rick Dudley, who was a decent scrapper during his nine seasons in the NHL and WHA. Dudley points out there are two game features that guarantee NHL fans will stand and watch: penalty shots and fights.

"It is a part of the game," Dudley insists. The Maple Leafs' Darcy Tucker plays the game today a lot like Rick Dudley did in the 1970s and '80s. Tucker had his best goal-scoring season ever in the year after the lockout. He potted 28 goals, racked up 100 penalty minutes, and had his share of fights. (Dudley's best year was 31 goals and 116 penalty minutes in 1974–75 in Buffalo.) Dudley says he understood that if he wanted to make it as a player in the NHL, he had to fight from time to time. Tucker seems to have come to the same conclusion. I always assumed that a guy who plays with such reckless abandon and is prepared to drop the gloves actually enjoyed it. Not so.

"I never liked fighting," Tucker insists. "I just did it out of necessity to stay in the league." Joe Nieuwendyk, who retired from the Florida Panthers last year, almost never fought in his career. And still, he would not ban hockey pugilism.

"It's just not a huge factor any more," he says. "I think there's still some people who enjoy seeing that, and it will never leave the game entirely."

Colton Orr is convinced that if fighting were banned from the game, players would simply find another form of intimidation and it would be worse.

"I think teams would take liberties. There'd be a lot more slashing and hacking," he says.

When it comes to fighting, European players have always been at a distinct disadvantage in the NHL. Fighting is banned in international hockey. If you fight, you don't simply sit in the penalty box. You're gone—out of the game. So for the past 30 years, when European-trained players came to the NHL, they had almost no fighting experience.

Take the case of Alexei Ponikarovsky. Born in Kiev, Ukraine, 27 years ago, the 6'4" 220-pounder certainly has the vital statistics to be able to hold his own in battle. But having come to the Toronto Maple Leafs from Moscow Dynamo, he never learned how to fight. He admired Russian players such as Alexander Mogilny and Pavel Bure, both of whom left Russian hockey to become huge stars in the NHL and were much smaller than Ponikarovsky. Neither player fought much at all. During his first full season with the Leafs, Ponikarovsky was assessed 52 penalty minutes in 86 regular season and playoff games—in other words, well under 1 minor penalty on average per game.

One night, during a particularly heated moment in a game between Toronto and Buffalo, Ponikarovsky's teammate Bryan McCabe collided with a Sabre after the whistle. Next thing you knew, everybody was pairing off and Ponikarovsky found himself with Rob Ray, the Sabres' own version of Tie Domi. Ray played more than 900 games in the NHL, most of them with the Sabres, amassing more than 3200 penalty minutes.

Ponikarovsky survived the encounter. "He can't reach me because he had a short reach," Ponikarovsky recalled. "I have longer arms, so I tried to keep him on distance and just threw a couple of punches and tried to wait for him to get tired." The strategy worked. Ponikarovsky and Ray fought to a draw. It still represents the Leaf forward's only fight in nearly 300 NHL games with Toronto.

"I still think that there are guys and moments in a game when a fight is the best remedy," says Blues assistant Brad Shaw, who was also an interim head coach of the New York Islanders. Shaw is an intelligent man, who usually does not resort to the rucksack of clichés that most coaches use when talking to the media. "Very seldom do these big guys hurt each other," Shaw says. "They both are so skilled at what they are doing that they do nothing but tire each other out and they can barely stand up after a minute and a half."

"But I think the pure guys, where they did nothing but fight ... I don't know if we'll ever see those guys again."

That would suit James Cullingham just fine. Cullingham is a professor at Seneca College's School of Communication Arts in Toronto. He is a former executive producer at the Canadian Broadcasting Corporation and has spent 20 years as an independent and network producer, writer, and documentary filmmaker. He is the kind of person Don Cherry has in mind when the outspoken former coach talks about the left-wing, espresso-sipping, downtown-Toronto crowd of hockey haters. Of course, Cullingham does not hate hockey at all. He loves it. But if Cullingham were commissioner, he would ban fighting outright.

"I think it reduces professional hockey in North America to the level of professional wrestling," he says. "It bespeaks our sort of weird, colonized sense of ourselves, that this national game has to feature fighting because that is what real men do. Well, actually, the best Canadian hockey players are women. And they don't fight."

The NHL has declined to ban fighting over the years, essentially for three reasons:

- First, hockey is the only major sport played in a relatively small, enclosed area, by combatants who are skating at each other at speeds unseen in any other sport. Bodies collide with incomparable ferociousness and when that happens, it is natural from time to time for tempers to flare.
- Second, despite the instigator rule, fighting is an important law-enforcement tool. If the league's superstars do not have bodyguards, the super-pests will take advantage of them with

impunity. The threat of being on the receiving end of a Tie Domi or Colton Orr punch is one of the few things that inhibits the pests from taking a run at Jason Spezza or Jaromir Jagr.

- Third, and most evident whenever a fight breaks out, the vast majority of fans in the building love watching a fight. They don't just tolerate it. They love it. They rise out of their seats. They cheer. The bloodlust kicks in. And if the hometown scrapper wins the bout, he is hailed as a conquering hero all the way to the penalty box.

James Cullingham takes issue with every one of these assertions. As to the first, he points out that football, like hockey, is a very violent game. Fighting is banned in football. Anyone who throws a punch is ejected. As a result, you almost never see any fights on the gridiron.

Acting as a devil's advocate, I counter Cullingham's argument by pointing out that there is so much more violence permitted under the rules in football that players do not have to resort to throwing punches. During the course of a typical football game, players are permitted within the rules to dive through the air at each other and pound their opponent mercilessly into the turf, which may look like a grassy field, but feels more like a concrete parking lot. The typical football play lasts only a few seconds. Then the play stops. The whistle blows. Everyone regroups. There is no flow in football as there is in hockey. As a result, the temperature of a football game does not typically rise as it does in a hockey game. Football does not unravel into fisticuffs very often as hockey indeed does, because so much madness and mayhem is already permitted by football's rules.

Cullingham is not convinced. As the father of three daughters, he thinks the NHL's tolerance of fighting sends a terrible signal to young people.

"I think that allowing fighting in professional hockey is inexcusable," he says.

Cullingham is distressed that on too many occasions, his students come to class and rather than discussing an impressive goal, they would prefer to rehash "that scrap they saw last night."

The broadcasters, he says, are just as guilty of fostering a climate where the fighter is admired more than the superstar. He points to simultaneous events that took place in March 2006 as a prime example. On the same day that the Leafs celebrated Tie Domi's 1000th NHL game, the Montreal Canadiens retired Bernie "Boom Boom" Geoffrion's number 5 at the Bell Centre. Geoffrion was one of the game's all-time greats, sometimes credited with inventing the slapshot, and at that moment, was confined to a hospital bed in Atlanta, where he was dying of stomach cancer. The Montreal ceremony, with Geoffrion's family in attendance, was moving, historic, and dramatic. And no one west of Montreal saw it on *Hockey Night in Canada*. Instead, they got the Domi celebration. Geoffrion's family attended the 40-minute ceremony in Montreal as Boom Boom died the same night.

"That says to me a lot about what the emphasis of the game has become," Cullingham said with evident disgust.

How about the notion that Wayne Gretzky's achievements would have been much more modest without his bodyguard Dave Semenko watching out for him on his left wing? Cullingham disagrees. He insists that with effective refereeing, bodyguards would be unnecessary. Furthermore, he says so many of today's fights are not at all spontaneous, but rather the result of two battlers jawing at each other, almost choreographing the fisticuffs to come.

"It is staged, like professional wrestling," he says. "The two guys decide, 'Okay, at some point we are going to go.'"

Steve Milton, the excellent hockey reporter for *The Hamilton Spectator,* did some research on hockey bouts and discovered that in the first year after the lockout, fighting was down 42 per cent, "proving once again that most brawls are scripted and not spontaneous."

New York Rangers assistant coach Mike Pelino thinks the new rules have taken care of the brawlers. Fighting is "down, still a part of the game but not a focus of the game. And that is just the way it should be…. It is more instinctive now as opposed to maybe, in recent years, it was a little bit more premeditated."

Evidence that the role of fighting has declined was put before Toronto hockey fans on October 30, 2006. That night, the Atlanta Thrashers were visiting the Air Canada Centre to play the Maple Leafs. The Thrashers were the better team on the night, peppering the Leaf net with 33 shots, compared to just 22 for the home side. But it was the Leafs who held a 4–2 lead late in the game. With just 20 seconds left, Thrasher defenceman Shane Hnidy (6'2", 210 pounds) took a run at the Leafs' Michael Peca (5'11", 190 pounds). Hnidy caught Peca looking the wrong way and tossed a vicious, blindside elbow at Peca's head. The Leaf forward collapsed to the ice. In the old days, that kind of cheap shot would have resulted in some kind of scrap if not a bench-clearing brawl. What happened on this night? Absolutely nothing. Hnidy was assessed a two-minute penalty for unsportsmanlike conduct, and the Leafs' largest player, Hal Gill (6'7",

240 pounds), who happened to be on the ice at the time, skated over to Hnidy and had a quiet word with the miscreant. And that was it. After the game, I asked Peca whether he was disappointed that no teammate punished his tormentor.

"It was too late in the game to do something about that," he insisted. "I felt a bit like the *Titanic* in open waters. I could see the iceberg coming, but couldn't get out of the way fast enough."

Peca added that there was no point risking a suspension or injury by having a teammate mete out frontier justice.

"You've gotta pick your spots these days," he added. "Besides, I know who did it. It's a long season."

I asked the Leafs' coach Paul Maurice about the incident. His answer smacked of new-NHL-speak.

"The referees are paid to protect the players," he said. "Peca's fine. The game's over. You've got to be a patient man."

"So, will someone have a conversation with Hnidy next time?" I asked.

Paul Maurice is a great interview, particularly when his team wins. He understands the theatre of the post-game press conference, the give-and-take between the coach and reporters. Even when reporters make silly or inane statements (as opposed to actually asking salient questions), he doesn't try to show anyone up, but rather responds almost always with a thoughtful comment. And when Maurice wants to be, he's funny, too. This was one of those times when he wanted to be.

"Michael Peca's fine," he repeated. "The game's over. There's no sense hanging over the boards and yapping at the other team with 20 seconds left."

Then, referring to his first comments when he did suggest the Leafs would be aware of Hnidy's number next time the teams played, Maurice added, "Now, I gave you a gift. There is no regifting here." In other words, "Paikin, I've said all I'm going to say on this," as the other reporters looked on and laughed.

Two days later, I spoke to the Leafs' general manager, John Ferguson, Jr. He also adopted the less-is-more approach.

"We've still got three more games against the Thrashers," Ferguson said, leaving it at that.

Except, the next time the Thrashers and Leafs met, it was one month later in Atlanta and despite badly outshooting the Thrashers, the Leafs lost 5–0. Even worse, Shane Hnidy's name was all over the official play-by-play sheet, having blocked opposing shots, taken three of his own at the Leaf net, launched some decent bodychecks, and been on the ice for one of Atlanta's goals. Doesn't sound like the Leafs exacted much revenge. One week later, the Thrashers defeated the Leafs again, this time 5–2 in Toronto. Hnidy was apparently so intimidated by his previous experience in Toronto that he blocked three shots, took three more on the Leaf net, and was on the ice for two of the goals his team scored against the Leafs. So much for "It's a long season."

NOW THAT TIE DOMI has retired, the "tough guy" duties on the Maple Leafs have fallen overwhelmingly to Wade Belak.

"Life without Tie?" Belak asks himself rhetorically, when I inquire about how the team is different without number 28. "When I first came here when I was 25 or 24, I learned how to take on that role from Tie. When the right time is to do it, he'd say, 'Be smart about it.' Now that he's gone, I feel I can use his knowledge to further enhance myself."

Keeping in mind that Belak is one of the class clowns on the Leafs, you can sense that when he utters the phrase, "use his knowledge," it is a little bit tongue in cheek. He's trying to make a serious point, but he also respects a dressing-room culture that says, "Don't get too serious when answering a serious question, particularly when there's a teammate watching." In this case, Darcy Tucker is right alongside Belak. You can feel the Abbott and Costello routine about to develop, and Belak is right on cue.

"Tie was a vocal part of our dressing room. Wouldn't you say so, Darcy?" he asks his teammate, who is now laughing and enjoying the show. "Tie usually threatened Darcy's life once a game. Tie's one of those guys who threatens people once a game. He was one of our vocal guys, one of our leaders in the room. Me and him kinda shared the duties. We don't miss him because he's on TV now. Hope he doesn't rip on us too much like some ex–hockey players do."

And has Belak heard how Domi likes his new life as a television commentator on TSN?

"He called me after the Ottawa game," Belak continues, now on a real roll. "He says it's good. Says it's frickin' easy. A cushy job. I don't blame him. Probably a lot easier than being a hockey player."

In case I still wasn't getting the picture, Belak happily explained the Mutt 'n' Jeff routine that is a feature of every hockey dressing room.

"Every team I've played on, everyone busts each other's balls pretty good," he says. "I think you need that atmosphere, where you can't take everything so seriously. You have to have fun and get in each other's kitchen and razz each other pretty well. Tie was always razzing us and we were always giving it back to him."

JAMES CULLINGHAM has stopped watching hockey. I tell him that's a shame, that the new rules have changed the game dramatically, and fighting is down significantly in the regular season (less than one fight on average per game now) and virtually non-existent in the playoffs.

"I think that is a good trend," he says. "I would still suggest doing away with it altogether. I would start watching hockey again because I love the game." Until that happens, Cullingham says, he'll stick with baseball.

"That's an ironic choice," I tell him. After all, there are more player brawls in baseball now than hockey. And if baseball has returned to the North American consciousness after its lost season in 1994, it did so in no small measure because lots of players cheated by using steroids.

Whether fighting does or does not have a place in hockey, this much is clear: there is very little pressure from society to get rid of it and Cullingham knows it.

"I think that there are a lot of people who would be fans, who could be brought back in (if fighting were banned), but I can't say there are a lot of people who share my views," he admits. "They clearly decided, with the crisis around the lockout, that speed was imperative, that opening up the ice was [paramount]. And I can't see how allowing fighting is consistent with that."

Detroit Red Wings' coach Mike Babcock has this reminder for those who would officially ban fighting from the game. Babcock was there, at the Joe Louis Arena, on January 2, 2007, when the Wings retired sweater number 19 for their brilliant captain Steve Yzerman. "Stevie Y" retired as the longest-serving captain of any team in NHL history. He won three Stanley Cups in Detroit, played for over two decades, all of it for one team, another extraordinary feat in pro sports today.

There were a number of Red Wing dignitaries at the ceremony to celebrate Yzerman's career, including the legendary Gordie Howe, Ted Lindsay, and Alex Delvecchio. However, Babcock asks, which player received the second-loudest cheers next to Yzerman? The answer was not Howe, who scored 1850 points in the NHL (and 508 more in the WHA). It wasn't Lindsay either, who played more than 1000 games in the NHL, most of them in a Red Wings uniform. Rather, the second most tumultuous crowd roar came after the introduction of a player who scored only 384 points in 935 games, but spent 3300 minutes in the penalty box and may have been the greatest fighter in NHL history: Bob Probert, fifth on the all-time list for penalty-minute leaders.

"Tell me anything you want," Babcock says about fighting. "I just listen to the people."

If the new rules were designed, in part, to reduce gratuitous wrestling-style fights in the NHL, then league officials have succeeded beyond what the vast majority of observers thought was possible. Tie Domi was the last of a breed. Colton Orr, whose fighting skills are among the best but goal-scoring prowess among the worst, spends most nights in the press box watching his team play. He appeared in only 35 regular season games and just one playoff game in the first post-lockout season. He no doubt was an intimidating presence on the ice. But on the score sheet, he contributed just 1 assist in those 35 games. Teams apparently can no longer afford to dress players like him.

Even though it has not been banned, as James Cullingham wants, fighting as an issue has gone away. Some observers think the NHL now needs to turn its attention to something far more urgent.

"I like a physical game," says Brad Shaw. "But I really think there are too many hits from behind, there are too many head shots and there are too many knees being stuck out on knees." Cheap shots and dirty play are the issue, he says, not fighting.

"The physicality is what I think appeals to the fans, and what appeals to me," Shaw says. "For a while this year, we kind of lost a little bit of that. I think it is coming back. But the physicality is something that always has to be there." Clearly, it will be. But without Tie Domi.

# THE UNITED NATIONS ON ICE

*Those who know nothing of foreign languages*
*know nothing of their own.*
—JOHANN WOLFGANG VON GOETHE

Imagine, if you will, being one of the very best in the world at your job. On a planet of 6 billion people, you are one of 700 who can do what you do. To perform your job effectively, however, it is essential that you be able to communicate instantly with your co-workers. The job is physically challenging. New problems requiring an urgent response emerge without warning. Now imagine not being able to understand most of what your compatriots are saying.

That is the challenge for a large number of players in today's National Hockey League.

The last time the Toronto Maple Leafs won the Stanley Cup, names such as Mikita or Toppazzini were still considered ethnically exotic. In those days, virtually all of the players in the NHL were born or raised in Canada. A small handful was from the United States. There were rare instances of well-known players, such as Stan Mikita of the Chicago Blackhawks or Ken Hodge of the Boston Bruins, who were born in Europe (in Mikita's case, Pardubice, Czechoslovakia; in Hodge's, it was Birmingham, England). But those players all grew up in Canada, spoke English as their first language, and no one considered them particularly foreign.

However, just as Canada became significantly more multicultural in the 1970s, so did the NHL. After their last, unlikely Stanley Cup victory in 1967, the Maple Leafs' fortunes went right into the dumper. Their mediocre status, however, may have made them more open to experimentation. One of the notions they considered was that every player in the NHL did not have to be born and raised on some farm in rural Canada. So the club risked further ridicule by welcoming a tall, wiry defenceman named Borje Salming from Kiruna, Sweden. And, as part of the same package, they also imported left-winger Inge Hammarstrom from Sundsvall, Sweden.

Swedes? In the National Hockey League? Sure, they played hockey in Sweden. But hockey over there certainly was not NHL calibre. And because the European ice surface was so much wider, the players almost never inflicted those punishing body checks on one another that NHL players were renowned for. And, of course, they never ever dropped the gloves.

It was a painful and difficult adjustment for the two players. In fact, physically, they were among the strongest players on the Leafs. (Rumour had it that Hammarstrom, despite his short stature, could outwrestle anyone in the dressing room.) But before long, other players and fans were calling them "chicken Swedes" because they refused to engage in NHL-style fighting. Even the Maple Leafs' owner, the always quotable Harold

Ballard, was frustrated at the tandem's unwillingness to fight. He accused Hammarstrom of being the kind of player who could go into the corner with six eggs in his pockets and emerge with not a single one cracked. (This was typical of the kind of "positive reinforcement" Ballard enjoyed using to get the best out of his players.)

But to almost everyone's surprise, Salming and Hammarstrom kept their heads down and simply took the abuse from their owner, the fans, and opposing players. Their persistence in the face of this ridicule made an important and lasting impact on the Leafs. Salming played 17 seasons in Toronto, scoring 794 points, and eventually retired from the NHL as the Leafs' all-time scoring leader for defencemen. But when he was elected to the NHL Hall of Fame in 1996, it was as much for being a pioneer in leading the European invasion of the NHL as it was for what he achieved on the blue line. Salming also became a second-team all-star, the first Leafs defenceman to be so honoured since Tim Horton. And while Hammarstrom did not leave the footprint that Salming did with both the Leafs and the league, he did score 116 goals and managed a very nice 7-year career in Toronto and St. Louis.

If the Salming–Hammarstrom experiment had failed, who knows how long other teams might have waited before venturing into foreign waters? Because their NHL careers were of varying success, before long other Europeans were making their way across the pond to play in the world's best hockey league. Sometimes, the circumstances were as dangerous and thrilling as a good John Le Carré novel.

In 1980, the Quebec Nordiques managed to sneak two marvellous hockey-playing brothers out of communist Czechoslovakia.

It was an intricately planned, dangerous mission that required the young men to hide in the trunks of cars and sneak through border checkpoints during the worst of the Cold War. Had the Nordiques' plan been foiled, the brothers would certainly have seen the inside of a jail cell, their hockey careers ended, and their families harassed. But ultimately, Peter and Anton Stastny (along with older brother Marian one year later) defected to the West and played some spectacular hockey for the Nords. Peter Stastny was inducted into the Hockey Hall of Fame in 1998, having scored 1239 points over 16 seasons.

Other players would follow, both by conventional means and through more cloak-and-dagger defections, to the point where Canadians make up just 62 percent of National Hockey League players today. Roughly 30 percent of NHL players come from Russia, Sweden, Finland, the Czech Republic, Slovakia, Ukraine, Lithuania, Belarus, Kazakhstan, Switzerland, and France. And most of them arrive with terrific hockey skills and less-than-stellar English.

I have often wondered how this sport can be played at such a high level when so many players on so many teams speak so many languages—English, French, Russian, Swedish, Finnish, Czech, Slovakian, and the list goes on. It is just another of the things that makes hockey unique—it's the United Nations of popular professional North American sports.

To be sure, pro football is more complicated than hockey. Players are required to memorize hundreds of plays, and many more of variations on those plays. But virtually every player comes to both the National Football League and Canadian Football League through a college or university program and English is their first language. The same is true of pro basketball, where the lion's share of players still come through a U.S. post-secondary education feeder system. However, it is interesting to note that basketball is now experiencing at the dawn of the 21st century the beginnings of a foreign invasion that the NHL initiated more than 30 years ago. The first overall pick (by the Toronto Raptors) in the 2006 National Basketball Association entry draft was Andrea Bargnani, who learned the game playing for Benetton in northern Italy. The NBA has also seen a decent-sized handful of exotic stars from far-flung places such as China's Yao Ming, Nigeria's Hakeem Olajuwon, Dikembe Mutombo from Congo (then Zaire), Manute Bol from Kenya, and Vlade Divac from the former Yugoslavia. But these players are still the exceptions in an overwhelmingly American game. The only other major pro sport in this part of the world that remotely comes close to hockey in its international flavour on club teams is baseball. (Soccer is another matter, but it's not yet a mainstream professional sport in North America.) For decades, but in particular over the past 25 years, Major League Baseball has put out the welcome mat for Latino players. Many of the game's biggest stars now have Spanish as a first language. But virtually all of them come to the big show with some knowledge of English, having played their minor league baseball in rural America. The newest wave of baseball players that might remotely resemble what hockey is experiencing comes from the Far East. Players such as Japan's Hideki Matsui of the New York Yankees, Ichiro Suzuki of the Seattle Mariners, or the latest phenom, Daisuke Matsuzaka of the Boston Red Sox, conduct their post-game interviews through interpreters. These men and a few others from Japan and Korea still represent just a tiny percentage of the more than 800 Major League Baseball players.

No, hockey is unique.

One thing that surprised me in talking to many NHL players about their ability to speak English was how readily they were prepared to talk about it. These players, like all professional athletes, are asked the same stale questions day in and day out ("How did it feel to score the big goal?" "What will you do now that your backs are to the wall?" "Are you going to have to gut it out in Game 7?"). For a change, they actually seemed to enjoy talking about one aspect of their game they have not yet mastered, namely their ability to communicate with their teammates and coaches in hockey's international language.

DARIUS KASPARAITIS is a pest. When he came to the NHL from his native Lithuania in 1992, he quickly established himself as a force to be reckoned with. Although not that tall for a defenceman (he is listed at 5'10") he is well known as a punishing body-checker—definitely not the kind of guy you want to skate into with your head down. Some opposing players have tried that, only to end up in a hospital ward recovering from a variety of broken bones.

Kasparaitis, born in 1972, is no longer the player he once was. His legs are still as massive as thick tree stumps. But he missed 15 games for the New York Rangers in the first post-lockout season thanks to an annoying groin injury that just refuses to heal. On this game day in March 2006, he takes part in a light afternoon skate. But it becomes quickly apparent that he is not healthy enough to be pencilled into the night's lineup. When I see him in the Rangers' dressing room after the practice session, he sports an enormous tensor bandage on his right thigh. In 2003–04, he missed more than half the season to injuries. When the body begins to break down at this stage of an athlete's career, the whispers begin. Am I on the downside of my career? Is this body ever going to heal? Do I actually have to consider retirement? The more serious the questions get, the lighter the tone in the dressing room becomes. So, when I ask Darius Kasparaitis, in the Rangers' dressing room, where he learned to speak English, his first response is to poke fun at the teammate next to him.

"He was my first teacher," he says, gesturing to the fellow beside him.

"I make all his musical selections too," the teammate says, referring to the boom box that is omnipresent in any professional sports locker room.

"Yeah, that's why I'm still listening to Styx and Journey," Kasparaitis replies, referring to a couple of rock 'n' roll bands whose best years were roughly 30 years ago.

The repartee may not be Burns and Allen, but it is instructive in this sense: before leaving Europe for the United States, Darius Kasparaitis did not speak one word of English. Not a word.

"I learn in locker room," he says. "I never took English lesson in my life."

(Because newspaper editors clean up the grammar in most every quote, not just those of foreign-born hockey players, readers probably have no sense of how hard these players have to struggle with their second language on a daily basis. We will not clean up the quotes, so you can read on hearing their authentic voices.)

Kasparaitis used to carry an English-language dictionary with him everywhere except on the ice. As was the case for all European players, he was matched up to room with a North

American teammate when his first club, the New York Islanders, went on the road. For five years, Scott Lachance, another defenceman, was his Isles roommate.

"I asked the question, 'What's that mean?' and 'Show me,'" Kasparaitis recalls of those early days. "And I just try to learn from people, you know?" One thing Kasparaitis had going for him that many foreign-born players do not is one of the game's most outgoing personalities.

"I was not shy to talk, you know what I mean? I look at my first interviews with Stan Fischler," he says, referring to the prolific New York author and journalist. "When I was playing for Islanders, my English language was so bad that it makes me laugh. But, you know, you have to go through that."

There are 30 head coaches in the National Hockey League. Twenty-eight of them were born in Canada. The other two are from the United States. Nearly one-third of the head coaches are francophone and so French is their first language. Of course, they all speak English as well. However, none knows anything more than "hello" and "goodbye" in any Scandinavian or Slavic language. Coaches coach in English and only English. So how did Kasparaitis get it?

"Well, it was tough in the beginning," he says, suddenly looking serious at the memory of it all. "We were just a sign language most of the time."

Vaclav Varada also remembers a much more difficult time in his hockey career. Like Kasparaitis, Varada has had a reputation of being one of the league's super-pests. He is not a particularly prolific scorer. But when he does score goals, it is usually the result of some mayhem he has caused in front of an opposing team's net or in the corners.

For 11 seasons, Varada played for the Buffalo Sabres and Ottawa Senators, before signing with Davos in Switzerland's top hockey league in August 2006. Varada first came to North America in 1994. His initial stop was Tacoma in the Western Hockey League. Season two saw him move north to the Kelowna Rockets in British Columbia.

"I was playing junior hockey and I couldn't even say anything," Varada recalls with a sensitivity I have never seen in him before, and certainly never on the ice. "So, it was difficult couple of years in junior for me."

How did he communicate?

"Pretty much didn't, you know?" he admits.

The coaches continually gave Varada special attention, pulling him aside, diagramming plays on their Magic Marker boards. When that did not work, Varada tried being anonymous.

"I try to hide in the lines and wait, you know, go as the last guy not to screw up the drills, you know?" he says sheepishly.

Varada received no formal English lessons from the Sabres, his first NHL team. His English teachers were his teammates.

"I just picked up from the guys in the room and I learn it on my own," he says.

His first roommate, Dallas Thompson, was also an enormous asset. Thompson is now the general manager of junior hockey's Prince George Cougars in the WHL.

"I stay in contact with him still and, you know, he was my big brother," Varada says.

Kasparaitis, too, would always let the other players go first when it came to practising drills he could not initially understand. Between the coach's diagrams and the example set by his teammates, eventually he figured it out. Plus, assistant coaches (whose sole job is to analyze video and point to flaws in one's game on a television monitor) often help to get the point across.

Are there ever moments when, even with the assistance of a coach's diagram or video screen, a player still has no clue what is going on?

"I think that even happens to the guys who are really good at English," says Alexander Steen of the Toronto Maple Leafs, whose father Tomas was one of the first Swedish players to make the NHL. The elder Steen played from 1981 to 1995 for the Winnipeg Jets and was the first European-born player to have his number retired (an honour bestowed in Winnipeg just before the Jets moved south to Phoenix).

Kasparaitis's head coach with the New York Rangers is Tom Renney. Originally from Cranbrook, British Columbia, Renney coached Canada's 1994 men's Olympic hockey team. He might legitimately be regarded as the secretary-general of this year's United Nations of the NHL. More than half of his players were born outside North America, giving the Rangers one of the highest Euro-quotients in the league.

"There is sort of a philosophy around the Swedes. There is a philosophy that the Finns embrace. There is a philosophy that the Russians play with. There is a philosophy that the Czechs play with," Renney explains.

Renney's significant international hockey experience has given him insights into the various European styles of play, and going further, the European player's mindset. Does Renney speak any other languages?

"No," he says. "I have some phrases here and there in most languages, but that is about it."

Most NHL players have what one might call the classic hockey player's build. They are tall and muscular, with the unusual combination of massive legs and big, soft hands. Even most fighters have soft hands. But, for all their obvious toughness, in this macho environment of towel-snapping young men, it is worth remembering that almost all of them, at some point in their hockey careers, have suffered from homesickness, particularly the European players.

Even Canadian hockey players suffer from homesickness. Barely into their teenage years, they are plucked from cities and small towns across Canada, and sent to billet with other families, often hundreds of miles from home. The junior hockey system prepares the best and luckiest of them for a career in the NHL. However, at least those young Canadians speak the language and understand the culture in their new homes. Foreign-born players have no such advantage. They find themselves thousands of miles from home, with only a few rudimentary English words, and suffering from complete culture shock. Most of them, upon arrival, have never used an ATM before. There is a lot to adjust to.

"Nothing I could do about it," Vaclav Varada remembers of the feelings of homesickness at the beginning of his North American hockey adventure. "I just battled through it."

Darius Kasparaitis also faced bouts of homesickness, first when he left his native Lithuania for Moscow, and then after he moved to New York to play for the Islanders. Fortunately, the large Russian community at Brighton Beach in Brooklyn was only half an hour away from the Islanders' home arena, the Nassau County Coliseum.

"Any time I want to go have Russian food or Eastern European food, I used to go there and shop there, and buy stuff,"

Kasparaitis recalls. "Everybody spoke Russian. That was kind of close to home … close as you can get."

Kasparaitis now has a 9-year-old daughter who lives in Florida with her Russian-speaking mother. Like her father, Kasparaitis's daughter will be trilingual: she speaks Russian, English, and Spanish.

While I would never suggest foreign-born players are more anxious than their North American teammates to see the season come to an end, one has to acknowledge that they must look forward to the off-season even more than the Canadians and Americans. Some of them have now made Canada or the United States their permanent homes. However others cannot wait to reconnect with their family and friends in the Old World. Ales Kotalik of the Buffalo Sabres is one such player.

"Oh, yeah," he smiled, when I asked whether he was going back to the Czech Republic at season's end. "I'm catching the first flight to go home." Kotalik has neither a wife nor children awaiting his return to Europe. He just wants to go home.

Where Darius Kasparaitis found himself a decade and a half ago, Rostislav Olesz finds himself today. The Czech-born forward could not understand a thing when he was made the Florida Panthers' first-round draft pick in 2004. He was utterly clueless when his coach barked out instructions. Now, he says, "I don't have problem understand what he wants and what he means."

Olesz did study English in school but it was British English, not the U.S. version. One of the first things he grasped when he came to the States was that Brit and U.S. English are indeed very different.

"Is big different than what I learn in school," he says. "It was just basic and a couple of words which I don't need here."

Olesz, like so many National Hockey League players today, builds extra time into his off-ice schedule to take English lessons. The Panthers arrange for as many as three hours a week of instruction, the team's travel schedule permitting. Where the use of English for most teams is important for obvious reasons, it is even more important in places such as Florida, where players have the added responsibility of selling the game to a community that is largely unfamiliar with hockey.

Olesz's coach, Jacques Martin, impeccably bilingual in French and English, points out that "some of the terminology, in hockey is universal."

The Sabres' Kotalik agrees. The Czech native from Jindr Hradec, two hours south of Prague, came to North America in 2001, knowing all the important words: *skate, shoot, score, face-off, icing,* and *stickhandle.*

"The first things what you hear what you learning over here is like hockey, hockey, hockey," he says. "Hockey words."

When Alexei Yashin joined the NHL with the Ottawa Senators in 1993, he was representative of the kind of Russian player whose skating, puck-handling, and shooting skills were a joy to behold. He also had his moments when he was in a fog after hearing his coach's instructions.

"Like, for example, he tells you, 'We're going to have a scrimmage today.' And 'scrimmage,' I didn't understand what a scrimmage was," Yashin recalls. "But you learn very quickly." Yashin adds that European players are particularly dependent on their roommates to help them over the language bumps. In his case, Mark Lamb and Dave McIlwain of the Senators were his guides.

(Ironically, one of the gains some players made in the most recently negotiated collective agreement may represent a step backwards for English proficiency. More players are now entitled to a private hotel room when they go on the road, thus potentially ending the custom of the anglophone roommate tutoring his foreign-born teammate.)

The Maple Leafs recently have gone far beyond Scandinavia in their search for new talent. For the past several years, they have featured a player who grew up, of all places, in Kazakhstan. When he was a child in Ust-Kamenogorsk (not too far from the Chinese border—not your typical hockey outpost), Nik Antropov spoke Russian at home, but took English lessons two or three times a week in school. At least, he was supposed to.

"I didn't really pay attention to them," he now confesses. "When I came over here, I said I should have learned, but I didn't."

Antropov is one of those players who has tested the patience of Maple Leaf fans. He is a strapping 6'5", but has never developed into the dominating player he occasionally shows he is capable of becoming. Numerous knee injuries have hampered his progress. In 2006–07, yet again, Antropov missed nearly 30 games due to injury. But when he returned, he played perhaps his best hockey as a Leaf, finishing with 18 goals—impressive enough for the Leafs to give him a new 2-year contract at season's end.

However, one wonders whether his inability to understand anything his coach or most of his teammates were saying had something to do with Antropov's slow development.

"My first two, two and a half years, I was just so shy, like most of the players who is coming over here, just shy to pronounce some words," Antropov says. "If you do pronounce them and it is wrong, you kind of close it up in yourself."

As was the case with Kasparaitis, Antropov's teammates both teased him mercilessly for his troubles with English, but also helped him get better. He also has had as many as seven teammates who speak Russian and could also help translate. Today, at age 27, he speaks with a thick Russian accent, but confidently, if not always with grammatical precision.

Antropov left his Kazakh home in 1998 for a year's stay in Moscow. The Leafs then brought him to Canada, where he has lived full-time ever since. He speaks only Russian at home with his wife and two young children, whose English is already better than his.

Antropov's teammate, Alexei Ponikarovsky, began taking English lessons at age 10 in his native Ukraine, and unlike Antropov, he came to North America having paid attention. Ponikarovsky's birthplace is Kiev, his passport is Ukrainian, his first language is Russian, his second Ukrainian, and his English is good as well. He can also speak smatterings of Finnish and Czech because teammates from those countries have tried to teach him the odd expression or two. And since Polish is close to Ukrainian, he can dabble in that as well. There have been moments in practice when he failed to grasp something the coach was saying. But within a year and a half, he understood everything. Perhaps coincidentally, Ponikarovsky's play has improved more than Antropov's during his time in Toronto.

And how would Antropov and Ponikarovsky's teammates evaluate their progress in the language department?

"With the exception of Tomas Kaberle, everyone speaks pretty good English," says Wade Belak, referring to his Czech-born defensive colleague. "Kaberle's English gets worse every year. I think he's been here eight years. We razz him all the time about it." In fact, one of the rarest sights in the Maple Leafs' dressing room is Tomas Kaberle giving interviews. This is not because he lacks accomplishments. He was the highest-scoring defenceman on the Leafs in the 2005–06 season, and in February 2006, was re-signed to a huge 5-year $21.25-million contract. But he has yet to master the sound bite for TV sports. One Leaf teammate who could not be razzed for his English was the team's backup goaltender in 2005–06. Michael Tellqvist, originally from Sundbyberg, Sweden, began taking English lessons in the third grade. He came to North America in 2001 and supplemented his formal education by checking out U.S. television programs such as *Friends, Seinfeld,* or *American Idol.* "I watched those shows and read the subtitles," he says. Today, his English is as good as any native-born Canadian or American. (I was astonished at how rapidly he answered my questions and how unaccented his English is.)

When your dressing room resembles the United Nations, locker-room razzing quickly focuses on ethnicity. Alexei Ponikarovsky is an ideal target. Born in Ukraine, ethnically Russian, with a teammate and friend from Kazakhstan, his lineage is a frequent subject for satire.

"Because it used to be USSR, now everybody separated," Ponikarovsky explains. "So it's all a whole bunch of other republics. So it is kind of confusing for them to understand."

In several different NHL dressing rooms, I asked dozens of different players born outside North America whether the ethnic teasing ever goes too far. It's possible to imagine that some players may be sensitive about where they come from. After all, one of the league's best players, Jaromir Jagr, has always worn number 68 on his back, a reference to the year Russian tanks invaded his native Czechoslovakia and put down the democracy movement that was known as Prague Spring. "I was very close with my grandmother, and my grandfather died in 1968 during the revolution," Jagr told me. "I decided to wear the number if I have the choice. The communists took everything from us, so I knew all the history."

It seems reasonable to ask whether, for example, Czech and Russian players ever have difficulty getting along. Or Czech and Slovak players. Or Swedish and Finnish players. Every player with whom I raised this possibility looked at me with the same confused look. "No. No. No. No. That never happens. It never happens," says an incredulous Swede, Alexander Steen.

I remind him that in the early 19th century, Russia invaded his ancestral homeland. Does he have no residual discomfort with Russian-born players?

"No. We don't look back at history like that. No, no, no. That's a million years ago."

"The game is the common denominator," says Tom Renney, Jagr's coach in New York. "The jersey that you wear that particular night is what it's all about. I have always been very, very impressed with the respect the European players show each other."

In fact, Darius Kasparaitis sees the plethora of nationalities as a strength for his New York Rangers.

"Our team has so many cultures, it is so good because of that, you know?" he says. "Yes, sometimes we make fun of nationalities but most time you just bring the best hockey you can bring to win a hockey game."

And how does he make fun of others players' nationalities?

"Like, Swedish, you know, we call them meatballs," Kasparaitis says. "And I usually make Russian people, say 'borscht,' 'vodka.' Playing with food."

The first post-lockout season of NHL hockey was also an Olympic year, so the Swedish players would razz the Finns, who would razz the Canadians, who would razz the Russians, and on it went.

The beauty of hockey is that, as much as coaches want to teach systems and diagram plays, a great deal of what happens on the ice is improvised. The game's fluidity and speed ensure that a lack of facility in English need not be the end of the world.

"Once the puck drops, you just see a guy open, you pass it to him," says former Sabre and Senator Vaclav Varada. "You just pretty much need to know the name of the player you're playing with and kind of build a relationship like that."

"The common denominator is respect," adds Tom Renney. "Just understand that they are very, very good hockey players, they are good men, and if you treat them that way, more than likely your investment in time and effort and trouble usually pays dividends."

"When you make a commitment to understand somebody, you will," Alexei Yashin says. "It doesn't matter like what kind of language they speak, you know?"

If only the real United Nations worked that smoothly.

# SELLING HOCKEY
# WHERE THERE'S NO ICE
# BUT COOL CUSTOMERS

*Snobbish Canadian hockey fans (even myself) refer to Raleigh*
*(North Carolina) as NASCAR Country. Why would hockey*
*succeed in a place that is known to us for watching people*
*drive around an oval and turn left for three hours?*
—JES GÖLBEZ, HOCKEY RANTS BLOGGER

It is a constant annoyance to hockey fans north of the Canada–U.S. border. Hockey is our damned game, and yet no National Hockey League team based in Canada has won the Stanley Cup since the Montreal Canadiens in 1993.

It would be one thing if teams in Boston, New York, or Chicago were winning the Cup. If that were the case, we could take some solace from the fact that true hockey fans, who have followed those teams for up to eight decades, were welcoming the arrival of the most impressive trophy in all of professional sports to their well-established hockey towns. But the sad truth—at least, sad for traditionalists of the game—is that some very un-hockey-like locales have been vying for, and becoming the custodians of, Lord Stanley's mug in recent years.

It all started in 1996 when the Colorado Avalanche captured the trophy. Three things didn't sit right about that. First, the team was moved to Colorado only because the Nordiques couldn't make a financial go of it in Quebec City. They played in a small arena (Le Colisée), which, while usually full, couldn't generate the revenues needed to keep up with escalating player salaries. And so, what rightly should have been a triumph for Quebec, whose hockey roots go back a century, instead turned into a very nice party for Denver, which had supported its champions for a grand total of one year. That just did not seem fair.

Second, the Avalanche defeated—wait for it—the Florida Panthers four games to none in the Stanley Cup final. The Florida Panthers? What in heaven's name was a team, only three years old, playing in an antiquated arena in Miami, doing in the finals? That just did not seem right.

And finally, what was Colorado doing with a hockey team anyway? They had been awarded a franchise before—and it had failed. The Kansas City Scouts moved to Denver in 1976, were renamed the Colorado Rockies, and continued to flounder. (At least they floundered with pizzazz, as they hired the inimitable Don Cherry to be their head coach for 1979–80.) But in 1982, with little local interest and losses mounting, the team left the Rockies for East Rutherford, New Jersey, and became the Devils, where they have prospered on the ice, winning three Stanley Cups. How could the hockey gods allow Denver, a city that had already rejected hockey once, to enjoy a Stanley Cup championship in the first season that the transplanted Canadian team played there?

Definitely not fair.

But something curious was happening in the central and southern United States, not just in Colorado. In the mid-1990s, the North Stars took "North" out of their name, left Minnesota, and relocated deep in the heart of Texas, becoming the Dallas Stars. In 1999, yet another southern team transplanted from a northern hockey city, won the Cup, as the Stars defeated the Buffalo Sabres four games to two.

It gets uglier. The worst franchise in all of professional sports, the Tampa Bay Lightning, got a whole lot better and defeated the Calgary Flames to capture the Cup in 2004. Tampa Bay as the centre of the hockey world? Give me strength.

But the hockey gods weren't finished messing with us. The Cup then went to Mayberry. In 2005–06, the first post-lockout season, the Carolina Hurricanes became champs by defeating the Edmonton Oilers, in another thrilling seven-game series. It wasn't even the Hurricanes' first trip to the finals. They had actually been there before in 2002. Two trips to the Stanley Cup final in four years for a team south of the Mason–Dixon Line? And I haven't even mentioned the fact that Stanley moved west to California in 2007, thanks to a superb playoff performance by the champion Anaheim Ducks.

For traditionalists, this was just about enough. Of the 10 Stanley Cup winners in the period from 1997 to 2007, only the three-time champion Detroit Red Wings could be said to represent a real hockey town. The New Jersey Devils won two Cups in the same period, but the horned ones are always an afterthought in the tri-state area. When you think hockey in New York, New Jersey, or Connecticut, you think of the Rangers or the Islanders. One tends not to think of East Rutherford, New Jersey, and the same will be true even when the Devils move to Newark for the 2007–08 season.

Five times in the last decade, Stanley has gone south—I mean both deep south and out west—to parts of the United States where there's generally no snow or ice, and hockey is less popular than professional football, high school football, arena football, baseball, basketball, auto racing, horse racing, bowling, and probably tiddlywinks as well.

By all rights, hockey should be popular in the American south. Above all else, folks stateside love a winner and the Carolina, Tampa, and Dallas teams have, at various times, been winning. And yet, hockey's hold on the Sunbelt is tenuous at best.

Like any politician running for president of the United States, NHL decision-makers have long held that the key to the league's future prosperity is a "southern strategy." For decades, the most consistent truism of U.S. presidential politics has been that you cannot take the White House without winning the South. The NHL has taken that message to heart. The league knows it can be a successful national operation in Canada, and a regional operation in the northeastern United States, and chunks of the rest of the U.S., such as Chicago and Denver. But to be considered a genuine American sport such as football, baseball, or basketball, hockey has to create a significant fan base in places such as Atlanta, Nashville, Phoenix, Raleigh-Durham, Tampa Bay, and Fort Lauderdale. Hockey in the Sunshine State? It seems laughable. But if the NHL is to remain a 30-team, big-time professional sports league, it must learn not only to survive but also to prosper in the southern states.

Florida is one of the fastest growing of the 50 American states and Broward is the fastest-growing county in the state. Half an hour west of Fort Lauderdale, along Highway 595, you take the exit for Northwest 136th Avenue and arrive in Sunrise, a picturesque little town of about 90,000. A 10-minute drive off the interstate brings you to a spectacular yet typical South Florida scene: a beautiful, winding boulevard lined with tall palm trees, magnificently manicured lawns and not a single scrap of garbage. Because the boulevard snakes back and forth, South Florida's hockey palace sort of sneaks up on you. You turn a corner and, suddenly, there it is in a huge open area with parking for thousands of cars. Not exactly Maple Leaf Gardens, which was in the middle of a bustling downtown area, right at the intersection of a subway and streetcar line. But beautiful in its own South Florida kind of way.

Oh, and one more thing: The temperature is an un-hockey-like 32 degrees Celsius. Are these the conditions in which hockey was meant to be played?

Okay, maybe I should keep my snobbish, Canadian attitudes about hockey to myself and try to have an open mind. Could it be a good thing to play hockey in what we traditionally think of as suntanning weather?

I first put the question to Gary Roberts, arguably the quintessential Canadian hockey player.

Born in Toronto's northern suburb of North York in 1966, Roberts still strikes fear into opposing players with his punishing forechecking. He won the Stanley Cup in 1989 with the Calgary Flames, wearing number 10 in tribute to his favourite player, the Montreal Canadiens' Guy Lafleur.

Roberts also spent 4 years in Toronto where he switched to number 7—his regular number 10 had been taken by Gary Valk. "I am not the type of guy that is going to ask [a new teammate] for his number," Roberts says. So he called former Maple Leaf star Lanny McDonald, with whom he had played on the victorious Calgary team, and asked the moustachioed one if he objected to Roberts borrowing McDonald's old number 7. McDonald said he would be honoured. Roberts became a fan favourite, scoring 83 goals over 4 seasons in blue and white and helping lead a string of Leaf playoff runs, even if they never made it to the finals.

Roberts surprised and disappointed Leaf fans when, before the 2005–06 season, both he and teammate Joe Nieuwendyk skipped Toronto for the sunny south.

"I didn't ever think I wouldn't be a Toronto Maple Leaf," Roberts says. "But, unfortunately, John never gave me that opportunity."

"John" was the Leafs' rookie general manager John Ferguson, Jr., who would have kept Roberts with the team at the right price, but was less interested in the talented but injury-prone Nieuwendyk. The pair, lifelong friends, wanted to stay together. Florida's general manager at the time, Mike Keenan (Calgary's newly minted head coach for 2007–08), thought Roberts's grit and experience, combined with Nieuwendyk's three Stanley Cup rings (for three different teams—Dallas, New Jersey, and Calgary—an NHL first), would give a much-needed boost to his young and inexperienced Panther team. So he snapped up the pair, leaving Ferguson wondering what had hit him.

Keenan's faith in the tandem was well placed. Although Roberts lost 24 games to injury, he still managed 14 goals and 40 points in his first season in Florida, while providing leadership in the dressing room. And all the 39-year-old Nieuwendyk did was score 26 goals—not bad for a guy the Leafs felt was washed up.

"It has worked out great," Nieuwendyk confirmed at the time. "It has been nice to be playing somewhere with your lifelong friend, and I think we have gelled nicely here.... This team has a lot of young players so any kind of leadership we can provide for them and some of our past experience has been beneficial."

Roberts and "Nieuwy," as he's nicknamed, played together on the ice and also lived close to each other off the ice.

"I went over to Joe's and we had a barbecue and, you know, it's 75, 80 degrees at 6 o'clock at night," Roberts says, acknowledging the off days are far more enjoyable. "You can have a hot tub outside and lounge by the pool."

Roberts was with the Flames when he temporarily retired from the NHL after playing just 8 games in 1994–95, and 35 more the following year. His long sabbatical—much of 1995 through 1997—ultimately did him a world of good. He successfully recovered from a broken neck. And his workout program took his physical condition to a new level. Roberts now says the best thing about the weather in Pantherland is what it can do for your body between games—as long as you're careful.

"Sitting out in 80-degree weather all day and having to play a hockey game isn't the healthiest thing for you either," he says. "But definitely, I find it is easier to regenerate between games when you have a nice sunny day out there and you can go home and enjoy it a little bit."

Nieuwendyk agrees: "I prefer that [the warm weather] at this point in my career over the alternative of the minus 20s and the slushy snow," he says, still wearing the familiar number 25 he first wore at Cornell University.

Is the weather that big a deal in Florida? Sean Burke, the veteran Canadian goaltender, who has played in both Phoenix and Tampa Bay, observes, "Once you get to the rink and you get in closed doors, everything is the same. It is just nice when you come out of the building."

But the Florida sun can play mind games with you. It just doesn't feel like hockey weather.

"As a player you wake up in the morning and you look out and it's sunny and warm and to me that kind of energizes you," says Panthers coach Jacques Martin. "I think that is a positive side of the game for a player."

What does his counterpart for the New York Rangers say a day after flying in from the frigid north to the sunny south? "I wasn't so disappointed that it was cloudy and a little bit rainy last night, to tell you the truth," jokes Tom Renney, meaning that any advantage the Panthers might have enjoyed by being used to the hot weather had disappeared. However, Renney adds, "Actually, when I drove in to the practice this morning, about 7:30, after a wake-up call with clear blue skies, you know, I wasn't so disappointed with that, either."

If you turn on Fox TV in South Florida on game day, you'll encounter the smiling face of Denis Potvin. Potvin won four consecutive Stanley Cups with the New York Islanders from 1980 to 1983. Until Paul Coffey came along and surpassed Potvin's individual achievements, many hockey people considered Potvin the second-best offensive defenceman of all time, behind only Bobby Orr. When Potvin's former general manager on Long Island, Bill Torrey, came to Florida to assume the presidency of the brand new Panther franchise, he urged his former stalwart on the blue line to join him as the colour commentator on the Panther broadcasts. Potvin had spent 23 years in the New York area both as a player and as a broadcaster. He was ready for a change.

It was an odd adjustment for Potvin, who grew up in Ottawa, still speaks fluent French, and returns to Quebec with his New Yorker wife and children during the summer off-season. He came to Florida in 1993 and has been a part of every Panther game-day broadcast since then. He recalls what it was like the first day he got dressed for work in his suit and tie in his air-conditioned home.

"And by the time I got to the car I was already perspiring," Potvin says. "And I thought, 'This is awful.' But I have gotten used to it now and the blood has thinned out a little bit and I think it is a wonderful way to make a living, don't you?"

IT IS MARCH 2006 and a great time to be following the exploits of the Florida Panthers. Despite getting off to a terrible start in this first post-lockout season, the Panthers have transformed themselves into an exciting, cohesive, up-and-coming hockey team that's put together the league's best winning streak. Instead of languishing near the bottom of the Eastern Conference, they're now making a genuine bid for a late-season playoff berth.

Professional sports teams can come up with a multitude of reasons for losing but the Panthers' explanation was unique. Eleven games into the season, Hurricane Wilma struck Florida. The club had to cancel some home games and was forced to spend an extended period on the road. The players, who crave focus and abhor distractions, simply couldn't concentrate on the task at hand.

"For a lot of the players' wives and kids, that was difficult to handle," recalls Jacques Martin. But eventually, order was restored, and the team regrouped and started putting a scare into their opponents.

The Panthers will have a busy week here in Sunrise, hosting three games over five days. Tonight, their cross-state rivals, the Tampa Bay Lightning, are the opponents. Then the Washington Capitals come to town. The Caps are one of the worst teams in the NHL this year. But they feature a sensational Russian player, Alexander Ovechkin (who will claim the Calder Trophy as the league's best rookie over his archrival, Sidney Crosby of the Pittsburgh Penguins). Then, the week ends with a real treat—not just an Original Six team, but the New York Rangers, who have a solid fan base of their own in South Florida, and are surprising everyone with their strong play.

When I look at the game against the Lightning from a sportswriter's point of view, a few important storylines are apparent. The all-Florida battle is a good angle. The fact that the Lightning won the Stanley Cup the last time hockey was played should also pump up interest. And there is a survival angle. It is Tampa Bay that stands between the Panthers and the final playoff spot, which the Lightning now possess. All the elements are in place for a memorable hockey experience this night.

Except for one thing. With less than an hour to go until game time, there is absolutely no buzz around the arena. There is no gauntlet of ticket scalpers outside the arena to wade through. No hot dog vendors. No one peddling souvenirs. There is no noise. No sense that something urgent is about to take place inside this colossal building. It is just so damned serene, my hockey antennae are completely discombobulated.

"You know when it's game day in Toronto," says Gary Roberts. "You can feel the buzz in the arena, you can feel the buzz around the Air Canada Centre. It isn't the same buzz down here. I think, mentally, it is even tougher to come to the rink and prepare yourself to play."

Several weeks later, when the Panthers' travels take them to Toronto, I ask Whitby native Joe Nieuwendyk to compare the buzz in southern Ontario to southern Florida.

"There is definitely a different atmosphere in Toronto," Nieuwendyk says. "You can't escape hockey here. It is in the papers, it's in the media. There's a lot of kids walking around with jerseys. Hopefully Florida will get that way as well."

Early in the day, Roberts and his Florida teammates get put through their paces in an early afternoon game-day skate at the ACC. It is unlikely there is a single person watching this practice who doesn't recognize number 10. That is not always the case at his home arena in Sunrise, where on two occasions the security guards refused to grant Roberts entry to the facility because he had forgotten his identification badge and they had no idea who he was.

"That didn't happen in Toronto," Roberts laughs.

The home of the Panthers is called the BankAtlantic Center. It is a dull name for a fine facility. The building seats almost 19,000 spectators. The sightlines are all good and the amenities are just what you would want for a night out with the family. Two years earlier, this same building was called the Office Depot Center. Its original name was the National Car Rental Center. Apparently, the days of one building having one name are over.

Game time arrives and the BankAtlantic Center is only half full. Nevertheless, the home side puts on an inspired performance, worthy of a team fighting for its playoff life. After two periods, the Panthers lead 5–1 and appear to have the game fully in hand.

I strike up a conversation in the press box with injured Tampa goalie Sean Burke. I point out that despite the fact his team is going to lose, it has actually been a pretty entertaining game.

"We can come back," he insists. "We've got the offence to do it."

I'm thinking, of course, he has to say that. But his team is on the road, down by four goals with only one period left to play, and facing one of the best goalies in the league in Roberto Luongo. This game is over.

As we continue our conversation, the Lightning's Martin St. Louis pops in a pair of goals fairly early into the third period. It is now 5–3.

"Well, at least your side is trying to make it interesting," I say to Burke.

And then the unthinkable happens—at least for the home side. Florida allows two more goals and suddenly the game is tied 5–5 with 9 minutes still to play. Tampa continues to pound the Florida net and at the end of regulation time, it is the home side that should feel fortunate to still be alive.

While we wait for the overtime period to begin, I cannot resist asking Burke whether what he said earlier—that he felt his team could come back—was really a reflection of what he believed at the time. He smiles and shakes his head. And yet, here we are, going into overtime. Comebacks are also a part of the new NHL.

With less than two minutes to play in overtime, the Panthers' best player, Olli Jokinen, bursts in on the Tampa goal on a break-away and calmly fires a wrist shot between the pads of Lightning goaltender Gerald Coleman. Game over. Home side wins the sixth of its last seven games. The playoff dreams remain alive. Panther coach Jacques Martin will joke after the game that his team is supposed to be in the entertainment business and there is no denying the game was entertaining. It was also the kind of game that gives coaches grey hair.

Management might be getting grey hair too. There were almost 8000 empty seats at the BankAtlantic Center for an important game against the Panthers' intra-state rival. All those who doubt that hockey can make it in Sunrise just got a major boost for their side of the argument.

"It is a matter of us being a competitive team, being an elite team, and I think the fans and the corporate people are going to support us," says Jacques Martin optimistically, although not totally convincingly.

Having seen this before as a member of the Dallas Stars, Joe Nieuwendyk is unperturbed.

"I have noticed in the one year that I have been here, there are more and more kids playing hockey on the streets out where I live, and I see the rinks filling up with minor hockey kids," he says. "It was the same way in Dallas. And now you go to Dallas and there are rinks everywhere and there is minor hockey everywhere."

Martin Gelinas, now a Panther, but a former member of the Carolina Hurricanes, has seen the same thing happen in the Raleigh-Durham area.

"My neighbours knew nothing about hockey," Gelinas recalls. "They came to a game. And now some of the kids in the neighbourhood are playing hockey. They know quite a bit about hockey; they are becoming knowledgeable about the game. They will learn."

"It is tough to go out there and see empty seats, no doubt about it," admits Gary Roberts. "Hopefully, this organization is going to do some things off the ice and bring the kind of people into this organization that they need to bring in order to draw more fans."

THE FLORIDA PANTHERS entered the National Hockey League in 1993 thanks to the enormous effort (and bank account) of Wayne Huizenga. At the time of the team's inception, every time you rented or purchased a video from Blockbuster, you were putting more money in Wayne Huizenga's pocket. He eventually sold Blockbuster, which he founded, for $8.4 billion. His corporate empire has also included Waste Management Inc., the largest waste-disposal company in the world, and AutoNation, the largest car retailer in the United States with annual sales of $19 billion. But Huizenga, like many extremely wealthy North Americans with a healthy ego, learned that it's hard to be famous if the businesses you own deal in garbage. But, buy a professional sports franchise and suddenly every word you say may as well have been delivered from Mount Sinai.

Huizenga now owns the most important sports franchise in Florida history, the Miami Dolphins of the National Football League. The Dolphins have won two Super Bowls, and competed in two more, although not while Huizenga owned the team. He bought the Dolphins in 1994 for $138 million. Today, *Forbes* magazine estimates the franchise's value at $856 million. He also used to own the Florida Marlins of Major League Baseball, but sold them when he couldn't convince Miami's politicians to spend public tax dollars to build him a new stadium. When the NHL rolled out its southern strategy, Huizenga bought in. His first call was to Bill Torrey, who had been the brains behind the New York Islanders' four consecutive Stanley Cups in the 1980s.

After the Islanders were sold, Torrey, who was pushing 60, left the club, bought a place in West Palm Beach, and planned to ease himself into retirement.

"And I was here, I think, eight or nine days when I got a call from Mr. Huizenga saying he wanted to meet with me and talk about putting a team down here," Torrey recalls. So much for retirement. Huizenga made Torrey the president of his new South Florida expansion franchise.

What was the reaction in the Torrey household? "I have four sons," Torrey says, "and they said, 'Dad, you're crazy. Hockey in Florida?'"

But the more Torrey thought about it, the more he asked himself, "Why not hockey in Florida?" True, there was virtually no puck history to speak of, no recognition of the game among those who had lived in the South for decades. But that was a declining part of Florida's demographic makeup. The fact is, hundreds of thousands of transplanted northerners were now calling Florida home. They knew hockey and many of them loved it. Not only that, but on any given night at any given sporting event, a significant percentage of ticket buyers would be tourists—again, many from the north.

"You have to understand one thing," Torrey explains. "Down here, you are not necessarily always the home team. There are a hell of a lot of out-of-towners that are attending every event here."

What about the admonition of former Toronto sports mogul Jack Kent Cooke, who left Canada for California more than 40 years ago? Convinced that transplanted Canadians in southern California would make hockey a sure thing, Cooke founded the Los Angeles Kings during the NHL's first major expansion in 1967. After a few years of red ink, Cooke finally figured out why the Kings were failing. "The half a million Canadians who live in L.A. hate hockey," he famously said. "That's why they left Canada."

(The old joke about Kings games in the 1960s and '70s went like this: A hockey fan calls the Kings' box office and asks, "What time does tonight's game start?" The ticket seller answers, "What time can you get here?")

"That is not true, here," Bill Torrey insists. "When the Panthers are competitive, they draw."

The Panthers played their first season in a lovely, smallish art deco arena near downtown Miami called simply Miami Arena. These were the very last of the good old days before corporate naming rights blighted the sports landscape.

But Miami Arena had its problems. It was built in the days before anyone had heard of luxury boxes. There wasn't much parking and what did exist was owned by private operators, not the hockey team. The facility was a few thousand seats shy of what the NHL typically wants arena capacity to be.

Miami Arena was also located in a rough part of town. The parking lots had huge chain-link fences around them, and coil after coil of barbed wire on top. They more resembled prison fences than a place to leave the car on hockey night. Over the years, I attended several Panther games at the old arena, and never saw a building empty more quickly after a game. Literally within minutes of the horn sounding to signify the end of on-ice hostilities, the streets would be empty. While the fans enjoyed themselves, they also couldn't wait to get out of that neighbour-hood and return to safer havens.

There was another quirky feature in those early years of the

Panther franchise. Many of the fans didn't know the difference between a blue line and a chorus line.

"The first couple of years, we were very conscious of telling people what an icing was and what a blue line was, and things of that nature," recalls Denis Potvin.

Still, in spite of all those handicaps, the Panthers enjoyed one wonderfully memorable season on the ice. At the end of the 1995–96 season, they found themselves—a franchise in just its third season—in the Stanley Cup final. They were backstopped by former New York Ranger goaltender John Vanbiesbrouck, whom the Rangers declined to protect in the expansion draft (which was designed to stock the new Panthers and Anaheim Mighty Ducks). The "Beezer" put together one of those magical playoff runs where the puck suddenly resembled a beach ball and almost nothing got behind him. The bubble burst in the final round, as the Colorado Avalanche swept the Panthers in four straight games, the Cup-clinching victory taking place in Miami Arena in a thrilling triple-overtime finale.

Their early success meant that the Panthers were no longer just a quirky expansion experiment, but instead were contributing to what was turning into Titletown USA. Their marvellous playoff run was followed the next year by baseball's Marlins winning the World Series, and the diamond team won another Series in 2003. The National Basketball Association's Miami Heat also started to improve, culminating in a championship for that franchise in 2006 with the incomparable 7'1", 325-pound Shaquille O'Neal at the helm.

But Huizenga understood that the economics of playing hockey in the Miami Arena were not going to allow him to realize the kind of revenues his team would need to compete with

Detroit, Toronto, New York, and other hockey hotbeds of the league. He hired market researchers, demographers, and did some public opinion polling. The future, they told him, was not in downtown Miami, but more than 90 minutes north and west of the city—a part of Florida where experts predicted the population would almost double over the next decade. That was where, they told him, he should build a new hockey palace for his team, in a small suburban community, close to a major shopping mall but not much else. He could design the new building with all the necessary amenities today's NHL required: luxury boxes, a private social club, the best confections, wider seats, fantastic sightlines, and, of course, he would have control of the parking lots (and their steady revenue stream) that would surround the arena. And so, Wayne Huizenga said goodbye Miami. Hello Sunrise.

And then he sold the team.

Making the Panthers a hit entertainment attraction in South Florida is now the responsibility of a new ownership group led by Alan P. Cohen, the CEO of the generic drug maker Andrx. There are six partners in the new consortium, including Bernie Kosar, the former University of Miami and Cleveland Browns star quarterback, who has a small piece of the action. Kosar spends most of his time running his restaurant in Coral Gables. The entertainment group is responsible for business development, keeping the corporate boxes full, and booking as many concerts and other shows into the BankAtlantic Center as possible. That part of the equation is working well. In July 2006, the trade publication *PollStar* ranked the BankAtlantic Center as the tenth-busiest arena in the United States thanks to appearances by the likes of the Rolling Stones, Billy Joel, Tim McGraw and Faith Hill, and Cirque du Soleil.

The other part of the equation—putting a winning hockey team on the ice—was led (at least until the end of the 2005–06 season) by one of the most controversial figures in NHL history. Like many people who have lived in Florida, Mike Keenan is a transplanted Canadian. Unlike Floridians, he has a Stanley Cup ring from a dream 1993–94 season when he coached the New York Rangers to their first championship in 54 years. But he is also a polarizing figure in the hockey world. Despite an impressive array of accomplishments, the Panthers were Keenan's seventh team in his NHL coaching and managing career (and he's now with his eighth club in Calgary).

In some respects, Keenan was a logical choice to lead the hoped-for resurgence of a franchise in the Deep South. His hockey roots in that part of the United States went back more than 30 years. After playing for the University of Toronto Varsity Blues, Keenan quickly realized he did not have what it took to succeed as a player in the NHL. But he still loved to play and his journeyman career took him to the Southern Hockey League, where he toiled in Virginia, Georgia, and, yes, Florida. Keenan was invited to the first training camp of the Atlanta Flames, one of the NHL's expansion franchises in 1972, but he failed to catch on.

If Keenan was unable to make much of an impression on the ice, this was never the case behind the bench or in the front office. During his first 10 years in the NHL, he was associated with 4 teams that went to the Stanley Cup finals, and participated in 6 semi-finals, before finally winning it all with the Rangers in 1994. But over the years, Keenan has somehow overstayed his welcome in virtually every job he has ever had. His career is a case study in the vagaries of professional sports.

At 6'7" and 240 pounds, Toronto Maple Leafs defenceman Hal Gill
has had to make a tough adjustment to the new, faster NHL.

The Leafs' Wade Belak describes himself as a "family man,"
but he's still one of the toughest customers in the league.

Michael Peca missed more than half the 2006–07 season due
to injuries. Here, he signs autographs with his left hand.
An ice bag covers the hand he normally writes with.

Toronto GM John Ferguson, Jr., thinks wealthier teams
such as the Maple Leafs should get more credit for agreeing
to the new economic system that has dramatically
levelled the playing field in the NHL.

Panthers general manager and coach Jacques Martin has a big job ahead of him, trying to make hockey popular in South Florida.

Gary Roberts was one of the veterans brought in to make hockey a bigger game on the South Florida sports scene. Here, he's interviewed by Leafs TV's Paul Hendrick.

A scrum of reporters and videographers awaits the arrival of goaltender Ed Belfour on the occasion of his first return to Toronto in a Panthers uniform.

Belfour holds court in the visitors' dressing room after the Panthers win over his former team, the Maple Leafs, 7–3 at the Air Canada Centre.

Detroit Red Wings goaltender Dominik Hasek made a spectacular
return to the new NHL in the 2006–07 season at age 42.

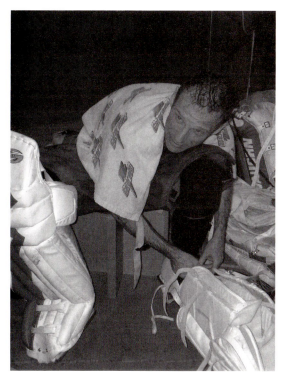

Dominik Hasek
removes his
equipment after a
Red Wings practice
at Joe Louis Arena
in Detroit.

Veteran forward Martin Gelinas has played in two
non-traditional hockey markets (Carolina and Florida).
Above, he meets the press after a practice with the Panthers.

Whether hockey
succeeds in South
Florida will depend, in
large measure, on stars
such as Finland's
Olli Jokinen.

Despite implementing several innovative measures in its hockey broadcasts, NBC's hockey viewership numbers in the United States are still abysmally low.

Heroic Leaf defenceman Bobby Baun approves of the new NHL. "I think we're finally starting to see the game as I'd like to see it right now," he told the *Toronto Star*'s Randy Starkman (left).

Eight-time Stanley Cup champion Red Kelly was part of the last
Maple Leafs team to win the Cup in 1967. He is being interviewed
here by *The Hamilton Spectator*'s Steve Milton.

The Maple Leafs' legendary former captain Dave Keon
returned to Toronto for a 40th-anniversary reunion
of the 1967 Stanley Cup champions.

Keenan first made a name for himself at the University of Toronto, where in 1984, he coached the Varsity Blues to a Canadian university hockey title (the last time U of T has reached hockey supremacy). His teams were the talk of the inter-collegiate hockey scene. He had tenure. He could have stayed in the academic athletic world as long as he wanted to. Instead, he gave it all up and moved two hours east of Toronto to become general manager and coach of the OHL's Peterborough Petes.

"I left a secure environment," Keenan told me in the spring of 2006, while still general manager of the Panthers. "You know, it's high risk and high return."

Keenan's next stop was the Rochester Americans of the AHL, whose most famous previous coach was one Donald S. Cherry.

Eventually, he made it to the National Hockey League where he has established some kind of record for frequent relocations.

Every city had a different story. He was "changed out" or made "tenuous," as he puts it, in Philadelphia, Chicago, New York, and St. Louis, despite compiling a creditable record at every stop. He left St. Louis when the ownership changed to go to Vancouver where he found himself, once again, a pawn in a front office game of musical chairs. Back on the merry-go-round. Next stop: Boston. Long-time Bruins general manager Harry Sinden hired Keenan to coach with the understanding that he, Sinden, would soon retire. Keenan presumed he would have a good shot at the general manager's job. But no, it went to Mike O'Connell, "and he wanted his own guy," says Keenan who would be on the move yet again.

His next stop was Florida. The Panthers wanted him to be their head coach in 2001, even though they did not have a general manager at the time.

"Maybe I should learn my lesson," Keenan says. But he didn't. (It could be called Keenan's Law: don't take a job where you're not the unanimous choice of those above you.)

For a while, things seemed to work out well in Florida. When the general manager's job opened up, Keenan was bumped upstairs. The team's ownership then hired the recently deposed coach of the Ottawa Senators, Jacques Martin, to be the head coach. On the surface, it seemed like a good match. Keenan and Martin shared considerable history. They last worked together in Chicago from 1988 to 1990, with Keenan as the team's head coach and general manager, and Martin as an assistant coach. They also worked together when they led Peterborough's junior hockey team to the 1980 Memorial Cup Final. Keenan and Martin also played hockey together at St. Lawrence University in Canton, New York.

But history caught up with "Iron Mike" once again. In September 2006, on the verge of what he hoped would be a breakthrough season for the Panthers, Keenan was on the move again. The details behind this coup are still murky. The Panthers said he resigned. At the time, Keenan told TSN's Michael Landsberg, "There's a lot more to it than that." He reported that his agent, rather than the team, called him to deliver the bad news. He called it a major shock and acknowledged he wasn't sure whether he and Jacques Martin were still friends. Martin was given Keenan's old general manager's position.

Some sources speculate there was a power struggle between Keenan and Martin, and that the coach won. They cite Keenan's desire to trade Gary Roberts to the Maple Leafs after the 2005–06 season (Roberts wanted the trade to be closer to his daughter, who goes to school in the Toronto area). But Martin is said to have gone over Keenan's head to get the trade vetoed. If that's true, it's a turn of events no general manager could accept.

One month after Keenan's departure, I asked Martin what the state of his relationship with Keenan was like.

"I haven't talked to Mike lately," he said brusquely.

"Are you still friends?" I asked.

"I don't want to deal with that issue."

Regardless of what went down behind the scenes, it brought more tumult to a franchise that has had five head coaches in the past six years—traditionally, not a sound method of building a winner.

"I've been a controversial figure," Keenan says in understated fashion. The average tenure of an NHL coach or general manager is less than three years. Keenan has had almost a quarter century in the game. He has worked in big markets (New York, population 10 million) and smaller ones (St. Louis, population 1 million). He has enjoyed the rare thrill of hoisting the Stanley Cup over his head, and taken the call from a general manager who told him not to let the door hit his derrière as he was leaving. Before he left Florida, Keenan was in the midst of what might have been his biggest challenge yet—selling hockey in South Florida with one of the smallest payrolls in the league.

In theory, the NHL's new economic system gave Keenan a chance to compete on a more level playing field. But for the 2005–06 season, the ownership in Florida gave him a budget that was well below the $39-million cap. Keenan would say at the time that his payroll was in the bottom 20 percent of the league. Another source said the Panthers had the smallest budget in the Eastern Conference that year—a paltry $22 million (the salary cap permitted teams to spend as much as $39 million but did not obligate them to spend that much). The difference between what the Panthers and teams like the Rangers were spending was the equivalent of three or four quality players. Plainly and simply, the Panthers had to be smarter than everyone else. In 2006–07, the second season under the new economic system, their ownership did give the club a significant budget increase. With the NHL salary cap at $44 million, the Panthers were spending $41 million on players—still below the cap but not nearly as much. They had to judge talent more effectively. They had to hope they could sign their players to more modest contracts. And as is always the case in sports, they had to get lucky, avoid injuries, and hope some of their underrated players would have unanticipated breakout years.

Things did not break for the Panthers; not during Keenan's tenure, nor since his departure. Florida, once again, failed to make the playoffs in 2006–07. Keenan did, however, make huge waves in South Florida by trading one of the league's best goaltenders in Roberto Luongo to the Vancouver Canucks for Todd Bertuzzi in June 2006. Money appeared to be the reason behind the trade. In Keenan's opinion, Luongo wasn't committed to staying in Florida. Rather than have the goaltender leave after becoming a free agent, Keenan traded him and at least got something in return. Luongo, meanwhile, became a legend in Vancouver where they rolled out the welcome mat for him. And why not? He finished the 2006–07 season as one of three nominees for the Hart Trophy as the league's most valuable player (ultimately won by Sidney Crosby). By February 2007, Bertuzzi was on his way to Detroit, having been grounded by a back injury in Florida. He scored only one goal in a Panthers uniform.

Can hockey survive in Florida over the long haul? Can it compete against other major professional sports such as football, baseball, and basketball, not to mention other leisure activities such as golf, tennis, boating, fishing, and just lazing on the beach?

Denis Potvin is convinced the game is here to stay.

"I kind of turn my nose up at a lot of those pundits who said during the lockout, 'Well, some franchises may not survive and maybe there shouldn't be hockey in some states,'" he says defiantly.

Bill Torrey thinks writing off the entire Sunbelt is a mistake. "There are markets in the South, which are probably not good markets, and they never will be," he says. "But this is a different market because of the makeup and the nature of it," he says, referring to the three high-growth areas of Miami, Fort Lauderdale, and West Palm Beach all within a 90-minute drive of each other.

How about Torrey's kids, all of whom still live on Long Island? Do they still think he's crazy?

"No!" he laughs. "They understand, because now they are at an age where they like to come down here and when they come down here they want to see a hockey game."

For Joe Nieuwendyk, who saw the Stars establish themselves in Dallas, this is déjà vu all over again.

"I don't think it is any different here or in Atlanta or in any other place," says Nieuwendyk. "They like to get behind a winning team. And so that is the key, and that is the challenge for all the organizations that play in the South."

Martin Gelinas has played all over the NHL, in long-established hockey towns such as Edmonton and Vancouver, and in places where the learning curve is a lot steeper, such as Carolina and now Florida. "The fans that come to this market and come to learn the game really appreciate the game, love the game, love the intensity, the physical part of it, the finesse, and so on," he says. "I think it will take off."

"I think it has gotten to be such a global game across the world, let alone in the southern part of the U.S., that people understand there is a place for hockey everywhere," says Rangers assistant coach Mike Pelino, who used to play for Mike Keenan's U of T Varsity Blues in the 1970s, then coached with Keenan in Florida before the lockout.

"I think that the idea of having hockey in places like Florida, southern California, Texas, and Phoenix is just outstanding for hockey and outstanding for the people to be exposed to this great game," he adds.

BUSINESS HAPPENED to take Canadian documentary film-maker and television show producer Karen Pinker to Charlotte, North Carolina, on the night of the seventh game of the 2006 Stanley Cup Final. As she waited for her flight to leave from the Charlotte Douglas Airport, her husband called, reminding her to bring home to Dunedin, Ontario, a souvenir, anything at all, from the Hurricanes' memorable season. Pinker wandered all over the airport, from gift shop to souvenir store, and could find absolutely nothing to bring home. Not a key chain, not a sweater, not a T-shirt—nothing. And yet, the Hurricanes' home arena was a mere two-and-a-half-hour drive away.

"And if that weren't bad enough," Pinker recalls, "the TV set in the departure lounge had a baseball game on. It was unbelievable."

Almost as unbelievable were the ticket prices in the playoffs for the Hurricanes' home games. If you paid $85 for your seat to a first-round game at the 18,730-seat RBC Center, you paid $125 for the same seat in the next round, and $180 per seat for the Stanley Cup final. Ouch. *The Charlotte Observer* quoted one season's-ticket holder as saying, "It's clearly a case of let's grab the money while it's there and next year be damned."

Nevertheless, the Hurricanes can legitimately claim that winning hockey is taking root in North Carolina. Although the club had not reached its goal of 15,000, season-ticket sales in 2006 after the 'Canes won the Stanley Cup were up 60 percent. Another positive sign was NBC TV's decision to televise two Hurricanes games nationally, while Versus (the new name for the Outdoor Life Network, which holds the U.S. cable rights for the NHL) would broadcast four Carolina games.

Interest in hockey may be up in South Florida, too, but it is still a rare day of the week that NHL news isn't relegated to the back pages of the sports section of the local newspapers. Even when he was still working there, Mike Keenan admitted to having doubts about the future of hockey in the Sunbelt.

"I don't know if it's permanent," he said. "This franchise hasn't turned on the community as it did when it went to the finals in 1996."

Fans are getting accustomed to travelling to a completely different location for home games—way out in the suburbs rather than downtown. And the club may be engaged in some practices that at first blush seem penny-wise but pound-foolish. The team now collects all parking revenues from lots adjacent to the arena. They normally charge $15 to park close to the arena, $10 for season's-ticket holders. However, some fans trying to save a buck began parking across the road at a shopping mall. As a result of this practice, the team says it intends to build a fence around the arena and environs. Anyone who wants to come through that fence on game day will be charged $5. These are the things financial wizards in the team's front office love, but which fans, who feel nickel-and-dimed to death, hate.

Perhaps Denis Potvin does the best job of putting hockey in the Sunbelt into perspective.

"It is not going to be the same as in Canada—it never will be," he says. "New York is not the same as in Canada—it never will be. Canada is very unique. But the southern markets are there. I think that the game is much more transportable now than it ever was."

"If you win, you'll fill the building," Keenan says, reminding me that even the much-beloved Dolphins play to half-empty stadiums when they lose. "If you don't win, you'll have a difficult time."

Yes, winning matters. This is professional sports after all.

# JACKIE AND WILLIE

*The air has finally gotten to the place
that we can breathe it together.*
—SEPTIMA CLARK (1898–1987),
AFRICAN-AMERICAN TEACHER AND CIVIL RIGHTS ACTIVIST

Everyone knows Jackie Robinson.

Robinson broke the colour barrier in Major League Baseball when he stepped up to the plate on April 15, 1947. He was playing his first game for the Brooklyn Dodgers (having already starred the previous season in the minor leagues with the Montreal Royals). The Dodgers' president and general manager, Branch Rickey, picked Robinson because, he said, "I'm looking for a ballplayer with enough guts not to fight back." Despite encountering intense, soul-destroying racism wherever he went, Robinson proved to be just that player. In 1962, he was inducted into baseball's Hall of Fame.

Decades earlier, in 1904, halfback Charles Follis signed a contract with the Shelby Athletic Association in Ohio, making him the first known black pro football player. (Coincidentally, one of his teammates was Branch Rickey.) Follis, who was nicknamed the "Black Cyclone from Wooster," has held a less illustrious place in sports history for a couple of reasons. First, when he played, the National Football League did not yet exist. Second, once the league was born, it too, like baseball, eventually adopted a tacit policy of racial segregation. The people who ran the football leagues reasoned that, with the United States in the throes of the Great Depression, scarce pro football jobs should be reserved for whites. The NFL actually broke the colour barrier a full year before baseball did—in March 1946. The Los Angeles Rams became the first integrated team in the NFL when they signed tailback Kenny Washington. (Another coincidence: Washington played football at the University of California at Los Angeles where one of his teammates was Jackie Robinson, who was such a good athlete that he played baseball and football and was a track and field star as well.)

In Canada, Lew Hayman was the Branch Rickey of the Canadian Football League. And just as Montreal (with Jackie Robinson) was the city where baseball began to reflect the diversity of its population, so would it be in football. Hayman ran the Montreal Alouettes. In 1946, the league ended a policy of forbidding "imports" (read: Americans) from playing in the CFL. The policy was not explicitly racist. But the effect of preventing imports from playing north of the border meant no blacks played pro football in Canada.

Hayman saw what Jackie Robinson was doing across town with the Royals and signed Kentucky State's Herb Trawick, a lineman who played both offence and defence. Trawick spent 12 years in Montreal and eventually became a Canadian citizen and a CFL Hall of Famer. Like Robinson, he encountered his share of racism and abided it with his talent and good-natured personality.

Three players simultaneously broke the colour barrier in the National Basketball Association in 1950. But basketball did not have nearly the hold on American society that baseball and football did so desegregation on the court seemed less historically significant than on the diamond or the gridiron.

As these North American sports leagues gradually opened their doors to black athletes, where was the National Hockey League? The answer is miles and miles behind.

Blacks were certainly playing organized hockey as early as the 1940s. In the Quebec Senior League, at that time considered just a notch below the NHL, Herb Carnegie led an all-black forward line for the Quebec Aces. Carnegie was so good—he was known as the black Jean Béliveau—that Maple Leafs owner Conn Smythe said, "I'd pay $10,000 to turn that boy white." Carnegie never got the chance to play in the NHL.

It was not until 1958—more than a decade after football and baseball—that the NHL saw the arrival of its first black player. Willie O'Ree was born in 1935 in Fredericton, New Brunswick, and played a grand total of two games for the Boston Bruins toward the end of the 1957–58 season. After that, he spent two years in the minors. The Bruins recalled him in 1961, and he played 41 more games for them. O'Ree never played another game in the National Hockey League. The next black player in the NHL would not appear for more than another decade.

Two things made O'Ree's tenure in the NHL noteworthy. One, of course, was his colour. The other was that O'Ree was blind in one eye, the result of a prior hockey injury. He told no one, fearing the disability would give league officials another reason to keep him off the ice.

O'Ree's experience in the white-dominated game was as difficult as one might expect. Other players took gratuitous shots at
him to see how tough he was. One night in Chicago, the
Blackhawks' Eric Nesterenko nailed him with a butt-end, the
very illegal and dangerous practice of using the top of the hockey
stick as a battering ram. O'Ree lost two teeth and his nose was
broken in the fracas. He responded by applying his stick to
Nesterenko's head, cutting him open for 15 stitches. (These were
the days before helmets, of course.) At other times, particularly
in U.S. cities, O'Ree heard taunts such as "Go home and pick
cotton." (There is not much cotton to be picked in New
Brunswick.) But like Jackie Robinson, he kept his head down
and persevered. O'Ree just wanted to play hockey, which he did,
almost all of it in the minor leagues, until he was 43 years old.
Unlike Robinson, he has said that he never was refused service at
a restaurant or hotel, and had good teammates in Boston and the
minors, who generally accepted him.

Why was hockey so far behind the other major sports in
North America? In fairness, pro hockey probably cannot be
judged by the same standard as the others. Unlike football, baseball, and basketball, almost every single player in the NHL half a
century ago was Canadian and the vast majority of Canadians
were white. Sports historian William Humber notes that blacks
made up a tenth of 1 percent of the Canadian population in the
1950s. And the 6-team NHL provided jobs for only 120 players,
as opposed to nearly 700 today. In addition, there were not, for
example, legions of blacks playing in separate "Negro Leagues"
as was the case in baseball (although in 1900, blacks did form the
Colored Hockey League in Nova Scotia, where most of Canada's
black population lived). Canada also did not experience

anything close to the racial divide that has so defined the United States. For all these reasons, and perhaps because hockey just simply was not as important in most of the States as the other major sports, even *The New York Times* failed to do a story on Willie O'Ree's breaking hockey's colour barrier.

Still, it's hard to explain the gap of almost 15 years between the end of O'Ree's NHL career and the arrival of the league's second black player. Mike Marson was born in Scarborough, Ontario, in 1955. He played his junior hockey in Sudbury and in 1973–74 was good enough to lead his team, the Wolves, with 94 points and was named team captain. He was drafted that year by the Washington Capitals in the second round, the 19th pick overall, and his first game in the NHL in October 1974 was the first game in Capitals' franchise history, too. Marson clearly had the scoring touch in junior hockey, but it did not follow him to the NHL. He played a full season in Washington, but over the next several years bounced up and down to the minors, playing for teams such as the Baltimore Clippers, Springfield Indians, Hershey Bears, Philadelphia Firebirds, Binghampton Dusters, and Dundas Merchants. All told, in just five seasons in Washington (and three games with the Los Angeles Kings), Marson scored only 48 points, but racked up 233 penalty minutes, suggesting he was a tough combatant.

The next black players to break into the NHL had a lot more impact on the ice than their two predecessors, one by putting the puck in the net, the other by keeping it out.

In 1978, the Buffalo Sabres drafted a 6'1", 200-pound forward named Tony McKegney, who would become the NHL's first black player to record significant achievements at the offensive end of the ice.

McKegney's backstory is remarkable. His biological father was a Nigerian engineer, who left McKegney's mother to raise their baby alone in Montreal in 1958. Soon after, she gave up the baby for adoption. McKegney never saw his mother again. He met his biological father once, after he turned 18 years of age.

If life started in a dramatically bad fashion for Tony, it got better in a hurry. He became one of three black children adopted by a white Sarnia family that already had three children. Lowrey McKegney, the story goes, was a Royal Canadian Air Force officer. Having seen orphans in Europe suffer through the ravages of war, he returned home determined to help orphans in Canada.

"My parents made us all feel like family," McKegney said in a 1980 interview. "Their children made us feel like family. We were taken young and grew up with them and seldom even thought about black and white."

McKegney's career got off to a lacklustre start. He was a major presence for the OHL's Kingston Canadians, scoring 92 points in 55 games in his draft year of 1978. The year before was even better—135 points in 66 games. Those numbers should have entitled McKegney to be drafted higher than 32nd overall. However, he had announced his intention to play in the upstart World Hockey Association and this may have scared NHL teams away. But McKegney never did join the WHA. The official story was that his contract demands were too high. But it was a team in Birmingham, Alabama, that had initially expressed interest in signing him, and speculation was rampant that racist fans in the Deep South put pressure on the team's owner (Toronto's John F. Bassett) to keep him off the roster. McKegney, shocked by this turn of events, signed with the Sabres.

McKegney made his NHL debut in October 1978 and it was a night to remember. He scored Buffalo's first goal of the season. His 13 years in the NHL eventually took him to Quebec, Minnesota, New York (Rangers), St. Louis, Detroit, and Chicago. McKegney enjoyed eight 20-goal seasons—the NHL's benchmark of consistent quality. He bagged 40 goals and added 38 assists in 1987–88 in St. Louis—the best season on record for a black player until Jarome Iginla tallied 96 points in 2001–02. McKegney's career tally of 639 points in just over 900 games meant that black players could no longer be marginalized.

At the other end of the rink, another black man—coincidentally, also adopted—from Spruce Grove, Alberta, was set to turn the hockey world on its ear by becoming a huge part of an emerging dynasty. Three years after the Buffalo Sabres drafted Tony McKegney, the Edmonton Oilers selected a diminutive goaltender from the Western Hockey League's Victoria Cougars.

Grant Fuhr was born in 1962. He was only 5'8" when he turned professional. But his on-ice acrobatics allowed him to stick around the NHL for 19 seasons and win both the Vezina and Jennings trophies for excellence in goaltending, and capture four Stanley Cups in the process. (Technically, Fuhr won five Cups, but he was injured for Edmonton's fifth and saw no action in that playoff year.) His lifetime goals-against average of 3.38 does not seem particularly impressive, until one remembers that Fuhr played most of his career in the 1980s during the era of "firewagon hockey" when final scores of 9–4 or 8–6 were not uncommon. His Oilers scored a lot of goals, but Gretzky and company often left Fuhr alone in his end of the rink to fend for himself.

Fuhr's name is all over the NHL record book. At the time of this writing, he holds the single-season marks for most games played by a goaltender, with 79, and most consecutive game appearances, with 76. And Fuhr shares the single-post-season record for most wins by a goaltender with 16. One of the more remarkable statistics in Fuhr's career is the 14 assists he recorded in the 1983–84 season, and that is also an NHL record. By the time he was done, he had played in 868 regular season games and another 150 in the playoffs. Despite 10 great seasons with the Oilers, Fuhr's overall career win totals are more modest than they might have been, thanks to too many years with mediocre teams in Toronto, Buffalo, Los Angeles, and Calgary. Still, Fuhr was good enough to notch 403 career wins, making him only the 6th goaltender in NHL history to surpass the 400 mark. He is 9th on the all-time wins list. In 2003, Fuhr became the first black player inducted into the Hockey Hall of Fame. Today, he is a goaltending consultant with the Phoenix Coyotes, reunited with his old friend Wayne Gretzky, the team's coach and part owner.

Perhaps because McKegney had preceded him by a few years, or maybe because he was just so very good, it seemed that few hockey observers made much of a point of noticing Fuhr's colour. Like McKegney, he was raised by a white family and experienced little racism growing up. However, there were exceptions. When he played for Buffalo, Fuhr was at first denied entry into the Transit Valley Country Club, of which many Sabres were members. The explanation was an "incorrect and incomplete" membership form. Eventually, the club reversed itself, offering Fuhr both a membership and an apology.

Before the NHL locked out its players and lost the entire 2004–05 season, there were 17 black players in the league—roughly

2.5 percent of the players. However, given that only 18 people of colour played in the NHL between 1958 and 1991, it is safe to conclude that hockey is making some inroads into a community not traditionally associated with the game. Next to Grant Fuhr's exploits with the Oilers, perhaps the proudest moment for Canada's various black communities came in the 2003 World Championship in Finland. With Canada and Sweden tied 2–2 and both teams having played nearly 14 minutes of the overtime period, Scarborough, Ontario, native Anson Carter skated down the right wing on Sweden's goaltender Mikael Tellqvist. Carter went wide around the back of the net, and then sneaked the puck between Tellqvist's right pad and the post. Off-ice officials spent several minutes watching and rewatching video replays before they and the referee confirmed that the entire puck went in the net. The goal meant gold for Canada. It also meant one of the more important goals in Canadian hockey history had been scored by a black man. The new face of Canadian hockey excellence was black, and with dreadlocks no less.

Sadly, Carter also was the target in an incident that was one of hockey's sorrier moments. In December 2004 during the lockout, several NHL players, including Carter, travelled to St. Petersburg, Russia, to participate in an exhibition tournament. When Carter was on the ice, some fans twice threw a banana in his direction.

"It happens in the world," Carter said at the time, adding it was the only racist incident he had experienced since he had played four years of college hockey at Michigan State. "My parents always warned me about it."

There have been incidents involving other players. Fans in Buffalo taunted former tough guy Peter Worrell (19 goals and more than 1500 penalty minutes over 7 seasons) by calling him a "monkey."

Ted Nolan, a former coach of the year with the Buffalo Sabres, now head coach of the New York Islanders, has heard his share of racial insults as well. Nolan was born on the Ojibwa First Nations reserve near Sault Ste. Marie, Ontario. In December 2005, he found himself the target of questionable fan behaviour while coaching the Moncton Wildcats of the Quebec Major Junior Hockey League. The crowd in Chicoutimi, Quebec, reportedly shouted racial slurs at Nolan, pretended to shoot bows and arrows, and did tomahawk-chop imitations.

"I thought this stuff happened in the 1940s," Nolan said at the time. "The racial slurs that we listened to throughout the game were just disgusting. It was really a bad night."

Nolan's experience in Quebec echoes that of Tommy Kane. As a kid in the early 1980s, the Montrealer had loads of hockey talent, and often outscored the likes of Mario Lemieux at tournaments. However, racist taunting became too much for Kane, who quit playing hockey. Athletic ability was hardly the problem. Kane would go on to become a successful wide receiver with the NFL's Seattle Seahawks.

And, of course, racism in hockey is not limited to blacks or First Nations people. Sean Avery, now of the New York Rangers, once took exception to a hit inflicted on his former Los Angeles Kings teammate Jeremy Roenick by the Phoenix Coyotes' Denis Gauthier. Avery told reporters after the incident, "It was typical of most French players in our league, with a visor on, running around and playing tough, and not backing anything up." Numerous observers remarked how you-know-what would have hit the fan had Avery replaced the word *French* with *black* or

*Jewish.* Avery later apologized but escaped punishment by the league.

On another occasion, the Ottawa Senators' Vaclav Prospal, who was born in Czechoslovakia, called the Montreal Canadiens' Patrice Brisebois a "fucking frog" during a close game. Prospal eventually apologized and was forced to take sensitivity training by the league.

"While all NHL players are staunch competitors, the heat of battle does not justify the type of behaviour displayed in this instance," the NHL's deputy commissioner Bill Daly said at the time.

One of the most blatant and outrageous examples of racism in hockey came at the junior level. In March 2003, former NHL goalie John Vanbiesbrouck, then the coach of the Ontario Hockey League's Sault Ste. Marie Greyhounds, referred to one of his own players as a "nigger" in front of other members of the team. He later explained his conduct as a bad attitude he must have picked up while growing up in Detroit. The OHL banned Vanbiesbrouck, but he ended up quitting anyway, and selling his share of the team out of embarrassment.

Canadians can rightly take pride in the fact that their country is a much less racist society than the United States. And professional athletes, including Jackie Robinson, have for decades confirmed the impression that Canada is, and has been, a more welcoming country to athletes of colour than the United States. Nevertheless, some of the above examples suggest we ought not to get too smug.

OF COURSE, there is no reason that hockey should be exempt from society's problems. But the question remains, is the progress that visible minorities are making in society also reflected in the makeup of the National Hockey League's 30 teams?

To help answer that question, I went to the Air Canada Centre in Toronto to watch the New York Islanders go through their midday drills in preparation for that night's game against the Maple Leafs. Amid the organized chaos of skating, shooting, and passing drills, two men calmly positioned themselves near centre ice, both on one knee, engaged in conversation. They were the Islanders' star goaltender Rick DiPietro and the team's goalie coach. Normally, there would be nothing unusual about that. Except that the Isles' coach in question was born and spent the first six years of his life in Trinidad, before his family immigrated to Canada.

His name is Sudarshan Maharaj—"Sudsie" to his friends. His is the only non-white face on the ice. Actually, he may be the only non-white face in the building. So it's not just the goalie skates covered in thick white impenetrable plastic that set him apart from everyone else. There are no other coaches or players in the entire league that look like Maharaj, or bring his particular life experience to the game.

Maharaj grew up in Couva, population 120,000, on the west coast of Trinidad. (The island itself is just off the northern coast of Venezuela.) His childhood was a happy one, but also economically difficult. For example, he recalls fashioning his own kite by catching the large dragonfly that is indigenous to the Caribbean, then wrapping a piece of thread around it.

By 1969, Maharaj's father had had enough of the island's poverty. His brother, who had seen more of the world, recommended that he move to Canada. So he did. He moved to the south end of what was then Etobicoke, Ontario—now south-western Toronto—and got a job cleaning cars. He sent money back home to Trinidad, where Sudarshan's grandmother and uncles helped fill the parental void. It was a real family affair. A year later, Sudarshan, his mother, and two older brothers also moved to Etobicoke.

They then did something a lot of families in Canada did. They flipped on their television set and watched a young kid from Parry Sound, Ontario, revolutionize the way hockey was played. That player's name was Bobby Orr, and the destiny of the Maharaj family would be inalterably changed thanks to number 4 and his big, bad Bruins.

"My parents fell in love with the game right away," recalls Maharaj.

What came next was pure Canadiana. A couple of years later, the family moved into a neighbourhood where there were lots of kids and many opportunities to play road hockey. Then the neighbours urged him to learn to skate, something he had never tried before. "The next thing I know I am playing in the local house league and away we went from there," he says. Maharaj was 8 years old.

One of the most memorable Stanley Cup finals at this time was the 1974 classic between Orr's Boston Bruins and the Philadelphia Flyers. The Flyers became the first post-1967 expansion team to win the Stanley Cup, and they did it in large measure because of remarkable goaltending from a 29-year-old Montreal native named Bernie Parent. One of Maharaj's brothers admired the way Parent played, and suggested his younger brother give the position a try.

He did. Something clicked. And Maharaj would spend the next two decades of his life between the pipes.

Maharaj worked his way up the local hockey ladder. He must have loved the game, because at ages 14 and 15, he would schlep his equipment for two hours each way on Toronto's transit system every day just to get to the arena to play.

When it was time for post-secondary education, Maharaj enrolled at York University just in time to play backup for the 1984–85 Canadian university championship team (a group that, incidentally, defeated Mike Keenan's University of Toronto squad for the Ontario title on the way to the national finals). It was at this point that Maharaj realized what 99.99 percent of Canadian kids who play hockey eventually discover. He was not NHL material. He seems to have accepted that news with equanimity.

"I realized at a very young age that I wasn't good enough for the NHL," he says. "I wasn't going to delude myself that I was."

But hockey was not out of his blood. So he sent letters to professional teams all over Europe. A team in Sweden sounded interested. Mildly interested.

"The agreement was I would pay my own way, and all my expenses. If I made the team I got my money back," Maharaj recalls laughing. Two weeks later, the club offered him a contract to play goal for a whopping $30,000 a year. He spent the next six years playing professionally in the Swedish league. If Maharaj's dark complexion makes the North American hockey world of today do a double take from time to time, it is not hard to imagine what the much less diverse Sweden of the late 1980s must have been like.

"You know what? You heard the comments. You heard the racial remarks. You got the jeers from the crowd. You got all those things," he says with evident sadness. Maharaj may have been Trinidadian by birth, but Swedish hockey fans in opposing rinks had no idea what to make of him. As far as they were concerned, behind his mask he looked vaguely Pakistani, and some shouted "Paki" at him to rile him up. Opposing players did likewise. It was at those moments that perhaps the spirit of Jackie Robinson came to mind.

"A lot of the times you had to bite your lip because you didn't have a whole slew of people backing you up all of the time," Maharaj offers.

He was often amazed at how supportive his teammates were. And in the fast-paced cauldron that is the arena, the game does offer its opportunities for payback.

"You deal with a lot of anger," he admits. "At that time, you maybe lay a slash on the guy in front of the net or something like that. But you come to understand that, in life, at a very young age, not everyone is good and kind and that everyone has a positive outlook on you or life. And you learn to deal with the fact that this is something I am going to be facing if I choose to pursue this."

Did he ever want to just give up?

"No. No, I love the game. I love the sport," he says emphatically. "There was frustration. There was anger. But hockey wasn't the issue. It was the people around it."

Maharaj's goaltending career came to an end in Sweden. He returned to Etobicoke and got a good but challenging job as head of special education with the local school board. He worked with some of the toughest-to-serve kids from youth detention centres and street gangs, trying to get them to change their lives and become integrated into mainstream society. There were occasions when he was physically threatened. At such times, his background playing a sometimes-violent game came in handy.

Then there were the political battles. Maharaj returned to Ontario just in time to become a first-hand witness to the wars among the educational establishment, the teacher unions, and Mike Harris's newly elected Conservative government. He frequently dealt with kids he thought should have been in treatment facilities, but instead were in regular classrooms, terrorizing other students who actually wanted to learn something. The Harris Tories insisted they were improving the education system.

"That's why I spent a lot of evenings watching your show, when there were Conservatives on, and cussing vehemently," Maharaj laughs, referring to the former TVOntario current affairs program *Studio 2*.

Before long, however, hockey called Maharaj back. He rejoined his alma mater as the goaltending coach for York University, and spent two years there. Then, he became coach of the Caledon Canadians, a Tier II team in the Junior A Hockey League, located in York Region north of Toronto. While the team is now defunct, it survived long enough to kick-start a chain of events that would lead Maharaj, of all places, to the National Hockey League.

While in Caledon, Maharaj hooked up with some goalies who were looking for additional coaching. One of them was Stephen Valiquette, who would become a decent minor-league goalie, and play nine games over five seasons with the Islanders, Oilers, and Rangers. While Valiquette was with the Islanders during the 1999–2000 season, one of the other goaltenders there was Kevin Weekes. Weekes wondered where Valiquette had learned some of his training and technique, discovered it was Maharaj's doing, and decided to get some private tutelage as well. One week in the summer turned into two weeks, then two months, then three years of private instruction. Suddenly, Maharaj was gaining a reputation as a goalie guru.

Valiquette, who now runs his own goaltending school, introduced Maharaj to a young goaltending phenom in the Islanders' system, Rick DiPietro. The Massachusetts native was turning heads with the American Hockey League's Bridgeport Sound Tigers and seemed to have "sure thing" written all over him, as most first-overall draft picks do. So naturally, after their first meeting and an initial evaluation, Maharaj tore a strip off the young netminder.

"I kind of ripped him the first night and he didn't want to talk to me the second night," Maharaj says, smiling.

The coach told the protege an old native saying, that the longest journey we take in our lives is from here to here. Maharaj first pointed to his heart, then his head.

"And I told him, 'You haven't started that journey yet,'" Maharaj says.

Talk about chutzpah. Maharaj's efforts to become the goaltending coach to the stars could have been over right there. He essentially insulted the goaltender that would grab the Islanders starting job in 2000 and become the foundation for the franchise for the next two decades—at least, that's the Islanders' plan. But a day later, DiPietro told his colleague Stephen Valiquette that perhaps that goalie coach might have something to say after all.

Then, DiPietro and Maharaj had no contact for two years. And Maharaj figured, well, that's that.

As fate would have it, in 2003 the Islanders hired a new head coach, Steve Stirling. The coach asked his first-string goaltender an important question.

"What do you need to take the next step to becoming one of the truly elite goaltenders in the league?"

Rick DiPietro answered, "There's a guy in Toronto. I think I'd like to work with him." And with that, Maharaj was invited to Long Island for an interview. In September 2003, Sudarshan "Sudsie" Maharaj became the official goaltending coach for the New York Islanders.

"I think it was equivalent to lightning striking," he says, still marvelling at the sequence of events that made him responsible for ensuring the Islanders got the best return possible on their goaltending investment. And what an investment it is. Rick DiPietro is the only goaltender in NHL history to be selected first overall (in 2000) in the league's annual entry draft. In the summer of 2006, after just his second season as the Islanders' starting goaltender and his fifth in the NHL, DiPietro signed a 15-year contract for $67.5 million. It was now the job of his coach, Sudsie Maharaj, salary $75,000 a year, to help make DiPietro the best goalie in hockey.

It was Maharaj who set up a pre-game routine for DiPietro, getting him to do two seemingly contradictory things better: relax and focus. And while his teaching technique is key, much of what Maharaj brings to his coaching is an understanding of the unique psychological burdens of playing goal. He is a big believer in sports psychology books, and he has encouraged his pupil to build a library of recommended volumes. He looks for any resource that can help DiPietro prepare both physically and mentally for the task at hand.

"Everything from his ability to rebound from difficulties to his overall approach to the game," Maharaj says. "And, to this point, he has always said that is one thing that he is happy about."

"When things aren't going well, as a goalie coach, you've got to fix what's going wrong and pick that out," says DiPietro. "And I think he does a good job of realizing when I'm not doing things right and he makes up drills to fix [the problem]."

Former Islanders interim head coach Brad Shaw also saw the effects of Maharaj's influence.

"One of Rick's weaknesses would be his excitability and the fact that he tends to lose his focus and tends to let things affect him," Shaw said. "I think what Sudsie does is he, through his relationship, has an ability to calm him down. He has an ability to get him through the rough spots."

However, and not unexpectedly, it did not take long after Maharaj's hiring for the jokes to begin. After all, how many goalie coaches from Trinidad are there in the NHL? In January 2004, columnist Don Brennan wrote this in the *Ottawa Sun:* "The Islanders' goaltending consultant/scout is a gentleman by the name of Sudarshan Maharaj. Memo to self: Check media guide for Maharaj's resumé, if only to see whether he ever played any cricket." Then, during an Islanders game against the Flyers, one of the colour commentators on the Philadelphia broadcast made another remark about cricket. Maharaj called both references "distasteful."

"There's not a lot of diversity in the game of hockey, so you get a guy from the Caribbean islands as your goalie coach, he is an easy target," says Brad Shaw, who did his stint as interim head coach on Long Island in 2006 after the team fired Stirling. "We always joke he is the best Trinidadian goalie coach in the league. It's something that he is probably always going to have to battle. You are just not viewed as a hockey person."

Of the ongoing battle, Maharaj says, "It is better today. Are there still people with a lower IQ than there should be? Yes. But for the most part I can't say I run into those issues on a grand scale."

The NHL requires every player to enrol in a diversity-training seminar before each season. Insults about a player's mother may be in bad taste, but they are not illegal. Racially motivated verbal abuse, however, is. The league investigates all allegations of racism, although as we saw in the case of Sean Avery, suspensions do not always follow and observers are not always mollified.

Maharaj cites dollars, not racism, as perhaps the main reason that more ethnic minorities are not involved in hockey. After the seemingly endless list of demands for skates, sticks, equipment, team jackets, entry fees, and so on, parents can be set back thousands of dollars for the privilege of getting up at 5 A.M. and driving to a cold arena on a pitch-black winter morning.

Maharaj loved jetting back and forth between Toronto and Long Island. He also frequently made the hour-and-a-half drive from New York to Bridgeport, Connecticut, to work with the Islanders' AHL goalies. He took in numerous OHL games, trying to unearth hot prospects for the Isles. And he travelled overseas a bit, too. The week I caught up with him, Maharaj was about to fly to Sweden to scout the World Under-18 Championship.

Toronto is still home. He has two young daughters with Yvonne, his significant other of eight years. His older daughter, Alexandra, loves to skate but has yet to show an interest in hockey. And Katherine, the younger one?

"She is more of a bruiser and I think she may be the one that straps on the equipment," he laughs.

When he was a new Canadian more than three decades ago, Maharaj spent considerable time playing at the Lakeshore Arena in Etobicoke. Today, when he trains NHL goalies, he does much of that training in that same arena. The Toronto Maple Leafs also use that arena from time to time when they are not practising at the Air Canada Centre.

"It has a lot of great memories," Maharaj says.

If this were a Hollywood motion picture, the story would end here. But life has thrown Maharaj a nasty curve ball. In August 2006, Maharaj was fired as the Islanders' goaltender coach.

There were front-office changes galore when the team owner, Charles Wang, appointed Garth Snow to take the place of Neil Smith as general manager (Smith having served as GM for a mere 40 days) and brought in Ted Nolan as coach. The new Islander brass signed DiPietro to the aforementioned astonishing 15-year contract, but at the same time, they fired their goaltender's first choice as his own personal coach. It was nothing Maharaj was doing wrong. Nolan simply wanted his own guy.

"It's no disrespect to the previous person," Nolan told me after an Islanders' practice in November 2006. "Unfortunately, the relationship just didn't work out."

I bumped into Maharaj in October 2006 at the Air Canada Centre, while the New York Rangers were loosening up at a game-day skate before facing the Leafs.

"It feels very strange being here," Maharaj admitted, two months after his departure from Long Island. "I've purposely avoided NHL rinks."

Has he talked with DiPietro since the firing?

"Rick is beside himself," Maharaj said. "I'm purposely not watching Islander games so I can't be accused of anything."

The next time I see DiPietro in the Islanders' dressing room, I ask him about the change in coaches.

"It's been tough on me," he admits. "I had a really close relationship with him [Maharaj]. We still stay in touch pretty frequently. I can't say enough about him. Great guy. Great coach."

When I try a follow-up question, DiPietro cuts off the discussion.

"I really can't comment on the change," he says politely. "Thanks." And off he walked.

My sense was, DiPietro would like to have said a lot more about the situation. That was confirmed moments later when he approached me, after my tape recorder stopped rolling.

"I don't want to comment on it," he said with a pained look on his face. "I'll get in trouble."

The fact is, every coach in every professional sport is entitled to surround himself with his own people, with whom he feels most comfortable. But there is something particularly ironic about Ted Nolan, an Aboriginal Canadian, who was blackballed from coaching in the NHL for almost a decade and has dealt with his share of racism over the years, being responsible for firing another atypical member of the hockey fraternity, and one who has suffered his share of racist comments as well. If the irony was lost on Nolan, it certainly was not on Maharaj, who, when fired by Nolan, said to the new head coach, "You know what it's like not to be 'in the club.'" The observation apparently fell on deaf ears.

"I went out of my way to be courteous and respectful to everyone," Maharaj says, "so when my time came to go down, no one would stomp on me."

And no one has. In fact, Maharaj has fielded phone calls from many former associates checking in on him, including the entire scouting staff of the Islanders, and Brad Shaw, now an assistant with the St. Louis Blues. They have, to a person, offered to aid Maharaj's efforts to make contact with others around the league and build a new scouting service for young goaltenders eligible for the NHL draft.

"I've learned a lot of good lessons," Maharaj says. "If I get to come back, I'll be a better person and coach."

During the off-season, goaltenders are free to work out with whomever they choose. After Maharaj was fired, DiPietro could not have sent a clearer signal to Islander management that he was not happy. DiPietro rented the Islanders' practice facility and invited two others goaltenders (Kevin Weekes of the Rangers and former Edmonton Oiler Ty Conklin) to join him while Maharaj put them through their paces.

Sudarshan Maharaj finds himself in a bit of a time warp these days. The woman who replaced him at his old teaching job with the Toronto school board retired. So he has returned to northern Etobicoke to work, once again, with kids from grades 1 to 8 with severe behavioural problems.

"I'm ducking desks for a living again," Maharaj jokes.

For such a young guy, Sudsie Maharaj has already experienced a lot of the roller coaster that is professional sports. He is trying to maintain his connection to the game by starting a goaltending scouting service that NHL teams can purchase from him. Given his experience, the genuine respect others have for him, and the harder road he has walked and skated to get from Trinidad to the NHL, it seems a good bet that we will see Maharaj's name associated with the world's best goaltenders again soon.

BACK IN THE LATE 1980S, when the Edmonton Oilers were winning five Stanley Cups over a seven-year period, most of the hockey world was falling in love with Wayne Gretzky, Mark Messier, Jari Kurri, Glenn Anderson, and Paul Coffey.

But Kevin Weekes was engrossed with another player.

Just 9 years old when the Oilers won their first Cup in 1984, Weekes could not help but notice that one player on that team looked different from all the others, and more like him. That player was Grant Fuhr. As Weekes grew up, first in Toronto's west end around St. Clair Avenue and Christie Street, then in the Huntingwood area of Scarborough, he was determined to be like Fuhr. He started playing road hockey with all the Italian kids in his first neighbourhood, and lived and died with the Toronto Maple Leafs. In grade 1, he wrote in his public school notebook that he wanted to be a goaltender in the National Hockey League.

"So I pretty much outlined my goal fairly early," Weekes says.

Weekes played hockey as a kid with the Toronto Red Wings, one of the elite teams in the old Metro Toronto Hockey League. The club was founded in 1955 and over the years has sent more than 50 players to both the NHL and its now-defunct WHA rival. Junior hockey stops took Weekes to the St. Michael's Buzzers, the Owen Sound Platers, and the Ottawa 67's before the Florida Panthers made him their second pick, 41st overall, in the 1993 entry draft.

Like nearly all 18-year-old draftees, Weekes had a bit of a wait before he could show his stuff in the NHL. Once he got there, he needed a suitcase on permanent standby. He played three seasons each with the AHL's Carolina Monarchs and the IHL's Fort Wayne Komets. Then in 1997–98, the Panthers called him up to the big show. But Weekes spent only 11 games in a Florida uniform before being shipped off to Vancouver. From there, he was traded to the New York Islanders in exchange for one of his teenage heroes, former Leaf goalie Felix Potvin. He managed to play 36 games with the Isles, and then Weekes was packing his bags again, this time for the Sunshine State's other team, the Tampa Bay Lightning. He played 61 games, winning 20 for a very bad Lightning team, and registering a 3.14 goals-against average.

Weekes finally seemed to have found a home in the NHL. But then in a move that was brilliant for the team, but not so much for Weekes, the Lightning acquired Russian goaltender Nikolai Khabibulin in March 2001. It would turn out to be the most significant trade in Tampa's short history, one that ultimately led to a Stanley Cup Championship in 2004.

For Kevin Weekes, it was back to riding the bench. He played only 19 games for Tampa during the 2001–02 season, and then, he was packing his bags, this time for the Carolina Hurricanes.

Once again, things initially looked promising. Weekes dazzled the hockey world with his lightning-fast reflexes and superb play. When the playoffs came around in 2002, the Hurricanes made him their starting goalie. He led the 'Canes to surprise upsets of New Jersey and Montreal. But then his skills seemed to abandon him. Coach Paul Maurice put him back on the bench, and rode the team's other goalie, Arturs Irbe, all the way to the final, where Carolina fell to the Detroit Red Wings.

Weekes recaptured his starting job in Carolina, playing 51 games in 2002–03, then 66 in 2003–04. He also made a bit of history by becoming one of just two starting goaltenders in NHL history to improve his goals-against average for six consecutive seasons. Only Curtis Joseph had done that previously.

Weekes returned to New York in 2005–06, this time to the Rangers, where he was a valuable backup, getting into 32 games. With his 6th team in 8 years, Weekes signed a 3-year contract and, naturally, he now hopes to be in the Big Apple for a more extended stay.

Weekes studied many of the game's greats: Patrick Roy; Felix Potvin; Bill Ranford, who replaced Grant Fuhr in Edmonton; Mike Richter of the Rangers; and Soviet legend Vladislav Tretiak. But Fuhr was his favourite. When Weekes was just 14, he visited Maple Leaf Gardens while the Oilers were in Toronto. He had a chance to meet both Fuhr and Potvin.

"And that had a real big impact on me," recalls Weekes, who would also befriend veteran Leafs such as Glenn Healy, Curtis Joseph, Steve Thomas, and Tie Domi.

Obviously, it was more than just a shared love of goaltending that drew Weekes to Fuhr. Their shared ethnicity was a huge factor in Weekes choosing Fuhr as his role model.

The Rangers may be the 2006–07 season's best example of the United Nations on ice. There are more Czechs (8) on their 25-man roster than Canadians (7). There are also 4 Americans, 2 Swedes, 1 Lithuanian, 1 Latvian, 1 Russian, and 1 Slovakian. As cosmopolitan a team as the Rangers are, there is still only one black face in their locker room, and it belongs to Kevin Weekes. Does he ever think about that? He says almost never.

"I'm real comfortable in my own skin, but I'm also comfortable in any environment," he says. "My parents are equally as comfortable in hockey arenas, too, as we would be if we were at home among one another or back in Barbados. I think hockey people as a whole are really good people. They're fairly down to earth and I think their horizons are broadening when you see so many people from different places that play.

"Hockey transcends everything," he continues. "It's like art, it's like food. It transcends distance and culture. So one language and one belief that everyone has in here is hockey."

Mike Grier agrees. He once played on an Edmonton Oiler team where he was one of five black players (Anson Carter, Sean Brown, Georges Laraque, Joaquin Gage, and Grier himself). More often than not, though, he has been the lone black face during his travels through NHL locker rooms in Edmonton, Washington, Buffalo, and now San Jose. He has had good relationships with both black and white teammates, and encountered very little racist trash talking on the ice.

"I think the players have all been very professional," he says. "I think, as you get older, people grow and mature and realize you're just another player like everyone else."

Kevin Weekes is a nice guy. He is unfailingly polite during interviews. He thanks reporters after they have finished "scrumming" him in the locker room. As I was talking to him after a heartbreaking loss to the Florida Panthers in a shootout, someone from the Rangers' training staff handed him a drink and he stopped our chat long enough to thank the staffer. Weekes is now in his 30s and remains single. He still lives in North Toronto in the off-season, and calls his parents in Scarborough after every game he plays.

"It is not like minor hockey, driving home in the car with them, but it is as close as you can get," he says. "My parents will always be my parents and I will always be their kid."

However, there have been harsh moments. While playing for Carolina, Weekes suffered the indignity of having a fan toss a banana at him as he was leaving the ice. The incident did not happen in the Sunbelt, but in Montreal during the 2002 playoffs. It was a shocking reminder that, as much as Weekes likes to think of himself as just another Canadian kid who made it to the big time, there is still a segment of hockey fans that will never let him forget he is not just a goalie. He is a black goalie.

"To me, it's not a big deal," he told the *St. Petersburg Times.* "You're always going to have ignorant people. The arena in Montreal holds, what, 20,000 people? You can't expect them all to have class."

Weekes clearly does have class. His approach to the game he loves also appears to be mature beyond his years. Citing grizzled veterans such as baseball's Roger Clemens and basketball's John Stockton, he mentions how even the best players never stop learning.

"And that's a funny thing about sports that people don't understand. Even when it appears as though you've mastered it, you never really have," he says. "You can always make one more save."

Starting in the fall of 2007, Weekes will be making those saves on the other side of the Hudson River. He signed a 2-year contract with the New Jersey Devils for $1.375 million to back-up one of the game's best, Martin Brodeur.

AFTER WILLIE O'REE hung up his skates at the end of the 1970s, he moved to San Diego and dropped out of sight. He worked for a company that handled security for the NFL's San Diego Chargers and later worked security at a San Diego hotel. In 1990, he became a goodwill ambassador for the International Hockey League's San Diego Gulls. Six years later, some smart folks at the NHL asked him to come home. Today, the annual Willie O'Ree All-Star Game celebrates hockey's baby steps toward a more diverse game. On January 18, 1998—the 40th anniversary of his first game in the NHL—O'Ree was appointed the league's director of youth development for NHL diversity. That program offers scholarships to inner-city kids to attend summer hockey camp or local hockey schools. The league says the program has introduced more than 40,000 boys and girls to hockey. The program now has its first graduate in Tampa Bay goaltender Gerald Coleman, an Illinois native, who got into two games for the Lightning in 2005–06.

"I think all the minority players in the league, it is something that we all relish and try to do as much as we can and try to get the message out there," says Mike Grier of the Sharks, "that, with young inner-city kids, minority kids, black or Spanish or whatever kids, if they want to play hockey, it is something that they can do."

The league also sponsors the NHL Diversity Equipment Bank, aimed at getting people and manufacturers to donate used hockey equipment to so-called at-risk youth. The league says it's received $500,000 worth of equipment so far.

The NHL may have been the last major professional sports league to integrate, but the tangible signs of progress are everywhere. Black players run the gamut from goal-scoring champions (Jarome Iginla in 2002), to bruisers who can strike fear into an opponent (13-year-veteran Donald Brashear, with more than 2000 career penalty minutes).

Somewhere in San Diego, the septuagenarian Willie O'Ree is smiling.

# THE EAGLE AND
# THE DOMINATOR

*There is no position in sport as noble as goaltending.*
—VLADISLAV TRETIAK

They are two of the very best ever to have put on the pads. They are both Stanley Cup champions and Olympic gold-medal winners. Some day, they both will venture to a beautiful old building in Toronto at the corner of Front and Yonge, better known as the Hockey Hall of Fame, where their pictures and stupendous achievements will forever grace a wall of excellence.

Their careers have intersected in unique and distinctive ways. In fact, they are the answer to one of hockey's more unusual trivia questions: Name the only two National Hockey League goaltenders ever to have been teammates on a Stanley Cup finalist and also faced each other as opponents in another Cup final?

They are universally known as the Eagle and the Dominator. They have enjoyed fabulous success between the pipes. Now in their 40s, both have made comebacks from potentially career-ending injuries, and this past season, worked for a fraction of the money they made during their glory years. Both were determined to convince those who said they were all washed up that there was (and is) a lot more life left in their battered bodies. Other players, including some of the best, have retired. But they're still playing the game.

These netminders are Ed Belfour and Dominik Hasek. They are old men, at least as age is calculated in the world of professional sports. They both play in goal, arguably one of the toughest jobs in team sports. No other position requires such consistent athleticism, fast reflexes, and stoical endurance under pressure. They prospered in the old, pre-lockout league. Remarkably, they have adapted to the changes introduced when the lockout ended, and are thriving in the new, revitalized NHL.

A vast distance separated them in their early years. Dominik Hasek was born in January 1965 in Pardubice, a city of 100,000 people roughly 100 kilometres east of Prague, in the Czech Republic (then Czechoslovakia). Edward Belfour was born three months later in Carman, Manitoba, population less than 3000, about 80 kilometres from Winnipeg.

The paths that led them to the best hockey league in the world were somewhat indirect. Hasek was drafted by the Chicago Blackhawks in 1983, but not until the 10th round, 199th overall. If that seems a ridiculously low slot for picking a goaltender of his talents, one has to remember that this was before the fall of the Iron Curtain, and as a result, very few Eastern Bloc players made it to the NHL because they were simply not permitted to leave.

As a youngster growing up in Czechoslovakia, Hasek never missed watching the Czech national team play. Jiri Holocek, the country's best goaltender in the 1970s, was his hero. He didn't get to see any NHL games until the end of the 1980s, when satellite television finally made it to Eastern Europe. But apparently, he didn't need to: Hasek was named goaltender of the year in Czechoslovakia for five straight years, from 1986 to 1990. After the end of the Cold War, he emigrated to the United States and made his NHL debut with the Blackhawks in November 1990.

Hasek got very little playing time in Chicago because the first-string goaltender was a guy named Ed Belfour and he owned the job. Belfour had come to the Hawks via the University of North Dakota, also a less common way to get to the big leagues. In those days, most players came through the factory that is major junior hockey, rather than the U.S. college ranks.

Belfour had made a strong impression on Blackhawk management at the end of the 1989–90 season. The club recalled him from the Canadian national men's hockey team just in time for the playoffs. Belfour registered a respectable four wins and two losses, which stood him in good stead for winning the starting job the next season.

And what a season it wound up being—perhaps the best rookie season by a goaltender in NHL history. Belfour was between the pipes for 43 Chicago wins (an NHL rookie record) and 74 games in total (also an NHL rookie record). The Eagle won the Calder Trophy as the NHL's best freshman, the Vezina Trophy as the best goalie, and the Jennings Trophy for the best goals-against average. Now that's a debut. He was so committed to excellence that the Blackhawk staff, arriving in the morning, would sometimes find Belfour asleep in the trainers' room. He had been there all night long, working in his equipment, taping his sticks, and simply fallen asleep.

The following season, Belfour and the Hawks made it all the way to the Stanley Cup final, but lost in four straight games to Mario Lemeiux's Pittsburgh Penguins.

Belfour and Hasek were never really chummy in Chicago. In sports, it's hard to be friends with someone who wants your job. Their relationship may have been made more strained by the fact that Hasek spoke precious little English.

"I could say, 'Hi.' I could say, 'Thank you,' and 'Nice to meet you,'" Hasek recalls. He knew Russian from his school days in Czechoslovakia. Eventually, his English improved thanks to private tutoring and locker-room banter. But his relationship with Belfour never did improve.

"We were the same age, and he was the starting goalie," Hasek now says. "Of course, he felt I was his biggest competitor. So we didn't talk too much to each other."

And Hasek went largely unnoticed. "It was tough to get a handle on Dom," recalls Mike Keenan, who coached that Blackhawks squad. "Eventually, we put him on waivers but no one claimed him. No one knew him. The entire league turned him down."

Keenan hired the magnificent and legendary Russian goaltender Vladislav Tretiak as his goaltender coach, in hopes of getting a better understanding of what he had in Hasek. But given that the starting job was Belfour's and the Eagle didn't look like he was going anywhere, the Hawks eventually gave up on Hasek, who played just 25 games for Chicago over two seasons. Eventually, before the 1992–93 season, they sent him to the Buffalo Sabres where, once again, Hasek found himself playing second fiddle, this time behind Grant Fuhr.

But as is so often the case in professional sports, one player's misfortune becomes another's opportunity. Fuhr got hurt midway through the season; Hasek took over and never looked back.

In the Czech hockey league, Hasek wore number 9. When he arrived at Buffalo, that number was taken. He wanted to keep his connection to number 9, so for reasons he can no longer remember, he asked the Sabre training staff to put the number 3 before the 9. Thus, Hasek became the first NHL goaltender to wear the distinctive number 39.

(Several goaltenders in the NHL now wear his number, among them Cristobel Huet of the Canadiens, Rick DiPietro of the Islanders, and Nikolai Khabibulin of the Blackhawks. Despite the obvious implied compliment, Hasek jokingly complained about the phenomenon: "I don't like it. It should be only my number!")

In Buffalo, Hasek became the Dominator. He won both the Vezina and Jennings trophies in 1994 with a microscopic 1.95 goals-against average and 7 shutouts. It would not be the last time he had his name engraved on those trophies. He also became just the second goalie in NHL history to win the Hart Trophy as the league's most valuable player (Montreal's Jacques Plante was the other), and then the only one to win it twice.

It was in 1999 that the careers of the Dominator and the Eagle intersected again, this time in hockey's grandest showcase. Hasek lowered his goals-against average to an incredible 1.87, won his third consecutive Vezina, and was runner-up for the Hart (to fellow Czech Jaromir Jagr).

Belfour, meanwhile, had left Chicago, turning down a contract extension, and opted instead for the up-and-coming Dallas Stars. The Stars were the best team in the league at the end of the 1997–98 season, but could get no further than the Western

Conference final. The following season, the Stars again claimed top spot in the league during the regular season, and then Belfour's side defeated two of the game's best-ever goaltenders in Grant Fuhr and Patrick Roy during the playoffs.

That set up a Dallas Stars–Buffalo Sabres face-off in the 1999 Stanley Cup Final. The Eagle against the Dominator once again.

In 1999, the stars were perfectly aligned for Dallas. In one of the most memorable Stanley Cup–deciding games ever, Belfour and Hasek backstopped their teams into a Game 6 triple over-time in Buffalo. Belfour made 53 saves, Hasek made 50, until finally, with less than 5 minutes to go in the 3rd overtime period, Brett Hull scored arguably the most controversial goal in Cup history to give the Stars a 2–1 win.

Back then, the NHL had a rule designed to give goaltenders added protection. Attacking players were prohibited from parking themselves in the goaltender's crease. Video replays clearly showed that Brett Hull's foot was in the crease when he scored the winning goal. The second the goal went in, the Stars' bench spilled onto the ice in celebration—almost daring the officials to disallow the goal. The Sabres, meanwhile, argued vehemently that the goal should be disallowed. The Stars won the argument when the referee rejected the Sabres' complaint. The league later explained that the rule allowed a player already in possession of the puck to bring the puck into the crease to score. Since Hull scored on the third of three consecutive shots, the league ruled that Hull had possession of the puck and there-fore was allowed to pursue it into the crease. It was an explana-tion that Dallas fans didn't care about and Buffalo fans didn't believe. The stupidity of the rule became abundantly clear the following year, as the NHL simply eliminated it.

In Buffalo, they still call 1999 the year the Stanley Cup wasn't really won. But don't try telling that to Ed Belfour.

"I guess being part of a Stanley Cup team in '99 was my proudest achievement," he now says. "That was a dream come true."

Unfortunately for Belfour, that 1999 season would be as good as it got. The following year, the Stars made it back to the final but lost to the New Jersey Devils. Belfour was spectacular. He notched four shutouts on his playoff belt. One of those whitewashes—Game 5 of the final against the Devils—went into triple overtime.

The next highlight of Belfour's career came during a time of intense national pride, in which he barely participated at all. In February 2002, Team Canada won an Olympic gold medal in Salt Lake City, ending 50 years of championship drought in the most important international competition. But Belfour did not get into even a single minute of a single game. He was the team's third-string goaltender and by all accounts a model teammate. He prepared hard in case he was needed, but the New Jersey Devils' Martin Brodeur was a superstar in the nets. Team Canada's coach, Pat Quinn, who was then also coach and general manager of the Toronto Maple Leafs was impressed by Belfour's selfless attitude.

Five months later, the Stars were fading and management began to sour on Belfour. When his contract expired, they figured this 37-year-old goaltender had not much gas left in the tank and declined to re-sign him. Enter Pat Quinn. The Leafs had just been jilted by Curtis Joseph, the hometown boy (who was the second-string netminder for Canada at those same Salt Lake Olympics), when he left for Detroit. So in July 2002, Belfour signed with a Toronto team that loved to score but didn't play much defence. All Belfour did was stand on his head night after night, winning a franchise record 37 games in his first season as a Leaf. The fact that Joseph was flaming out with the Red Wings made the Belfour acquisition look even better.

Belfour followed up that performance with 10 shutouts the following year—a personal best. But in his third season as a Leaf, 2005–06, his back acted up and Belfour was able to win just 22 games. In spite of a Herculean effort on his part, the club failed to make it past the second round of the playoffs.

However, Belfour's tenure as a Leaf was not without its highlights. By the end of the 2005–06 season, he had moved past Terry Sawchuk, the last Leaf goalie to win the Stanley Cup (with Johnny Bower in 1967), into second place on the all-time wins list with an astonishing 457 victories.

"It was nice to see he got the record in Toronto," recalls Maple Leaf forward Darcy Tucker. "He's a guy who'll compete on a nightly basis like no one else I've ever seen."

Toward the end of that season, speculation was rampant in Toronto that the Leafs would decline to pick up the final option year of Belfour's contract. Essentially, the contract worked like this. If the Leafs wanted Belfour back, it would cost them another $5 million in salary. If they didn't, they could cut him loose for a $1 million buyout and have $4 million to find a cheaper (and younger) goaltender, plus tend to some other team weaknesses. In the old days, that decision would have been less difficult, since the Leafs could afford not to have to choose. But in the new NHL, a salary cap meant a tough decision would have to be made.

I asked Pat Quinn, at that point still the Leaf coach but no longer the general manager, what he would do if the decision were his.

"Ed Belfour is one of the best I've ever had," he said. "If his recovery [from back surgery] is a good one, he'll revert to form." The new general manager of the Leafs, John Ferguson, Jr., opted not to await the outcome of Belfour's surgery. He gave the netminder a cool million to walk away. In July 2006, at the age of 40 and coming off back surgery to boot, Ed Belfour signed with the Florida Panthers, one of the cheapest and weakest teams in the league. He took an 80 percent pay cut to occupy a back-up position. Everything suggested the days of Ed Belfour, Stanley Cup champion, Vezina Trophy winner, and the second-most victorious goalie of all time, were almost done.

MEANWHILE, Hasek's tenure in Buffalo was alternatively magnificent and miserable. When he was on his game, he took the team further than it had any business going—he was that dominant. But before the Stanley Cup run—during the 1996–97 season—Hasek became a divisive figure for both his team and the hockey world.

The relationship between Hasek and the Sabres' head coach, Ted Nolan, was tense. Nolan took a team consisting mainly of no-names and crafted them into an exciting, winning squad. The club's promise to outwork any opponent resonated in blue-collar Buffalo. But the one superstar on the team—its quirky European-born goaltender—often required special treatment, something that was anathema to Nolan, a First Nations Canadian who struggled for everything he achieved in his hockey life.

So when Hasek took himself out of a game in the first playoff round against Ottawa in 1997, complaining that he heard his knee "pop," reporters covering the team suspected there was more to the story than they were being told. Team doctors insisted his condition was "day to day," hockey parlance for an injury that needs constant re-evaluation, and the player could be fit to play at any time. Hockey writer Jim Kelley of *The Buffalo News* suggested that Hasek was purposely keeping himself out of the lineup to undermine his coach. After Hasek read the piece, he burst out of the Sabres' dressing room, looking for the reporter. Some observers say he attacked Kelley, ripping his shirt and attempting to choke him. Meanwhile, Hasek's backup, the unheralded Steve Shields, played some of the best hockey of his life in Hasek's absence, and the Sabres managed to eliminate the Senators from the playoffs.

The league suspended Hasek for three games after his confrontation with Kelley. (Would they have suspended an injured player?) In the fourth game of the following series against the Philadelphia Flyers, with the Sabres down three games to none, Hasek took the pre-game warm-up, only to leave the ice complaining that he felt his knee tweak again. The Sabres would go on to lose the series in five games.

What did Hasek think of the allegations that he exaggerated his maladies in a power play with his organization?

"Of course, it's definitely unpleasant," he said, his normally bubbly mood turning sour at the question. "It bothers you. It makes you uncomfortable. But I know I've always made the right decision. If you can't help on the ice, there's nothing you can do about it. It's tough to make these decisions, but in my mind, the most important thing is how I'm feeling myself."

If things were strange on the ice for the Sabres that year, they were even screwier off the ice. The club so overachieved in 1997 that several team officials won individual awards. The general manager, John Muckler (since fired after six years as GM of the Senators), was named executive of the year. The coach, Ted Nolan (now with the Islanders), won the Jack Adams Award as the league's best coach. And Hasek hit the trifecta in winning the Vezina Trophy, the Hart Trophy, and the Lester Pearson Award (given by the players' association to their choice as league's best player).

And then Muckler was fired for feuding with Nolan. Nolan was fired for feuding with both Muckler and Hasek. And Hasek was miserable.

Hasek eventually got out of Buffalo. He was traded to the powerhouse Detroit Red Wings in time for the 2001–02 season, and this time, everything fell into place: 41 wins on the season (a best for his career) and a Stanley Cup championship—finally. Having reached the top of the mountain, Hasek announced his retirement.

"I was very proud of winning the Hart trophies," Hasek told me earlier this year. "But you don't celebrate that with your teammates. It's different when you win with your teammates. The whole city celebrates. The whole nation celebrates," he added, referring to the Olympic gold medal he won with the Czech Republic in 1998.

Hasek's achievements would have been enough for any *two* goaltenders in the NHL. But apparently, they were not enough for him. Retirement did not suit him. And so, after a year on the sidelines, he announced his return to the Red Wings. Sadly, the Hollywood script went awry at this point. The groin injury returned, and after just 14 games of the 2003–04 season (the last one before the lockout), Hasek was done. In an almost unprece- dented move in modern pro sports, he declined to accept his salary for half the season. He went home to the Czech Republic, had surgery, and wondered whether his body had finally given out on him.

The owners' lockout of the players and the cancellation of the 2004–05 season was a black eye for hockey but a godsend for Hasek. His body, which he had always pushed to the limit on the ice, appreciated the pause. And when the Red Wings decided not to re-sign Hasek once his contract expired, the Ottawa Senators decided to take a flyer on him. At the age of 40, could Hasek recapture even some of his old glory?

I decided to find out. I visited Montreal in January 2006 and watched the Canadiens host the Senators. Ray Emery got the start in goal for Ottawa, but was shaky early on, getting pulled while the game was still in the first period. In comes Hasek, having not expected to play, having had no warm-up to speak of, and with his team trailing 4–1.

Generally speaking, a 4–1 score is too one-sided to be considered great hockey. But this was not the case at the Bell Centre on that day. One could only marvel at the juxtaposition of bone-crushing hits and delicate passes. And once Emery had been pulled, both goaltenders—Hasek for Ottawa and Cristobel Huet for the Habs—were strutting their best acrobatic stuff. In the third period alone, Hasek made four "highlight reel" saves. On one occasion, he stood up to a repeated barrage of shots. He twisted his body so dramatically to stop the puck that his stick went flying through the air and ended up behind his own net. On another occasion, a Canadiens player at the point shot the puck toward Hasek, but there was so much traffic in front of the Ottawa net, Hasek could not have seen it coming. At the last fraction of a second, as the puck emerged through a maze of bodies, Hasek saw and stopped it, and again, sent his stick into orbit. A third time, the Canadiens had a power play and passed the puck briskly, trying to disrupt Ottawa's penalty-killing foursome. Eventually, defenseman Sheldon Souray was set up at the point in the middle of the ice for a perfect scoring opportunity. He wound up and launched a rocket at Hasek. The pride of Pardubice calmly skated through all the traffic around his net, came out to the top of his crease, made the save, and pounced on the rebound as well. Finally, with 3.7 seconds left in the game, the Canadiens got a breakaway. Hasek shut the door.

Hasek played 44 minutes and 27 seconds and allowed no goals. How does he do it? That is when Hasek becomes the Dominator. Critics, observers, opponents, even teammates are left wondering how such an unorthodox style of play—the flipping, the flopping, the saves while lying on his back—can still be so effective.

After the game, I ask his opponent on the night, Cristobel Huet, what he thought of Hasek's performance.

"He's great to watch, but you don't want to play that way," Huet says.

"Why not?"

"Only *he* can play that way," Huet responds.

For years, the Senators had been missing something. The club had been long on talent but short on clutch goaltending in the playoffs, when it counted the most. It seemed that Hasek would make up for what they lacked.

And then came the Olympics.

The Italians hosted the 20th Olympic Winter Games in Torino in February 2006. Hasek had already backstopped his native Czech Republic team to Olympic gold in 1998. Four years later, the Canadians stormed back to claim international bragging rights, while the Czechs fell to fifth at the Salt Lake City games. The hockey world could not wait for a rematch between Hasek's side and defending champion Team Canada.

Fans of both sides would be left heartbroken. The Canadians failed to capture a medal of any colour. And just nine minutes into the Czech Republic's first game against unheralded Germany, Dominik Hasek felt something very seriously wrong in his upper right thigh. He left the game and did not return for the rest of the Olympics. Without Hasek, the Czechs could capture only bronze.

Part of what has made Hasek's injuries so maddeningly puzzling is that they tend to take place on ho-hum plays. Hockey fans generally expect that players get hurt and are removed from the rink if there are plays that involve spectacular collisions, slap-shots that knock goalie masks off, or slashes that break sticks and bones. But none of Hasek's injuries has been caused in such obvious ways. When you watch the replays, it is often hard to see the cause of any injury at all. The 2006 Olympics were a perfect example: Hasek dropped to his knees to make what appeared to be a routine save, and then found himself incapable of playing for the next four months. Predictably, in a town whose politicians and journalists love to traffic in rumour and gossip, there was plenty of talk. Some people just couldn't see how such an innocently acquired injury could be so debilitating. Even when the playoffs came around, rumours persisted that Hasek would make a glorious return to the ice and lead the Sens to the Cup final.

Except he didn't. The Dominator didn't play another game that year. At the conclusion of the 2005–06 season, and in the wake of the immensely talented Senators taking yet another predictable powder during the playoffs, the club said goodbye and good riddance to Hasek. In a most unusual media briefing, head coach Bryan Murray announced it was time for the club to "move on" without Hasek. He made the comment without previously consulting either Hasek or general manager John Muckler.

Five months later, at the opening of the 2006–07 season, I asked coach Murray whether his team had put the Sturm und Drang of Hasek's time in Ottawa behind it.

"He was a top pro guy," the coach acknowledged. "Unfortunately, he wouldn't play when I asked him and the players asked him at playoff time. I think you have to have great trust in this business. I think that was lost."

Of his injuries, Hasek says, "I can say by far these are the worst moments. If you lose a game, it's disappointing but you play the next game. But injuries—it takes months and it's a very disappointing part of the game."

The ghost of Hasek still appeared to haunt Canada's capital city even as the team signed Swiss-born Martin Gerber to replace Hasek in July 2006. The new goaltender seemed all too aware of how tall an order that was.

"There are some special people in the league you can't replace," Gerber said. "He's been such a great player and still is."

Did Hasek's style influence the way Gerber plays his game?

Gerber laughs. "There's no way I can play like that," he says. "I don't think there's anyone who can play like that. His style is so unique."

Having played himself out of the Senators' goaltending job, Dominik Hasek's career options seemed awfully limited. The Florida Panthers general manager at the time, Mike Keenan, called Hasek's agent to inquire whether the Czech star might be interested in coming south. The answer was no. If Hasek were ever going to play again in the NHL, it would be for one team and one team only. Only trouble was, that team wasn't showing any interest.

And then it did. Just as the Panthers had taken a chance on Ed Belfour, the Wings decided to rehire Hasek. In July 2006, the Wings gave Hasek a one-year contract for $750,000—a pittance compared to the $8 million the Dominator once fetched. Even at that, skeptics called it a waste of money. But funny things happen in sports. Sometimes, for example, players make unexpected comebacks. Midway through the 2006–07 season and at age 41, Hasek had registered the league's best goals-against average (a remarkably stingy 1.85 goals against per game). In a season that saw the Wings lose two of their best all-time players (Steve Yzerman to retirement and Brendan Shanahan to free agency and the New York Rangers), Hasek was standing on his head like in the old days. In a season where most expected the Wings to deteriorate markedly, Hasek helped lead the team to the best record in the Western Conference. He was second in the league in goals-against average with a stingy 2.05, and second again in shutouts with 8, passing Lorne Chabot for 10th place on the all-time career shutouts list. Hasek doesn't play almost every game any more. But he was between the pipes for more than three-quarters of Detroit's matches and was still marking new achievements. During one stretch of play over four games in November 2006, Hasek held his opponents scoreless for 181 minutes and 17 seconds—the longest shutout sequence in the NHL that year and remarkably, given all his past success, the longest whitewash of Hasek's own brilliant career.

Not bad.

While the comeback from his Olympic injury was exceeding everyone's expectations, the question of why Hasek wanted to return to the NHL was still inadequately answered in my mind. The money, relatively speaking, wasn't that good. He had won every important team and individual honour available to him. So why continue to play and risk another serious injury?

Jim Bedard is the goaltending coach for the Red Wings. It is his job to make sure Dominik Hasek is as prepared to play every night as is humanly possible. That means putting Hasek through a strenuous regime of stretching exercises, drills, and workouts to reduce the potential for injury. That means poring over hours of video to look for tendencies of the other teams' best players.

"I feel my job is keeping him sharp, keeping him game-ready, to compete at this level," Bedard says. "You don't teach Dominik Hasek anything."

Bedard recognizes hockey genius when he sees it and Hasek's got it. "With older players like this, the panic level is so low," Bedard observes. "Some call it experience. I call it 'level of panic.' It's something you can't teach. It comes with experience and talent."

"He reads the game better than any goalie in the league," adds Detroit head coach Mike Babcock. "He knows where it's coming from. He just has unbelievable hockey sense as a goalie."

Bedard offers this insight in explaining why players such as Hasek—or his 45-year-old teammate Chris Chelios—continue to play a brutal game long after most have retired: "As you get older, you see the light at the end of the tunnel and you appreciate being in this environment and atmosphere," Bedard says. "You can't tell anybody who hasn't been in this atmosphere what it's like. It's a boys club. It's a group thing: the travelling, the bonding, things that go on in the dressing room that you just can't relate to the real world. Especially at this level."

"But what hasn't he seen? What hasn't he won?"

"I see the fire burning extremely bright in his belly," Bedard says. "He doesn't like to get scored on in practice. He's happy when he wins and is unhappy when he loses because he expects a lot of himself. He makes people better around him because of his work ethic."

I ask Hasek, what's left to prove?

"I want to prove to myself and my kids that I'm a competitor and can compete," he says. "It's all about winning, getting back on the ice, that I can play at my age."

Mike Babcock thinks it goes beyond that.

"I think he *does* have something left to prove," he says. "I think he thinks it didn't go the way he wanted in Ottawa. And the legacy he wants to leave is that he's the best in the game. You can't blame him for that. He's beyond competitive. He just wants to win all the time."

Even though his return to the NHL didn't lead to a Stanley Cup championship, Hasek had plenty to be proud of. He helped take the 2006–07 Red Wings to the third round of the playoffs, before bowing out in six games to the eventual Cup champions, the Anaheim Ducks.

OCTOBER 9, 2006: Two nights earlier, Ed Belfour had started for Florida against the Atlanta Thrashers and stunk up the joint. Coach Jacques Martin pulled him in the middle of the second period. Now, on this Thanksgiving Day in Toronto, the Eagle takes to the net for an afternoon practice. It is his first return to the Air Canada Centre since Toronto chose to buy him out of the option year on his contract and fans are looking forward to a confrontation between Belfour and his replacement. The Leafs' new goalie is Belleville, Ontario, native Andrew Raycroft. At $6 million over 3 years, he costs less than half as much as Belfour. And he does not have a wonky back like Belfour's. There is, however, as big a question mark on Raycroft's back as on Belfour's. While a member of the Boston Bruins in 2004, Raycroft won the Calder Trophy as the league's best rookie. But Raycroft's sophomore year was a disaster. He saw his goals-against average skyrocket from 2.05 to 3.71, his playing time cut in half, and much of the hockey world write him off as a flash in the pan. But that was then, this was now and the Leafs figured they would rather gamble cheaply on Raycroft returning to form than pay dearly for the privilege of hoping that Belfour could do the same.

Belfour is looking comfortable warming up on his old home ice. The Panthers start with breakaway practice, a play that was pretty rare in the old NHL. But with shootouts now used to break ties, teams are practising breakaways more.

Belfour's old Maple Leaf teammate Gary Roberts comes in on a break and blasts a shot that hits the goaltender right in the chest. Even from my vantage point in the seats 20 metres away, that shot stung. Roberts taps Belfour on the back with his stick as if to apologize, as he skates away.

After each shot, Belfour retreats into the net, like a turtle returning inside his shell. Then, as the shooter makes his approach, Belfour skates out to the top of the crease and prepares for a shot, a deke, or something else. You would never know Belfour's back was an issue until a pause in the practice gives him a chance to remind us that it is. He stands up straight, reaches behind him with both arms to grab the crossbar of the net, and then shuffles his feet back and forth while leaning backwards as much as he can. You can almost imagine him muttering to himself, "Come on, stretch, baby, stretch."

Apparently, on this day, Belfour's back is responding to the plea. He may be 41 and his previous game may have been a dud, but he looks terrific in goal, going hard on every shot, unwilling even in practice to give up an easy one to teammates. The slapshots are coming in at warp speed, but Belfour is saving everything. His reflexes still look lightning fast. Even on the drill where someone fires a shot from the point and two other teammates try to whack in the rebound, Belfour gives up nothing, although outnumbered three to one.

Half an hour later, the goaltender takes a break. But another two minutes go by and he is back in, taking more shots from close and far—wrist shots, snap shots, slappers, and everything except Roberts's earlier blast to the chest is hitting his pads or gloves.

Ed Belfour is in the zone.

Practice comes to an end. Belfour leaves the ice and heads to the dressing room. As he trudges to his stall, I approach him (politely of course) and ask whether he has a few minutes to chat.

"Not now," he says irritably. "Don't you know the routine?"

I do know that Belfour is a notoriously bad interview. He is renowned around the league for answering questions with the most stultifying, yawn-inducing answers. There is not a cliché he has failed to trot out in his plodding, monotone voice. I cannot say for certain that this is his intention, but it seems as if Belfour actually tries hard *not* to say anything remotely interesting. My brief experience with Belfour the Maple Leaf did nothing to move me from that view. One day, after a practice, I approached Belfour and sat beside him in the dressing room. I flipped my tape recorder on, started to ask questions. Every question was met with a one-word answer. It was not as if he was being hostile. He wasn't. He just seemed thoroughly uninterested in talking about anything related to his team, his game, his career, or his preparation. Lest I take it personally, Toronto's hockey beat reporters told me, "That's just Eddie."

But I figured, that was then, this is now. He has returned to Toronto for the first time as a Panther and surely he will realize how interested the hockey world is in that story. And happily, he followed up his initial, querulous response by saying, "Just let me get undressed and then I'll talk."

And then, one of the strangest things I have ever seen in a locker room of any sport took place.

As Ed Belfour sat at his stall, slowly and methodically removing his gear, the assembled members of the working press just waited and watched. Six cameramen formed a semicircle about a metre and a half in front of him. Then there was another ring of newspaper and radio reporters around the cameramen. And we all just waited and watched as Ed Belfour took his equipment off. No one said a word. The reporters were looking around the room, glancing at the television set in the corner, checking their BlackBerrys, trying to do anything but stare at Belfour, who was paying them no heed at all. The Panthers' public-relations guy elbowed his way in to toss Belfour, now dripping with sweat, a towel. With the stench of Absorbine Junior in the air, the waiting game continued. Off came the pads. Then the skates. It wasn't as if Belfour was dragging out the process. But on the other hand, he wasn't rushing to get changed either. And all the while, 20 reporters and cameramen were waiting.

Finally, Belfour is in just a T-shirt and underwear and there is a collective sense that our patience will be rewarded. But no. Belfour walks away. Without a word of explanation, he walks straight through the scrum of reporters toward the trainer's room, and is gone. He does not say, "I'll be right back." Nothing. I have staked out many political meetings in my time and I have never seen anything like it. Even ill-tempered cabinet ministers behave more generously.

Eventually, several minutes later, Belfour does re-emerge, holds court, and gives predictable answers to predictable questions. *Yes, it was great to play in Toronto, the fans were great, the guys were great, but stuff happens and now I'm in Florida, where the training staff is great and we're all workin' hard to get prepared to play again.* It's the standard Belfour repertoire of stale clichés.

The television people are the first to break away from the pack, having acquired their sound bites to punctuate the main story—Belfour's return to Toronto. The radio folks hang in a little longer. Oddly enough, by the time he turns his attention to me, Belfour is in a somewhat talkative mood. In fact, now that the grind of supplying quotes to the daily press is over, and virtually all the other reporters have gone, Belfour is actually getting as introspective as I have ever seen him.

The first thing I want an update on is that wonky back of his. In the spring of 2003, I spent a month in hospital recovering from complications related to a herniated disk in my lower back. I know what crushingly debilitating back pain is like and cannot imagine how anyone can play professional hockey with a back that refuses to co-operate.

"What hurts?" I ask him.

"Nothing right now," Belfour says. "I feel good. I'm just working on my game."

Next, I want to know why, with his achievements and health concerns, he continues to play.

"I always feel I have a lot to prove every year," he says.

What more can he have to prove?

Belfour talks about how the game is constantly in flux, particularly of late with all the rule changes. He notes that the younger players are faster. There are more power plays now that the referees are calling most every infraction. And because defencemen can no longer tackle attacking forwards in the goaltender's crease, there is simply a lot more action and distraction for puckstoppers to deal with.

"I still love playing the game and I'm a competitive guy," Belfour continues. "Ever since I was a little kid, I always wanted to be the best I could be, play the hardest I could. I guess I'm wired that way."

"Wired" is a good way to describe Ed Belfour. For those who have only ever seen the mild-mannered master of the cliché on television, that description will seem odd. But to the people who have played with Belfour, it will not.

"Yeah, he's an emotional guy when he's in the room," says Gary Roberts. "He's very vocal during the game and in the dressing room between periods. He screams once in a while. But that's good. You can't have too quiet a room."

Does Belfour confirm Roberts's description of him as a screamer?

"Only if things go really bad," he says with a smile.

Belfour admits he was a lot worse when he was younger. "But as you mature in the league, you learn how to handle things better."

He has not always handled things well. There was that incident in March 2000 when he played with the Dallas Stars. Police were called to a local Dallas hotel after patrons complained that a loud and apparently drunk Belfour was causing a ruckus. The goalie eventually pleaded guilty to resisting arrest after scuffling with police and security guards. He reportedly spat in the face of one officer and kicked two others in the chest. Eventually, the authorities required pepper spray to calm him down. Then things completely deteriorated when Belfour offered the officers money to make the situation go away. At first, the officers said he offered $100,000. Then he offered $1 billion. At the end of it all, Belfour was slapped on the wrist with a $3000 fine and 24 months of probation, during which time he was required to visit two Dallas high schools to warn students about the excesses of alcohol.

Sadly, this was not an isolated incident. In April 2007, Belfour was arrested outside a South Florida nightclub and charged with disorderly intoxication and resisting an officer. This came after security guards from the club asked police to make Belfour and his teammate Ville Peltonen leave the premises. According to police, Belfour refused, walked toward the officer "in a fighting stance," and pushed him. Police say Belfour then fell forward on the ground, kicking and refusing to submit to his arrest. Police add his speech was slurred, his eyes were bloodshot, and he smelled of alcohol.

Incidents such as these are titillating and cannot fail to attract the attention of the media. At the same time, it's obviously awkward to ask Belfour probing questions about whether or not he has an alcohol problem. His relations with the fourth estate are already strained, after all.

"He's very guarded with the media because he's been burned a few times," says Doug Stapleton, who handles Belfour's public appearances and manages his website.

But Stapleton insists Belfour has a good, although very dry, sense of humour. He recalls an incident during the lockout when Belfour was scheduled to sign autographs in Toronto. Belfour was supposed to show up at 1 p.m., and Stapleton called the goalie's cell phone just to make sure he would be on time.

"Are you close by, Eddie?" Stapleton asked.

"What do you mean?" Belfour asked.

"Your autograph signing," Stapleton said. "It starts in 15 minutes. Are you close?"

"Oh no," Belfour replied, sounding disorganized and like he'd just gotten out of bed. "I thought it started at 4. I just stepped out of the shower."

Stapleton started to panic. He had a store full of hundreds of hockey fans The Eagle was about to jilt.

"And just then," Stapleton says, "I look outside, and there he is pulling his car up." Gotcha.

Belfour has two children from his first marriage. His daughter Regan lives in Toronto with her mother, so while he is in town, a visit is in order. His son is a chip off the old block. On this Thanksgiving Day in October 2006, 17-year-old Dayn Belfour is a 6'0", 200-pound goaltender with the Winkler Flyers in Manitoba's Junior A hockey league. And the similarities with his father do not end there. Eddie the Eagle also played for Winkler, and for the same coaches now mentoring Dayn. The biggest difference between father and son is that Dayn wears number 1. He cannot wear his father's familiar number 20 because the Flyers have retired it in Ed's honour. But he does wear the same style mask, complete with an eagle painted on it, just like his father (although his teammates have nicknamed Dayn "the Beagle" just to bug him).

BELFOUR DIDN'T PLAY the night after I talked to him in October. Panthers coach Jacques Martin started Alex Auld instead. So Belfour's real return to Toronto was delayed until the next Panthers–Leafs matchup in December. In the interim, there had been another incident involving Belfour—early morning "horseplay" in a Uniondale, New York, hotel, after which Auld required stitches. Witnesses said Belfour was getting rowdy, Auld tried to calm him down, and things degenerated into a wrestling match. The team insists alcohol was not a factor. Whatever happened that night, Belfour had been even more reluctant to engage the media ever since.

How would the Leaf Nation greet Belfour on his return? After the Leafs' mid-morning game-day practice, I asked Toronto coach Paul Maurice whether he or his charges would be upset if the hometown fans cheered lustily for the visiting goaltender.

"Not at all," he insisted. "I'm sure our guys would have a positive view of that. They appreciate that the Leaf jersey may not be the last jersey they wear either."

Were the Leafs a tad spooked or intimidated by Belfour's return to Toronto? It sounded like it. "He's in a group of guys," Maurice said, "that if it's going for them, you won't beat them."

What remained to be seen was whether Ed Belfour would have it going for him on this night.

I looked for some hint of that at the Panthers' game-day skate. When it came time for the Panthers to practise their shootout drills, Belfour at first looked quite ordinary. In a drill where the goaltender has the advantage and should save the majority of shots, the first shooter put one through the five-hole. Then came a goal on the short side. And another one on a deke.

Sure enough, Belfour was only warming up. The next shooter lost the puck after Belfour poke-checked it away. Then a pad save. Then a glove save. Then a stick save covering the five-hole. The next player tries a deke to his forehand, but Belfour, now in the skater's head, perfectly anticipates the move and slides over leaving absolutely no daylight to shoot at. Twenty penalty shots later, having saved almost all but the first few, Belfour skates to the bench for a water break, having demonstrated he is still scary fast with his reflexes and impressive in instinct. Finally, he skates back and forth between the blue lines, clearly alone with his own thoughts. No other player approaches him. He is in his own world. Then, for what must be the millionth time in his career, he gets down on the ice onto his knees and stretches again and again and again. First the groin, then the left leg, then the right leg. And with that, he leaves the ice and disappears into the trainer's room.

Maybe it's the recent media boycott, or maybe it's something else, but on this trip to Toronto Belfour just doesn't look as if he is enjoying himself. I asked several of his teammates and they all assure me the Ed Belfour that the media know is not the same friend and teammate they associate with.

"I have dinner with him socially and he's very easygoing," says Gary Roberts (who was sent to the Penguins at the trade deadline). "But remember, he's a goalie. It's the toughest position in the game. Goalies have to be tightly wound up."

"He's not the most talkative guy and doesn't open up very easily," admits Martin Gelinas. "But he's a friend and I like him."

Defenceman Ric Jackman, 29 years old and fresh off a 2007 Stanley Cup win with the Anaheim Ducks, has played with Belfour in Dallas, Toronto, and most recently Florida. When I spoke with him, Jackman saw a veteran, whose focus and preparation may be misinterpreted as aloofness or unhappiness.

"He's as cheerful as any guy, but he doesn't joke around and throw tape balls at guys," says Jackman, a Toronto native. "He's constantly preparing and that's why he's so successful."

It's 7:30 P.M. at the Air Canada Centre and the Leafs and Panthers are about to take to the ice. The Leafs are coming off one of their best games of the season, a 9–2 thumping of the New York Rangers just two days earlier. It is the club's third consecutive win after suffering through a miserable seven-game losing streak. The team feels as if it has turned a corner. Public address announcer Andy Frost delivers the starting lineups in his pre-game spiel. Another ex-Leaf, Gary Roberts, gets a nice cheer when his name is mentioned. But Roberts has played in Toronto several times since leaving Ontario's capital city. Tonight, all eyes are on the prodigal goaltender.

"And starting in goal for the Florida Panthers, number 20, Ed Belfour," says Frost, to a decent but not overwhelming cheer (remember, this is game time in Toronto—half the people have yet to arrive).

Less than three minutes into the game, the Leafs are on a power play, and right-winger Jeff O'Neill walks straight in on Belfour from the goaltender's right and wraps the puck around him into the left corner. It's Belfour's first shot on goal of the night and, just like that, the home side leads 1–0. Belfour does not appear catlike in his reflexes; more like a deer caught in the headlights. I wonder if Ed Belfour is nervous.

Halfway through the period, the Leafs are on another power play. Captain Mats Sundin takes a pass on his off wing, gets a step behind the defenceman, and goes to the net untouched. This time, however, Belfour is there. He cleverly poke-checks the puck away from Sundin and to safety.

Still, the first period is looking not bad for the home side. Or, at least until the 16-minute mark, when the Leafs begin to fall apart. Czech native Rostislav Olesz sneaks one through the pads of netminder Andrew Raycroft, and the score is tied. Then, in the last minute of the period, two more defensive meltdowns result in a couple more goals, including one by Gary Roberts, who always seems to save his best games for Toronto. Suddenly, it's 3–1.

Just 28 seconds into the second period, yet another Leaf defensive miscue results in a fourth Panther goal, again by Roberts. The Panthers will tally the next three goals and take a 7–1 lead by the midway mark of the third period. Raycroft is now long gone, having been replaced by the Leafs' backup, Jean-Sébastien Aubin. Meanwhile, Belfour appears to be getting more and more comfortable by the minute. A second period blast by Bryan McCabe is deflected and changes direction a millisecond before it gets to Belfour. Somehow, he punches out his right pad and makes what appears to be an effortless save.

The Leafs score two goals late in the game—far too late to be meaningful. The final 7–3 score flatters the hell out of them. Each team fired 36 shots at the other's net. But Ed Belfour made a huge statement about how much hockey he has left in him. The significantly younger Raycroft has looked alternatively sharp and confused (sometimes on the same night) but the season is only half over and such judgments should be not be made hastily. The two ex-Leafs—Roberts and Belfour—were the first and second stars of the game, respectively. And when they walked into the visitors' dressing room after the post-game interviews, their Panthers teammates erupted in a spontaneous cheer.

A lingering post-game question for reporters was what form the dressing room choreography with the media would assume. Knowing Belfour's habit of retreating to the trainer's table, the media were lined up around his stall in short order. When Jim Lang of Sportsnet asked Belfour whether the assembled horde might have a moment of his time, Belfour, dripping sweat and wearing only a T-shirt and underwear, immediately skedaddled, muttering almost inaudibly, "I'll be back" to no one in particular.

Once again, we waited. And waited. And waited. The television reporters, who needed their sound bites for their 11 P.M. broadcasts, nervously wondered if the Eagle's "I'll be back" could be relied upon. Or was he just trying to get out of Dodge with as little fuss as possible? This may sound petty, but for the television folks, there are three all-sports channels in Canada, all competing to be best and first. Not to mention the local news programs, that also have a sports component after 11 P.M., and the radio and newspaper reporters have deadlines of their own. Ed Belfour was testing their patience in the extreme.

Suddenly, the trainer's door opened and out flew the Eagle, still unshaven but looking very sharp in a fine, dark pinstripe suit, white shirt, and purple striped tie. The questions were all predictable and so were the answers. Was he surprised the Leafs didn't try to re-sign him? "Maybe a little bit. But that's just part of the game and you move on." Anything special about beating your old team? "It's always exciting to come back. You want to do your best against your former team."

And on it went. Only when he was asked if he had been nervous in the early going of the game did he switch off autopilot. He immediately barked out "No!" with a vehemence that was absent in all of his other answers.

Belfour did stay and answer everyone's questions politely. And after giving the media their sound bites, he left the dressing room, patiently talked to some fans, gave autographs, and even posed for pictures. His job having been done and done well, Ed Belfour, it seems, could finally relax and enjoy what he achieved—career win number 463, good for third place on the all-time wins list.

Why does he still do it? I ask Paul Maurice, who instantly breaks out into a wide smile. "He absolutely loves it," the Leafs coach says. The question prompts another memory for Maurice—a quote from former forward Kevin Dineen who played more than 1000 games in the NHL, AHL, IHL, NCAA, and international hockey before retiring in 2003 just shy of 40 years of age.

"Kevin Dineen said once they'd have to drag him kicking and screaming out of the rink. And that's about what happened," the coach said. Sounds like Belfour is reading from the same playbook. Gary Roberts sees it too.

"Look at his preparation on game day," he says. "Watch his routine. He's as dedicated as anyone I've played with. He does a lot more than anyone else. Definitely comes to play and brings the competitive edge to the dressing room. He loves the game that much."

DOMINIK HASEK and Eddie Belfour are not friends. Belfour speaks of a deep respect he has for Hasek, and acknowledges that his own play improves when he is pitted against someone of Hasek's calibre. While Hasek's post-lockout return to the NHL turned out to be more successful than any hockey expert anticipated, the Florida Panthers, conversely, still seem mired in mediocrity. They managed only a 12th-place finish out of 15 teams in the Eastern Conference in the spring of 2007. Belfour's personal record was more than respectable: 58 games played (two more than Hasek), with 27 wins against only 17 losses. His 2.77 goals-against average ranked him 22nd best in the NHL, certainly nothing to brag about. Then again, unlike Hasek, the Eagle was not blessed with having the Detroit Red Wings playing in front of him.

Does Belfour read the sports pages to keep an eye on what Hasek is up to?

"Oh no, he's probably watching me but I don't watch him," he says, before letting out a big laugh.

And how about Hasek? Does he keep an eye on Belfour?

"Once in a while, I check the papers," he confesses. "I know when he's playing, when he wins a game. I follow his career." And if the hockey highlights are on in the Red Wings' dressing room and the video features Belfour, Hasek's teammates will razz him into watching.

"We talk about it," Hasek admits. "Oh look, Eddie's back," he mimicks his teammates' refrain.

Why do Dominik Hasek and Ed Belfour still play in the National Hockey League?

"Because I love the game," Belfour said without missing a beat. "I'd love another chance to be part of a Stanley Cup championship team. That'd be awesome."

Does Hasek feel what he, in fact, is—one of the oldest players in the NHL?

"I don't know, what does it mean to feel 42?" he laughs. "I feel good. I feel happy in Detroit. I don't know what age means. I don't know how I'm supposed to feel at 42. I feel good about myself."

At 42 years old, how long can Belfour keep playing?

"Chellie is going to be 45 this year [January 2007] and I've gotta keep up with him," Belfour jokes, referring to the Red Wings' ageless defenceman Chris Chelios, who still plays a remarkable 20 minutes a night.

"Might you play that long?" I ask Belfour.

"Ah, you never know," he says with a smile.

"You'd like to if you could?"

"Sure I would," says the Eagle.

Clearly, neither Belfour nor Hasek has anything left to prove in the NHL. Except each maybe does to himself.

# BROADCASTING

*Hello Canada and hockey fans from
the United States and Newfoundland.*
—FOSTER HEWITT'S OPENING LINES TO HIS
BROADCASTS ON *HOCKEY NIGHT IN CANADA*

Foster Hewitt became the voice of professional hockey in 1927, when he started broadcasting Toronto Maple Leaf games at the old Mutual Street Arena, not far from where Maple Leaf Gardens would be built in 1931. He covered his first game on television in 1952 and ever since, *Hockey Night in Canada* has been an enduring and popular Saturday night tradition.

Hewitt died in 1985 at the age of 82. Were he alive today, Hewitt would be amazed by the explosive growth in hockey broadcasting. A year before his death, Canada's first-ever all-sports television channel signed on to the airwaves. Today, The Sports Network (TSN) has 8 million subscribers. It is available in more than 80 percent of Canadian homes and has become one of the prime vehicles for both live hockey broadcasts and coverage.

Would one all-sports channel satisfy the Canadian sports fan's appetite? Apparently not. Before long, it was followed by two more. In 1997, Headline Sports opened for business offering highlights 24 hours a day, seven days a week, and a ticker at the bottom of the screen constantly updating scores. A few years ago, the channel relaunched itself as The Score: Home for the Hardcore. It also had its licence adjusted so the channel can now broadcast sporting events as well as highlights.

In 1998, Sportsnet entered the fray. It provides four distinct regional channels: East (Quebec and the Atlantic provinces), Ontario, West (Manitoba, Saskatchewan, and Alberta), and Pacific (British Columbia and Yukon). These regional services allow the channel to tailor its programming and game selection to each region's particular tastes. As a result, Sportsnet says it broadcasts more NHL games featuring Canadian teams than any other broadcaster.

And would Foster Hewitt have imagined this development: teams owning their own television channels, rather than selling game rights to conventional network broadcasters? The Maple Leaf hockey team had 70 regular season games last year televised on CBC, TSN, or Sportsnet. The 12 games those services did not broadcast were shown on Leafs TV, a special pay TV channel owned by the club. Leafs TV provides 24/7 coverage of the activities of "Leafs Nation." This includes replays of old games, coverage of the Wendel Clark celebrity golf tournament, and, more than anything else, talk, talk, and more talk.

And the Leafs are not alone. The Vancouver Canucks put 17 of their 2006–07 regular season games not televised by CBC, Sportsnet, or TSN on Canucks TV. The team's website also lists the dozens of neighbourhood bars across British Columbia where Canuck fans can watch Canucks TV if they don't want to shell out $11.95 for each game. Similarly, the Edmonton Oilers put 11 games on their own Oilers Pay-Per-View television. The Ottawa Senators broadcast five games, and so on.

The National Hockey League is often thought of as the weakest of the four major North American sports leagues because, unlike the National Football League, Major League Baseball, and the National Basketball Association, it has never been able to sign a lucrative U.S. network television rights package. That is not to say the NHL is not on television—there were 2460 regular season NHL games in 2006–07 and all but two of them were on TV somewhere, nationally, locally, or on a specialty station. But there is no doubt that hockey's television revenues pale in comparison to those of the big three North American sports leagues for the simple reason that hockey is about as popular in the United States as arena football, bowling, or curling.

Last year, hockey's lack of popularity was underscored when some U.S. newspapers stopped sending reporters to cover their home teams' road games. Even big newspapers such as the *Los Angeles Times* declined to cover any of the Kings' or Anaheim Ducks' road games in 2006–07. The *Toronto Star*'s Chris Zelkovich noted that newspapers from just 17 of the league's 30 cities bothered to send a reporter to cover the 2006 Stanley Cup Final between Edmonton and Carolina. The lack of coverage partly reflects the financial difficulties that the newspaper industry is experiencing, but it's distressing for those who want to see the game grow in U.S. markets.

As for broadcasting, a discussion of television rights fees really needs to be broken into two categories. In Canada, there is ample competition for NHL hockey among a variety of players. Of course, the CBC has been broadcasting games for more than half a century. More recently, TSN and Sportsnet have joined the action. While the CBC does not make public its numbers, it is believed the Mother Corp. records as much as $30 million in annual revenues through its hockey broadcasts. The NHL and *Hockey Night in Canada* are extremely important properties for Her Majesty's semi-public broadcaster.

So, Canada is not the problem. When hockey people talk about the league's difficulties attracting a decent television deal, they are always referring to what's happening south of the border.

It's not really surprising that most Americans have no instinctive affinity for hockey. There is no century-old tradition of playing the game in much of the United States, as there is in Canada. Hockey is a completely foreign sport in great swaths of the U.S. South, Midwest, and West. It is hard to justify charging networks big bucks for a product that the vast majority of consumers have never seen or cared about.

However, the issue also has been mismanaged over the years by some of the league's officials. Unlike the other major sports that were happy to make scheduling accommodations to television, for example, the NHL declined to do so at a time in its history when it could have made a difference. As early as 1963, CBS Television talked to the league about creating a "hockey game of the week" on Sundays. It proposed creating a full day of sports programming, with hockey coming on right after the network's NFL fare. The NHL had no interest. Saturday was hockey night, not Sunday. And so, the U.S. networks put their vast marketing resources into promoting football, baseball, and basketball on Sundays. It would be another decade before the league scheduled weekend afternoon games to accommodate

NBC's NHL game of the week and introduced the hockey world to Peter Puck, the animated black disk that taught the game to many Americans who had never seen hockey before. But by waiting until 1973 before acting, the NHL essentially gave the other major sports a full decade's head start in promoting their game and stars. The league has never caught up.

The kinds of broadcasting rights fees the major U.S. networks are paying the other sports must make officials in the NHL's head office green with envy. The NFL takes in nearly $4 billion a year in broadcasting revenues. The television landscape has been fractured by the hundreds of new channels that crop up every year, but these changes have never affected the value of the NFL property, whose rights fees have only ever increased. If all of the NFL's 32 teams failed to sell a single ticket for a single game all year, each team would still reap $100 million in revenues from TV money alone. Talk about a profitable venture. And, of course, the Super Bowl is still the single most important television event in any broadcasting season, where 30-second commercials cost $2.4 million according to *Advertising Age* magazine.

While neither baseball nor basketball comes close to the NFL's prosperity, each is still doing not badly. A given franchise in either of those two major professional sports can still look forward to receiving $20 million apiece in television revenues. In today's sports economy, that will still buy the services of a few stars. And those numbers refer only to national network revenues, not other local deals that all teams also have. By contrast, the NHL's latest television deal will pay each of the league's 30 clubs $2 million. That will pay the salary of one above-average player. Using another yardstick, *The Washington Post* estimates the NFL's television revenues account for a whopping 66 percent of the league's overall earnings. For the NHL, television income accounts for just 3 percent of its earnings.

Because hockey's numbers are so small relative to other sports, journalists have routinely dumped on every one of the NHL's broadcasting decisions. And rightfully so—the sad truth is, even the most generous observer would be baffled by the league's decision-making.

In February 1993, the league snagged the NBA's number two man away from basketball and made him NHL commissioner. At first, Gary Bettman's luck was good. In Bettman's second year on the job, 1994, the New York Rangers, having suffered for 54 years under the curse of 1940, finally recaptured Lord Stanley's Cup. Led by the incomparable Mark Messier, the Broadway Blueshirts won in seven thrilling games over a plucky Vancouver Canucks squad. The fortuitous mix of success-starved hockey fans in America's biggest market and overachieving Canucks from one of Canada's largest cities resulted in the highest all-time television ratings for hockey on both sides of the border.

That historic series should have propelled the NHL to the next level of success. Instead, the owners started the next season, 1994–95, by locking out the players for 103 days. The glow of good publicity for a well-fought final was replaced by negative headlines related to another typical sports labour dispute. And that was not the NHL's only blown opportunity. The error was compounded when, that same year, Major League Baseball players went on strike in August and, for the first time in more than 90 years, there was no World Series. What an opportunity for hockey to fill the void in New York, Chicago, and Boston, where fans were furious at the loss of their beloved Yankees, Mets, White Sox, Cubs, and Red Sox, not to mention the chance that was lost in the NHL's less traditional markets. Wouldn't it have been better if the Dallas Stars did not have to compete against the Texas Rangers, or the Los Angeles Kings against the Los Angeles Dodgers? Instead, hockey disappeared and returned only in January 1995. Advantage lost.

Making it all even worse was the fact that the league had just signed one of its most lucrative U.S. television deals. Rupert Murdoch's Fox Television burst onto the U.S. broadcasting scene and started buying up sports properties with a vengeance. Murdoch believed that only sports would maintain its value in the increasingly fragmented broadcasting market. And so, Fox paid huge dollars for Major League Baseball. It shocked the football world in 1994 by dramatically outbidding CBS for the rights to the NFL's National Football Conference games. Fox spent more than $1.5 billion on a 4-year deal, putting the Tiffany network on the football sidelines for the first time in almost 40 years. Local Fox stations also got in on the act, buying local broadcast rights to 20 of the 21 U.S.-based hockey teams. For example, in Dallas, Tom Hicks, who owned both hockey's Stars and baseball's Rangers, signed a 15-year, $550-million deal with Fox Sports to broadcast the games of both of his clubs. Then in 1998, not content with just purchasing television rights, Fox Broadcasting bought the storied Los Angeles Dodgers baseball franchise for $311 million (and sold them 6 years later for $430 million).

So when Fox signed a 5-year, $155-million deal with the NHL to broadcast hockey from 1994 to 1999, everyone had high hopes. The Fox deal represented the first major national network deal for the NHL in almost two decades. And while Fox's new approach definitely sent shivers down the spines of hockey purists (remember the blue flash every time a player took a slapshot? It was supposed to help new viewers find the puck more easily), the network pioneered some advances in game coverage that still seem fresh a decade later.

But even Fox's pizzazz could not overcome the lunacy of half a lost season in 1994. What made the lockout even more useless was that nothing was resolved by the action. The owners won some concessions from the players but not enough to alter the economic imbalances in the game. Salaries continued to go up. Too many teams continued to lose money. And hockey continued to fail at making the U.S. breakthrough the 1994 Stanley Cup Final portended.

As hard as Fox tried to sell hockey south of the border, nothing seemed to work. The blue streak following the puck earned the network the ridicule of every sports columnist and fan in traditional hockey markets. And yet it failed to make the game more accessible for people with no ties to the sport. So the NHL went in a different direction. Much to the consternation of Fox officials, the league next signed a new deal with ABC and its sports specialty channel ESPN for 5 years at $600 million. The league figured it had the best of both worlds. In ABC, its games would return to a traditional network carrier. In ESPN, the NHL was hitching its wagon to the foremost sports specialty channel in America. The deal seemed to make sense and made everyone, except the folks at Fox, happy. (Not everyone at Fox was miffed at being out of the national hockey-broadcasting business. Sportsbusiness.com reported that in a survey of Fox's 170-odd broadcast affiliates, station managers overwhelmingly expressed delight at the loss of the hockey contract. National, as opposed to local games, had awful ratings and the affiliates were content to lose the rights to hockey, rather than face an increase in rights fees.)

While viewership on Canadian channels continued to be strong, not even the double-barrelled power of ABC and ESPN was moving the ratings up in the States. Audience sizes continued to decline. Superstars such as Brett Hull complained that the game "sucked" and low ratings suggested most sports fans agreed. Finally, when the NHL locked out its players again in 2004, this time for an entire season, ABC and ESPN announced they would not pick up a $60-million option to continue broadcasting hockey. Hockey's efforts to convince everyone they were a major North American sport never looked sillier.

How did the NHL respond to the loss of ABC and ESPN? Rather than accept significantly lower rights fees in a future agreement, the league decided to give its product away. So in May 2004, the NHL signed a two-year "revenue-sharing" deal with NBC. The U.S. network now broadcasts between six and nine weeks of regular season games on Saturday afternoons, plus eight weeks of playoff games. But because NBC had such little faith in hockey's ability to deliver a sizeable audience, almost all the playoff games ended up scheduled on weekend afternoons. There are probably only 20,000 things Americans in Raleigh-Durham, Miami, Dallas, or Phoenix would rather do on a May or June afternoon than stay inside and watch hockey. But that is the best the league could do. NBC did agree to put games 3 through 7 of the Stanley Cup final in prime time.

Of course, the fact that NBC is paying the NHL nothing—not a cent—for the right to broadcast its games was indicative of hockey's status stateside. NBC is assuming all expenses related to producing the broadcasts, and the network and league are splitting advertising revenue. It is the same arrangement NBC had with the Arena Football League for four years, before the network determined the game was a ratings loser and ended its association with the league in mid-2006. Arena football games on average drew a 0.9 rating. Sadly, NHL hockey does not do much better. Having said that, NBC's commitment—more significant than ABC's—will put more games on a national U.S. network since Fox TV's efforts in 1998.

How has NBC done so far? Well, for its first week of coverage in the 2005–06 season, the network earned a 1.5 overnight Nielsen rating. The last year before the lockout, ABC registered a 1.7 for its first week—a drop of almost 12 percent. A few months later when April came along, hockey's ratings on NBC had dropped even further to a 0.7 rating. In a country of 300 million people, that represented about 800,000 households. By the time playoffs games were televised in May, NBC's numbers were 13 to 19 percent lower than ABC's anemic numbers a couple of years earlier. An exciting Carolina Hurricanes–New Jersey Devils playoff game on a Saturday afternoon in May drew fewer viewers than the surfing telecast that preceded it.

If you thought things might improve during the final round of the Stanley Cup playoffs, given the dramatic and engaging series between the Hurricanes and the Edmonton Oilers, think again. Raleigh-Durham, North Carolina, barely cracks the top 30 in market size in the U.S. and, of course, Edmonton may as well be Timbuktu for most sports fans south of the border. Despite the fact the series went the full seven games and was chockablock with entertaining hockey (thanks to the new rules), NBC's broadcast of the seventh and deciding game of the 2006 Stanley Cup Final earned a 3.3 rating. The last time hockey featured a

Game 7 was in 2004, the year before the lockout, when Tampa Bay defeated Calgary in another thrilling series. ABC snagged a 4.2 rating for that game, meaning NBC's numbers were down more than 20 percent.

By the time the 2006 playoffs were over, NBC's average rating was 1.1, 21 percent lower than ABC's 2004 numbers. There was no way to sugarcoat those numbers. They were awful.

A typical example of the troubles the NHL playoffs have on U.S. television occurred in late April 2007. In the second round, an all–New York State matchup featured the Buffalo Sabres against the New York Rangers—the quintessential "new NHL" team against the drawing power of Gotham.

The Sabres and Rangers were playing the third game of the series, and it was a thriller. The underdog Rangers eventually won in the dying seconds of double overtime. But much of New York City yawned. The game garnered a 1.8 rating on NBC in the New York area. Conversely, the Byron Nelson Golf Classic grabbed a 1.9 rating on CBS, and Tiger Woods wasn't even playing. Most curiously, the Nextel Cup auto race did the best of them all—a 2.1 rating on Fox. And New York City is hardly in the heart of the red states. Fortunately for the NHL, the Yankees–Red Sox baseball game had already ended by the time hockey started, or the Rangers–Sabres audience would surely have been even smaller.

On the plus side for the league, because NBC paid nothing for the rights, the network made money for its 2005–06 season. Given the revenue-sharing arrangement with the network, the NHL also turned a profit. And, as some observers noted, traditional hockey fans couldn't care less what the numbers are. They just want the games televised. In the evening.

The other major development on the U.S. broadcast scene was the departure of ESPN from the business of broadcasting hockey. Even on the foremost all-sports channel in America, hockey was barely making a dent in the difficult ratings game. In the last season before the lockout, only 416,000 homes on average watched NHL hockey on ESPN. The network also has a second channel, ESPN2 (nicknamed "the deuce"), where ratings for hockey were even worse.

While ESPN walked away from the table, another major player, Comcast, stepped up. America's largest cable television provider, Comcast signed a deal with the NHL worth more than $200 million to provide coverage for anywhere from 2 to 6 years. Comcast is a huge player on the U.S. cable television scene. It owns four regional sports networks plus a majority share of basketball's 76ers and hockey's Flyers, both in Philadelphia. It is broadcasting at least 58 games on Monday and Tuesday nights on a channel that used to be called the Outdoor Life Network, famous for its coverage of hunting, fishing, and the Tour de France bicycle race. The service rebranded itself in September 2006, changing its name to Versus, and plans to compete directly with ESPN.

While Versus was available in fewer homes than ESPN (63 million compared to 90 million), the NHL says the Versus deal is better for the league because hockey will be the most important sports property on Versus, whereas it was clearly a minor offering on ESPN.

"That is the type of treatment we have always coveted," NHL commissioner Gary Bettman told *The Washington Post* after signing the deal.

A year into the new arrangement, Versus saw its subscriptions increase to 70 million homes. It is unclear how much of that is due to its broadcasting of NHL hockey.

"In the short term, we gave up some TV subscribers," Bettman added. "In return, with patience, we will have better coverage, better production."

Patience will be required. During the 2006 playoffs, Versus (still called OLN at the time) averaged a 0.4 rating—ESPN was doing 0.7 at the same time in 2004. In the opening round of the 2007 NHL playoffs, Versus could notch only a 0.3 rating. Market penetration is still a big issue for the NHL. In Detroit, arguably the hottest hockey town in the United States, Versus is still only in 61 percent of homes. In Los Angeles, where there was some burgeoning interest in the Anaheim Ducks' 2007 Stanley Cup victory, Versus can be seen in only 59 percent of homes.

IF THE BAD NEWS is that hardly anybody is watching, the good news is that U.S. hockey broadcasters are doing a mostly top-notch job on the technical side. In fact, their innovations should put some of our Canadian broadcasters to shame. Given Canadian television's massive head start over the States in covering hockey, and the fact that we ought to understand the game better because it is in our blood, this seems particularly inexplicable.

It is May 7, 2006, and the Anaheim Mighty Ducks are hosting the Colorado Avalanche in Game 2 of the Western Conference semi-final. The hockey world is abuzz over the performance of Ilya Bryzgalov, the Ducks' Russian goaltender who is a month away from celebrating his 26th birthday. With his third consecutive playoff shutout, Bryzgalov has tied a mark set in 1945 by then rookie netminder Frank McCool. Bryzgalov is not even Anaheim's regular starting goaltender. That job is normally filled by Jean-Sébastien Giguere, who was the most valuable player in the 2003 playoffs. In that year, Giguere put together the kind of run Bryzgalov is now enjoying, where the puck looks like a beach ball and you guess right on every shot. The opposing players misfire, fan on shots, or hit the post when they've got you at their mercy. But coaches go with who's hot and, right now, nobody in the world is hotter than Ilya Bryzgalov. His shutout run will continue for 2 hours, 49 minutes, and 15 seconds—3 full games, plus all but 30 seconds of the 1st period of Game 3 against Colorado. At the end of the streak, only the legendary George Hainsworth (who played in the 1920s and '30s) stands above him on the consecutive-shutout-minutes list.

NBC is broadcasting this historic performance by the Ducks' goaltender and the network is doing an excellent job. When the game ends, the network immediately superimposes a graphic at the bottom of the screen telling viewers that Bryzgalov has now tied Frank McCool's record.

Naturally, Bryzgalov is the game's first star. He takes a curtain call, skating to centre ice and acknowledging the cheers of the Anaheim fans, and then heads back to the bench where NBC colour commentator Pierre McGuire is waiting for him.

McGuire may be the best in the world at what he does. He began his coaching career more than 20 years ago in the U.S. university hockey system. Eventually, he made his way to the NHL where he was a scout for the Pittsburgh Penguins when that team won its two Stanley Cups in 1991 and '92. He went on to become a head coach with the Hartford Whalers and an assistant with the Ottawa Senators.

What makes McGuire so good is not just his knowledge of the game, but also his ability to communicate it clearly with energy and enthusiasm. Bryzgalov arrives at the bench and McGuire begins to question him. But they are not the typically inane questions that make up so much of the conversation between athletes and journalists. The questions reflect an obvious understanding of what was required for Bryzgalov to have done what he just did. The content is great. And beyond that, it makes so much sense to be interviewing the game's first star while he is still on the ice, while the cheers of the spectators are still ringing in the background. Some television producer has not dragged Bryzgalov down a corridor to an interview spot away from the ice. Nor is the interview being done in an antiseptic studio. It's happening right where history was just made. The location just feels right and makes for good theatre.

Bryzgalov leaves and his place is taken by another Ducks star. Teemu Selanne is a couple of months away from his 36th birthday and still playing remarkably well. The "Finnish Flash" started in the league in 1992 with the Winnipeg Jets, scoring a sensational 76 goals in his rookie year. But his best seasons were in Anaheim in the late 1990s, when he came back from injuries to score more than 100 points twice. Eventually, he left Anaheim to play three years in San Jose and another in Colorado, before the Ducks brought him back for what was expected to be a modest swan song in 2005–06. Instead, Selanne put together a great 40-goal, 90-point season, and his game has not deteriorated one iota in these 2006 playoffs. Not bad for an "old" guy.

Selanne comes through the dressing room tunnel onto the ice, half undressed already. McGuire does another solid interview. When it's over, Selanne heads back to the dressing room, exchanging high-fives with team officials and fans en route. Again, great theatre, which is what sports is when it works best.

It is remarkable that it has taken a U.S. network with almost no experience of broadcasting hockey games to pioneer what seem to be obvious improvements in the way hockey is covered. Football, baseball, and basketball have used sideline or dugout reporters for years, and yet it has never to my knowledge been a feature of *Hockey Night in Canada*'s, TSN's, or Sportsnet's game coverage. But that is all about to change.

The credit for putting an announcer at rinkside generally goes to an executive producer at NBC named Sam Flood. Flood developed the coverage of one of the fastest-growing sports in the world: the National Association for Stock Car Auto Racing (NASCAR). It is a frequent feature of a NASCAR broadcast to run a clock in the corner of the screen to time the pit stops the drivers need to take. The audience for NHL hockey in the United States was so small that there was more, potentially, to gain by experimentation, than there was to lose by alienating viewers. So Flood sometimes put a clock in the corner of the screen for NHL broadcasts, too. In NASCAR broadcasts, announcers routinely reported from the pits during races. Why not adapt the same approach by situating commentators at ice level in a hockey game? Flood tried this too.

What started with NBC is now catching on with other networks. On December 1, 2006, TSN became the first channel ever to put both announcers—Chris Cuthbert and Glenn Healy—at rinkside when the Buffalo Sabres hosted the New York Rangers. Less than two weeks later, the voice of the Detroit Red Wings on Fox TV, Ken Daniels, did the play-by-play of the Wings–Senators game at rinkside as well (although his broadcast partner, Mickey Redmond, remained upstairs). In one respect, everything old was new again. Foster Hewitt's earliest broadcasts were done at ice level.

Whether this is the beginning of a whole new way of covering hockey is still an open question. Some see it as a one-time gimmick that will not stand the test of time. Jeff Paterson, sportscaster and talk-show host on Vancouver's all-sports radio station Team 1040, was unimpressed with the rinkside play-calling. Of TSN's experiment, Paterson wrote on his blog, "Putting a couple of schmoes between the benches may have been a kick for them, but it did absolutely nothing for the guy sitting at home watching the game. In fact, I would go so far as to say TSN's experiment did a disservice to the viewer."

This is a view not shared by the first announcer to attempt the innovation. Cussing players, screaming fans, and a multitude of other distractions make the task difficult, admits Pierre McGuire. But "you are really in the game down there, even though it is a very inhospitable place to work," he says.

Perhaps because he clearly knows his stuff, players, coaches, and general managers have been open to McGuire's role in this experiment. On one occasion, he mentioned on air that one player had just finished a particularly mediocre shift—and the player heard him say it. When the player gave McGuire a dirty look, McGuire fired back, "I wouldn't have to say it if you wouldn't float so much."

The role is not without its dangers. During Game 1 of the 2007 playoff series between the Sabres and Rangers, McGuire got clipped by an errant high stick. He sustained a nasty cut on his forehead for his troubles.

Can the commentator and announcers in the broadcast booth

maintain a rapport when they are so widely separated? How do they avoid speaking at the same time or stepping on each other's lines when they aren't in a position to read one another's body language? Remarkably, there wasn't a single glitch in the NBC broadcast I watched. McGuire is constantly in touch with a producer in the truck, telling him what highlights he wants edited, and when. That producer then communicates with Mike Emrick and John Davidson in the broadcast booth by saying, "McGuire can add …" This is a cue for the announcers to bring McGuire into the discussion, after which McGuire would break down the play even further with an edited highlight package. After a while, the three-way conversations became seamless. He and his other play-by-play partner, Gord Miller, demonstrated the same seamlessness on TSN's broadcasts.

Being so much closer to the players gives rinkside announcers access to some sensitive information, and McGuire acknowledges there are some things he will not share with his television audience.

"I won't tell you where a guy's hurt," he says. "You're an invited guest in a place where guys make their living, winning and losing. It's a privilege to be there."

The other new trick NBC has brought to its broadcasts is the stripe of information that goes across the top of the screen. It has all the basics—the score, the period, and how much time is left to play. But from time to time, another stripe drops down from the main one, showing who is playing on what line, how much ice team a particular player is getting, and other pertinent facts. For example, in the Colorado–Anaheim game, as Avalanche captain Joe Sakic skates back to the bench after a shift, the second stripe drops down to inform the viewer that Sakic's shift lasted 1 minute and 6 seconds. Then, Sakic's game total comes up. We learn he has played 12 minutes so far. Later in the period, another stripe will drop down indicating the shots on goal to that minute, hits by each team, goal-scoring chances, and so on. Midway through the third period, the second stripe tells us Teemu Selanne has just completed a one-minute-long shift for a total of 16 minutes and 38 seconds thus far—a long time for a veteran. In the 2007 playoffs, we similarly learned that Rangers' star forward Jaromir Jagr had been on the ice for more than 2 minutes—an eternity in an era of 30-second shifts. The broadcasters may not have mentioned it, but fans watching the game now had hard evidence that the Rangers were double-shifting their best player in an attempt to create more offence. This kind of information may seem irrelevant to the casual fan, but to the hardcore puckster, these are the statistics that enhance one's enjoyment of the broadcast. And remember, this is sport. All numbers are either fun or important.

It is not just the visual component that makes hockey so riveting. The sounds are unlike those heard in any other sport as well. Pucks bouncing off goaltenders, skate blades cutting up the ice, trash talking galore, players giving each other instructions, they are all part of the theatre of the game. Generally, television viewers have missed most of these elements, and only some of them have been experienced by fans in the arena. Television has provided novel camera angles but, up until now, it has not been particularly good at bringing the sounds of the game to the fan at home.

NBC has been experimenting with putting a tiny microphone on players to pick up more of the audio texture of the game. But on this day, either the experiment did not work well or the players had nothing interesting to say. Ever since former Flyers captain Bobby Clarke called referee Bruce Hood "a fucking queer" on a live *Hockey Night in Canada* broadcast many years ago, the networks have all been afraid of putting live microphones near the action. Their solution has been to record exchanges on the ice, edit them together, eliminate the profanity, and then broadcast the snippets moments later. During the Colorado–Anaheim broadcast, we got only one example of the "mike on the ice." Avalanche defenceman Patrice Brisebois made an utterly forgettable comment to a linesman after completing a pass. This is a good idea that needs further thought before it adds anything to the viewer's enjoyment of the game.

Among other experiments, NBC has installed tiny cameras on goaltenders' helmets to give a first-hand view of what it must be like to be on the receiving end of a 150-kilometre-per-hour slapshot. They have also liberally employed an end-zone camera, particularly on power plays, when all the action tends to be in one end.

If NBC is at the leading edge of the broadcasting spectrum in terms of its willingness to experiment, then the CBC is trailing far behind.

"Our overall philosophy hasn't changed over the years," says Joel Darling, the executive producer of *Hockey Night in Canada* since 2000 and an employee of CBC Sports for almost two decades. "The game is the thing. We pride ourselves on what the story is on the ice."

Darling and Flood could not be more different in their approach to hockey broadcasts. While Flood came to hockey from others sports, Darling cannot remember a time in his life when hockey was not a central feature. His late father, Ted, was the play-by-play voice of the Buffalo Sabres from the team's inaugural season and for the next 22 years. The press box in the Sabres' home arena is called the Ted Darling Memorial Press Box. Joel Darling, meanwhile, calls hockey "an unbelievable part of my life." The father of 11-year-old twins, he still plays hockey every Wednesday night.

Just as the two executive producers are nothing alike, neither are their programs. CBC appears to see itself as the anti-NBC. The thinking at *Hockey Night* seems to be not to mess up the broadcast with gimmicks. The show continues to shoot its game overwhelmingly from its mid-arena camera, going east to west with the flow of the action. You will not find sports tickers running throughout the game showing out-of-town scores, a feature that is omnipresent on all-sports channels. The use of the "lower third" of the screen to impart information is also very selectively used. Even the network's most popular feature, Coach's Corner with Don Cherry and Ron MacLean, is shot simply with two people and one camera on a locked-off shot for the entire segment.

"I worry about the clutter," Darling says. "There's a lot to be said for being traditional."

CBC has made some progress. They broadcast in high definition. For the 2007 playoffs, they replaced their difficult-to-read scoreboard in the top-left corner with the stripe across the top of the screen that all broadcasters now use. They were the first to feature a female colour commentator when former Canadian women's Olympic team captain Cassie Campbell performed that function during a *Hockey Night* broadcast in October 2006. (Harry Neale, the regular colour commentator, was snowed in that night.) And a few years ago during the all-star game,

*Hockey Night* put chips in players' helmets to see how fast they were skating.

Darling acknowledges part of the reason the CBC may be reluctant to try further innovations is because of the men who are still calling the games. Bob Cole and Harry Neale have been fixtures together on *Hockey Night* for more than 20 years. Despite complaints that Cole and Neale are not nearly as sharp as they once were, there are, in fact, no demonstrations in the streets to replace them. As a result, it is a safe bet that *Hockey Night* will not be reworking its broadcast too much until it replaces its broadcast team. (At the time this book went to press, there were rumours that Cole and Neale might be demoted to Hockey Night's "B" team, but so far, CBC has made nothing official.)

From a broadcaster's point of view, hockey has a distinct programming advantage because it has two intermissions to fill. Football and basketball have only one, and broadcasters usually use it to show highlights of the game they are carrying and others from around their respective leagues.

The CBC still features the best and worst of intermission programming. Whether you love him or hate him, Don Cherry's Coach's Corner is still must-watch television for hockey fans. Viewership surveys still indicate that the ratings for *Hockey Night* spike during the first intermission, as even casual fans tune in to see what the always-controversial former Boston Bruins coach has to say.

Contrast that, however, with the CBC's second intermission feature, the Satellite Hot Stove, which is very hit and miss. As its name suggests, the Satellite Hot Stove evokes the far-distant days when guys sat around a wood stove while listening to the game on the radio and talking hockey. Now, with the advent of satellite technology, the participants still do the sitting around, but usually they do it in three different cities. Ron MacLean anchors the segment, which, at its best, updates hockey fans on player movement, trade speculation, and other gossip. During the sixth game of the 2006 Stanley Cup Final, Canadian Press's Pierre LeBrun, *The Globe and Mail*'s Eric Duhatschek, and the CBC's Kelly Hrudey all speculated on impending free-agent movement, where players might end up, and who might be traded. Much of their informed speculation turned out to be accurate. They noted, for example, that then Florida general manager Mike Keenan planned to trade goaltender Roberto Luongo. On other occasions, however, the discussion is virtually unintelligible. The participants bump into each other, stepping on each other's lines, and sometimes the discussion becomes hopelessly technical and arcane.

NBC's intermission features are what you might expect from a large U.S. television network. Where the CBC sets are pedestrian, NBC's are spectacular. The NBC studio features a stylish hockey net and goalie mask as props in the foreground. Unlike the visually static Coach's Corner, NBC makes use of a wonderful high-angle establishing shot, taken from a camera attached to a "jib" or crane. (The crane alone costs more than $10,000: CBC and NBC are in different rent districts.) The ensuing graphics are extremely professional, with a "crawl" across the bottom of the screen listing the playoff goal, assist, points, and goaltending leaders. During the second intermission, the announcers diagram the "left-wing lock," a defensive zone scheme designed to blanket teams with strength on the left side (a system originally devised by the Czechs in the 1970s to counter the almost entirely left-shooting Soviet powerhouses), by having the left-winger drop back with the defencemen. It reminded me of the old days when Howie Meeker diagrammed various schemes on *Hockey Night* except the graphic look of the diagrams was light years beyond that. (Kelly Hrudey does some similar breaking down of the action in his Behind the Mask segment on CBC.) The three NBC announcers—Ed Olczyk, Ray Ferraro, and Bill Clement—are all ex-players and remarkably smart and articulate. And NBC runs some finely crafted commercials for the league entitled My NHL, narrated by U.S. television star and major hockey fan Denis Leary. It's a very polished product.

WITHOUT QUESTION, television has been the most important hockey medium for fans over the years, and it's likely to remain pre-eminent for some time to come. However, the NHL is now finally moving in a big way into the internet age. In November 2006, the league announced two significant deals with two of the most important players of the online world. The first deal, with Google, makes games available on Google Video. At the moment, the NHL is making both recent games and all-time classics such as Game 6 of the 1967 Stanley Cup Final between the Leafs and Canadiens available for free in hopes of boosting interest in hockey. The league is still trying to decide whether eventually to charge for these downloads or to sell advertising. The NHL is also exploring the possibility of delivering content through BlackBerrys, cell phones, and laptop computers.

In another significant deal, the NHL is now providing daily short-form video content—mostly edited three- to five-minute highlight packages of the previous night's games—to YouTube, again in hopes of attracting eyeballs that don't traditionally watch hockey. The NHL was the first North American pro sports league to do a deal with this extraordinarily popular website. In theory, internet users will be so intrigued by what they see on YouTube, that they will get into the habit of watching games on conventional television and gradually become more involved hockey fans.

Even with these deals, however, the NHL is still a long way behind its competitors on the internet. *The Globe and Mail* reported the league's website, NHL.com, had about 1.6 million visitors in September 2006. That pales in comparison with Major League Baseball's website, MLB.com, at 9.1 million visitors, and the National Football League's NFL.com at 16.4 million visitors.

IF THE BROADCASTING PICTURE in the U.S. still looks unsure, the same cannot be said about hockey's heartland. Earlier this year, the CBC and the NHL agreed to a 6-year rights package worth an estimated $600 million, according to *The Globe and Mail*. Richard Stursberg, the CBC's executive vice-president for television, said the deal continues the longest-standing relationship between a broadcaster and a league in television history.

Interestingly, the contract actually gives the CBC fewer Saturday night Maple Leaf games, the ones that garner the highest audiences. With TSN and Sportsnet prepared to pay 50 percent more for the rights to show their share of NHL hockey, and Toronto indicating they'll put as many as 20 games on their own Leafs TV channel, hockey will be virtually everywhere on Canadian television in the years ahead.

But then, this country's affection for hockey has never been the issue. We love our game.

# WHAT I LOVE
# ABOUT THIS GAME

*Canada is hockey.*
—MIKE WEIR

If I have heard it once, I have heard it a hundred times from journalists who cover the sports world far more intensely and frequently than I do. They have talked to football players, basketball players, baseball players, and hockey players. And to a person, every single journalist I have talked to agrees: the best athletes to interview are hockey players.

On the face of it, it's a claim that requires a double take. Wouldn't professional football or basketball players be better spoken? After all, nearly all of them are American, have English as their first language, and are university graduates. But, no, I have never heard a sports reporter say football players are the most forthcoming and articulate. (Admittedly, homebrew football players in the Canadian Football League, who have far more in common with hockey players from small-town Canada than they do with U.S. footballers, also get good reviews.)

I have never heard a baseball beat writer claim that baseball players are great to interview. Maybe this is because baseball games are played every day, and the constant exposure of reporter to multi-million-dollar player becomes problematic.

No, it is hockey players. Whether they are from Canada, the United States, Scandinavia, or other parts of Europe, hockey players get the most positive reviews.

There are many theories that might explain the judgment, but I suspect that hockey players are overwhelmingly polite and responsive with reporters because the vast majority of them come from two-parent homes with close families that were deeply involved in their upbringing. Unlike professional football and basketball, which are seen as outlets for poor kids, often from single-parent homes and bad neighbourhoods, playing hockey is a deeply traditional, middle-class recreation, no matter which side of the 49th parallel, or the Atlantic, you grew up on.

It certainly isn't formal education that makes hockey players different. Although more and more players are making it to the NHL from the university and college ranks, the junior hockey leagues of North America still represent the most significant entry point to the profession. Fully half the players taken in the first round of the 2006 NHL entry draft played for major junior teams in Canada. (Interestingly, the second-largest plurality came from Europe.) These players are not university graduates. Most of them are so focused on hockey that they are lucky to finish high school. So, it isn't their higher educational achievements that have made them pleasant to be with.

In hockey, it's rare for an athlete, coach, or general manager to get really angry at reporters. I'm surprised it doesn't happen more. Sportswriters and those on the television beat want to talk to hockey players for only two reasons: things are going very well, or things are going very badly. Hockey players are notoriously self-effacing. Wayne Gretzky's modesty while he was comprehensively rewriting the NHL record book was both amazing and sometimes stultifyingly boring, because he simply would not boast about his achievements and instead constantly gave credit to his teammates. Even lesser players have historically been inclined to talk about being in "the right place at the right time" rather than brag about their stellar achievements on the ice. They're embarrassed to be seen boasting in front of their teammates, and such modesty speaks well of them.

But, Ed Belfour aside, even hockey players who screw up badly on the ice are almost always generous with their time and prepared to face the unpleasant music of the post-game interview. In December 2006, the Maple Leafs had just come off a stunning 9–2 victory over the New York Rangers, when, three nights later, they absolutely stunk out the joint against the Florida Panthers. Hal Gill was the worst defenceman on the ice for the Leafs that night. He put passes on the sticks of Panther players instead of his teammates' and was on the ice when a bushel of goals were scored against his side. Before the game was over, Leaf fans were booing Gill every time he touched the puck.

But in the Leaf dressing room after the game, there was Gill, all 6'7" and 250 pounds of him, facing the microphones and answering everyone's questions. His teammate, the feisty Darcy Tucker, began to chastise the assembled media horde for picking on Gill, calling him "one of our best players all year." Tucker is a media favourite because he never ducks the microphones, always has a comment when asked, but is no camera hog. He always gives the impression he would rather be doing something other than giving interviews, but he understands the requirements of the post-game media machine and does his best. The first time I interviewed Tucker, I made the mistake of calling him a "plugger." I meant to distinguish his style of play—rugged, tough, in the face of his opponents, yet very effective—with that of other more finesse-type players such as Jason Spezza or Jaromir Jagr. But Tucker immediately took exception to my comment.

"Plugger? Plugger?" he asked me, his eyes starting to bug out of their sockets. "What kind of plugger scores 20 goals 3 of the last 4 years?" He was ticked off, no question about it. And then he stared daggers at me. Was I intimidated? You're damned right I was. I immediately acknowledged my faux pas, and tried to explain what I had meant. My hunch is, had he been a baseball player, he would have ended the conversation right there, got up, and left the room. But he is Darcy Tucker, a hockey player, so we continued and had a perfectly civilized conversation.

I believe the hockey players I spoke to while researching *The New Game* enjoyed having the opportunity to talk about something other than what passes for news in daily sports journalism. Generally speaking, reporters have access to players twice on the day of a game: once after their early skate, and again after the game that night. The players are less rushed, inclined to be more laid-back and expansive after the practices. The post-game interviews tend to be rather quick and focused because reporters have deadlines to meet, and the players want to go home. Regardless, the demands on their time are significant and the amount of content reporters need to feed the ubiquitous beast that is the 24-hour sports channel, all-sports radio station, or newspaper website is unending. It's why I found players, coaches, and managers happy to talk about something that did not require them to "take it one game at a time" or "give it 110 percent." They all were pleased to discuss the game of hockey and why they loved it so much.

My encounters with John Muckler have ranged from intense to uninteresting. As the recently deposed general manager of the Ottawa Senators, he may have had the second most pressure-packed job in Canada's capital, next to that of the prime minister. He led a team that had badly underperformed for several consecutive years in the playoffs, despite having extraordinarily talented players who excelled in the regular season. Unfortunately, the Stanley Cup is not awarded to the team having the best regular season. It goes to the squad that is best when it counts, in the playoffs. And until the Senators' remarkable playoff run to the 2007 Stanley Cup Final, the club had never been particularly good when it counted.

After finishing atop the Eastern Conference in the 2005–06 regular season, expectations were once again high for Muckler's team. The Senators did nothing to dampen those expectations when they dispatched the defending Stanley Cup champion Tampa Bay Lightning in just five games in the first round.

But in the second round, a supposedly inferior team from Buffalo felled the Senators in just five games. True, three of the games went into sudden-death overtime, including the decisive fifth game. But it was a series Ottawa should have won. Instead, they lost in remarkably dramatic fashion. In Game 1, the visiting Sabres scored a short-handed goal with just 1:37 left to play to tie the game. But the Sens immediately came back by scoring a power-play goal with 1:13 to play to retake the lead, 6–5 (it was not a night for the goaltenders). However, with 11 seconds to play, Buffalo managed yet again to prick Ottawa's victory balloon by scoring another tying goal to send the affair off to overtime. I have no recollection of how the goal was scored. But I remember well the television cameras cutting to John Muckler. He was so furious at his team's folding yet again, that he broke the long-held code of the press box (which requires a perfect and unyielding poker face) and slammed his hand so hard on the desk in front of him, I thought it would collapse on the spectators sitting below. One could read his lips mouthing something awfully profane.

Muckler's agony wasn't finished. Just 18 seconds into over-time, the Sabres scored the winning goal, stole the first game of the series in Ottawa, and broke the Senators' hearts. The Sabres eventually took a 3–0 series lead before eliminating the Sens in 5 games.

All of which is to say, until the 2007 run to the final, the public face of John Muckler was a largely unpleasant one during his years in Ottawa. Muckler did not appear to be the same man who was such an important part of the Edmonton Oiler dynasty of the late 1980s, when he was either an associate or head coach for five Stanley Cup championships. Ottawa's problems, and his constantly having to discuss them with reporters, were clearly frustrating him.

So, a few months after the debacle against the Sabres (and well before his ouster from the Sens in a June 2007 power struggle), when I asked Muckler what he loved most about hockey, something happened in him that I had not seen in a decade and a half. His eyes lit up. He smiled. And then he started reminiscing as if he had all the time in the world.

He talked about his love of the game itself, the people in the game, being part of a team, the excitement, the highs and the lows, the challenge every day. "The greatest part of winning a Stanley Cup is the hunt," says the man who ought to know. "After you win it, everything comes to a standstill and then you say, 'What do I do now?' All the activity is gone. All the challenges are gone. You're now a champion."

And then a week later, according to Muckler, you start thinking about the next hunt and how to get back to the Promised Land.

Despite his well-documented travails with the Senators, Muckler is actually quite an expert at winning. Besides the five titles in Edmonton, he can lay claim to being a part of championship teams in the Eastern Hockey League, the American Hockey League, and the Central Hockey League. Winning a championship as a general manager was the last mountain to climb.

"That's why I went into being a general manager," he says of his appointment in 2002 to the Senators. "To see if I could do it as a general manager. That's exciting to me, to be able to be the architect of a hockey club and watch all the people that you've employed put everything in place and get it all together."

Muckler, now 73, remembers putting skates on for the first time at age four, while living in Simcoe, Ontario. He quit skating after he turned 70, and even then only because a bad back forced him to give it up.

"I've got a disk problem," he says. "All players, all players have disk problems."

ONE OF THE PLAYERS on the University of Toronto Varsity Blues men's hockey team when I was a student there was Mike Pelino. During his years at U of T, he won three Ontario university championships, one Canadian university title, and was an Ontario all-star twice. I knew Pelino a little bit in those days, having interviewed him after practices and games numerous times. As terrific as Pelino's university career was, his professional career as a player just never happened. He didn't even get a cup of coffee in the NHL, but he has made an impressive mark as a coach. He was the longest-serving coach at Brock University in St. Catharines, Ontario. And Pelino spent enough time with Hockey Canada to win 11 gold medals at various levels, including, most memorably, the 2002 gold medal as an assistant coach at the Winter Olympics in Salt Lake City. Eventually, he made it to the NHL as an assistant coach for the Florida Panthers in 2003–04. Now in his mid-40s, he is currently an assistant on Broadway for the Rangers, clearly on a path to become a head coach in the NHL.

I had seen him only once or twice since leaving the U of T, but when I showed up at the BankAtlantic Center in Sunrise, Florida, one afternoon to watch the visiting Rangers practise in preparation for a game that night against the Panthers, I was welcomed into the arena by a booming voice, yelling at me from at least a hundred metres away.

"Hey Paikin!"

Of course, it was Mike Pelino. To my complete surprise, he welcomed me to practice by telling me he had followed my career with as much interest as I had followed his. I was both embarrassed and flattered.

I told him about this book project and wondered, since the Rangers had yet to take to the ice, whether we could do a formal interview about the new NHL. He agreed, and we sat down in the stands, both amused at the notion of the former Varsity Blue and former cub reporter for *The Newspaper* doing our first sit-down interview in a quarter of a century.

What did Pelino love about hockey?

"The synergy of the entire game and everything around it," he said. "The dynamics on the ice, the speed of the game, the passion you have to play with, and the compassion you have to have for your teammates and your whole organization. I think it just brings out the best in people."

I loved the answer. When was the last time you heard someone from the world of sports use the words *synergy, dynamics,* and *compassion* in one paragraph? Pelino went on to talk about the dual nature of the challenge of hockey—how every shift tests a player as an individual, and yet no team can be successful unless those individuals bond as a team.

"That's something that I think brings it all together for me," he added. "I think the complete package is what I love most about hockey."

Harder than being on the receiving end of any slapshot or recovering from a serious injury is the notion that these athletes will all face a day when they can no longer make their living playing hockey. I have heard politicians describe the effect of losing elections the same way. The opportunity to work so closely with others, as a team, and united in common cause is something that simply does not exist in most people's jobs. It does in hockey.

"The night in and night out intensity that is required and the battle that is there every night" is what Sean Burke loves about the game. "That is what people will never get to experience, that we get to experience—just how intense it is every night and what you have to bring to be able to stay in this league." Burke has played pro hockey for 18 years. When he failed to make the Tampa Bay Lightning roster for the 2006–07 season, he accepted reassignment to the team's AHL affiliate, the Springfield (Massachusetts) Falcons, where he fought for his share of the goaltending duties with two other netminders half his age. And then, as so often happens in sports, the Los Angeles Kings got into injury troubles and needed a reliable backup. So, off Burke went to the opposite coast. The former Marlie junior has played for the Devils, Whalers, Hurricanes, Canucks, Flyers, Panthers, Coyotes, Flyers (again), Lightning, and now the Kings (not to mention all those international stints for Team Canada along the way).

Sean Burke probably never unpacks his suitcase. But he is still playing the game he loves.

Once upon a time, Darius Kasparaitis was one of the better defencemen in the NHL. The Lithuanian native was renowned around the league for his punishing hits. Even after numerous injuries slowed him down, he still managed to lead the Rangers in hits in the 2005–06 season and was ninth overall in the NHL. But, as we saw in Chapter 5, the injuries have caught up to Kasparaitis and at 35, he is now struggling to stay in the NHL. On Halloween 2006, the Rangers sent him to their AHL affiliate, the Hartford Wolf Pack, to play himself back into condition. Two weeks later, he was back but was still on a pace to miss half the season. Kasparaitis knows there are fewer tomorrows than yesterdays in his NHL career. What will he miss the most?

"I think travelling, camaraderie, being around people, going to a game every night, and seeing 10,000 people, 20,000 people rooting for you, against you, you know?" he says. "And it is nothing you can replace with. It'll stay with you for the next 50 years."

Mike Pelino, confirms that even coaches can catch that fever.

"Nothing is the same as two players going to war together," Pelino says. "But if they know that their coach is with them as well, then that connection is made, and I think you really can share the experience."

Rick Dudley loved watching Gordie Howe play the game when he was a kid. Imagine what a dream come true it was for Dudley to play in the NHL and wear Howe's number 9 as well. His best years as a player were the six seasons he was with the Buffalo Sabres. That team went to the final in 1975.

"The year we went to the Stanley Cup final and lost to the Flyers in six games, that year, I never had a bad day," Dudley recalls with ample nostalgia and emotion in his voice. "It was just fun to be at the rink every day. They were guys that were like a family."

Dudley has had more good days than bad ones in a professional career that has lasted 40 years. As a general manager, he has put together teams that have gone to the finals eight times in three different leagues. Like John Muckler, he has done almost everything there is to do in hockey, including once owning a team (the Carolina entry in the East Coast Hockey League). All this from a guy who was never drafted as a player.

"Since I was 18 years old I have been in professional hockey and I have been able to exist in it, make a living in it and do pretty well in it, and I wouldn't trade it for the world," he says. "It has been fun."

"If you have ever laced on skates and if you have ever played it, I don't think you ever get it out of your system," adds Bill Torrey, the architect of the New York Islander dynasty of the early 1980s.

Toronto Maple Leaf defenceman Ian White was even more concise when asked what he loved most about hockey.

"Everything," he said.

That sounds about right.

THANK GOODNESS for the Chicago Blackhawks.

As long as the Blackhawks are in the National Hockey League, the Toronto Maple Leafs will not have to wear the goat horns as the most frustrated and frustrating team in hockey.

Once Mark Messier led his New York Rangers to a Stanley Cup victory in 1994, erasing 54 years of championship agony in Gotham, the road to the next longest Stanley Cup drought went through Chicago.

Not since 1961—the days of Bobby Hull, Stan Mikita, and Glenn Hall—have the Blackhawks won The Cup. But not far behind that championship ignominy are the Maple Leafs, whose last Cup win was in Canada's centennial year.

Leaf fans hold a special place in their hearts for that 1967 championship team. Coach Punch Imlach led a squad that was nicknamed the Over-the-Hill Gang. It was a troupe that had won Stanley Cups in 1962, 1963, and 1964, and by '67 was virtually held together with stick tape and a prayer.

Everyone knew it would be the team's last hurrah because 1966–67 was the final season of the old six-team NHL. The following year, the league would double in size by adding new teams in Los Angeles, Minnesota, Oakland, Philadelphia, Pittsburgh, and St. Louis. To stock those teams, the existing Original Six clubs would have to free up many of their established players. So, clearly, 1967 represented the last time out for Imlach's warriors.

Among the stars of that team were goaltender Johnny Bower (age 42), defenceman Allan Stanley (age 41), Red Kelly (age 39), Terry Sawchuk (Bower's goaltending partner) and legendary D-man Tim Horton (both age 37), captain George Armstrong and blueliner Marcel Pronovost (both age 36).

Somehow, this crew of oldtimers, mixed with some splendid up-and-coming players such as Ron Ellis (only 22 years old) and Dave Keon (age 27), defeated a superior Montreal Canadiens team in six games. Expo 67 was being held in Montreal that year, and numerous references were made to how marvellous it would be for that city to show off the country's most famous piece of hardware at the world exposition. But Lord Stanley's mug stayed in Toronto, the site of its then home at the Hockey Hall of Fame on the Canadian National Exhibition grounds.

The unlikelihood of Toronto's victory has only added to the lustre of that team over the years. So, on February 17, 2007, when today's Leafs decided they wanted to celebrate the 40th anniversary of those Leafs, it was one of the most eagerly anticipated events on Toronto's hockey calendar.

Adding to the spectacle of it all was the return of one of the all-time great Maple Leaf legends, Dave Keon. For more than three decades, Keon had been estranged from the team because of his mistreatment by former owner Harold Ballard. The origins of the feud seem almost irrelevant all these years later, but suffice to say, Ballard never showed Keon the kind of respect he deserved and almost certainly would have received had he played for the Montreal Canadiens. Give the Habs their due— they know how to celebrate their former stars.

Ballard figured Keon, at age 35, was washed up and offered him a new contract reflecting that opinion. As a result, Keon left Toronto in 1975, jumped to the archrival World Hockey Association, and played for another 7 productive seasons in Minnesota, Indianapolis, and Hartford. At age 42, having played a 78-game season for the Whalers, Keon finally retired, proving beyond any doubt that Ballard was quite simply wrong in his assessment.

But Keon's ire with the Leafs did not expire when Ballard died in 1990. Despite numerous efforts by any number of people associated with the organization, Keon continued to snub the Leafs' efforts to bring him into the family. Not even the closing of Maple Leaf Gardens in 1999 could get Keon out of Florida, where he now lived. He declined to participate in closing ceremonies that featured every significant Leaf still alive from the previous 60-odd years.

It was 17 years after Ballard's death before Keon finally came home. Why then? "This is one night, one weekend," he said to the assembled media horde at the celebration for the Leafs' 1967 Cup-winning team. "Let's just leave it at that."

Before the game began between the Maple Leafs and Edmonton Oilers, that '67 championship team came out to take a bow. Johnny Bower, 82 years old and still a huge fan favourite, received an enormous ovation. So did the last man introduced, the captain, George Armstrong. But the biggest cheer was reserved for the penultimate Leaf to take a bow. Public address announcer Andy Frost said simply, "The Conn Smythe Trophy–winner, Dave Keon.…" Out he came, looking fit and trim, wearing his familiar number 14 sweater. Keon received the ovation that was 30 years overdue.

If you were in your late 40s or older, and you had followed hockey for—lo!—these many years, it was impossible to witness the tribute without getting a huge lump in your throat.

At the first intermission of the game, the Leafs made many of the oldtimers available for media interviews. Keon, of course, was mobbed. So was Johnny Bower. In response to one questioner, he estimated he had received more than 200 stitches in his face, "But I'm so old now, the wrinkles cover them up," he said.

While most of the reporters were interested in pursuing the Keon-comes-home angle, I was more curious about what these older players thought about the new game. And interestingly enough, they all had strong feelings. They still watch.

So, for example, would Johnny Bower have wanted to participate in a shootout?

"If the Rocket didn't shoot at me, then yes, okay," he said, referring to Maurice Richard, and sending the assembled media into guffaws.

Frank Mahovlich, who played left wing for the Leafs and continues to occupy the same ideological territory for the Liberals in the Senate, still watches hockey and loves what he sees.

"Keon and I were pretty fast skaters," he said. "This would have been our kind of game. It was more defensive when I had to play. Now it's wide open."

Defenceman Larry Hillman observed that in his day, once a team had a lead, "you'd put the checking lines out and that was it. Now the lead can change hands two or three times per game."

Bobby Baun scored a winning goal in overtime during the Stanley Cup playoffs in 1964—on a broken leg, no less. ("I've got a lot of miles out of that goal. I won't deny it one bit!") He also likes what he sees today.

"I think we're finally starting to see the game as I'd like to see it right now," he said.

If there is one thing about the new NHL that rankles some of these veterans, it's the phantom penalties.

"I don't like the idea of just touching a guy and you get a penalty," admits Larry Jeffrey.

"We were taught to fight through our checks," adds Ron Ellis, who scored 332 goals in his brilliant career as a Leaf—more than anyone else except Mats Sundin, Darryl Sittler, and Dave Keon.

"If a guy puts two hands on the stick and pulls you back, well, yeah, that's a penalty. But if he starts reaching and has the stick on you, you're supposed to fight through those," Ellis added.

As much as these oldtimers enjoy reminiscing about the great Leaf teams of the 1960s, many also enjoyed discussing the buzz around the new rules, particularly the shootouts. Ties were far too frequent in the NHL they agreed.

Would Keon have enjoyed participating in a shootout? He paused and almost smiled for the first time that evening.

"That would be kind of fun," he said.

However, Ron Ellis, who was also a pretty fine goal scorer, looked downright appalled at the notion.

"I had a few breakaways and as long as I had someone bothering me from behind, I was pretty good," Ellis said as Larry Jeffrey smiled beside him. "But going in with nobody touching me, I was awful! When you've got a guy coming from behind giving you a little tug, you can get the shot away. But if you've got too much time to think, you can screw it up!" Both men howled with laughter.

Dave Keon. Frank Mahovlich. Ron Ellis. Playing the new game in the new NHL?

Now that would be worth the price of admission.

# ACKNOWLEDGMENTS

People often ask me, "How are your books born?" Here's how *The New Game* came to be.

After writing three books over a five-year period for Penguin—all about politics—I assumed my days of authoring were over. Professionally speaking, I looked forward to focusing solely on my TVOntario responsibilities and a saner work life.

But Penguin's new publisher, David Davidar, then told me to enjoy a few months away from writing and assured me we would be talking again. I assured David he could talk all he liked, but I would no longer listen. My days of book writing were over.

He knew better. I supposed I should have, too.

Before long, senior editor Susan Folkins approached me. "How'd you like to have lunch and talk about writing another book?" she asked.

"Not a chance," I replied. "I'm finally starting to get my life back to normal" (if you call working nights for 13 years normal). "Besides," I added, "I've really said everything about politics I want to say for now."

"Who said anything about politics?" Susan replied. "I want to talk to you about writing a book on hockey."

My ears pricked up. Instantly, I recalled Michael Corleone's line from *The Godfather: Part III:* "Just when I thought I was out, they pull me back in."

A book on hockey? Hard to resist.

Susan and I worked on an outline. We received further encouragement from Ed Carson (then president of Penguin Canada) and Diane Turbide (editorial director), and then I watched a dream come true—the dream of hanging around professional hockey arenas and talking to players, coaches, and general managers. The result of more than 100 interviews and 2 years of work is in your hands.

My thanks to Susan for getting the ball rolling (puck gliding?); to Jonathan Webb for his excellent editing suggestions; and to Joe Zingrone for his added layer of literary and quality control. I thought I knew a lot about hockey. Working with Joe has forced me, reluctantly, to conclude that he knows more. Nice working with you again, Joe: you shoot, you score.

THANKS AS WELL to Stephen Myers for his efforts at publicizing this book, and Diane Turbide and Tracy Bordian for making the whole thing happen.

In the hockey world, I owe an enormous debt of thanks to Pat Park, the Toronto Maple Leafs' media relations director, who allowed me to be a frequent, if unknown, presence at the Air Canada Centre. The world of pro sports has too many discourteous egomaniacs in it. Pat was always the complete opposite: very helpful and very decent, particularly to a guy who was unaware of the numerous rituals in the hockey world.

Thanks also to *The Hamilton Spectator*'s Steve Milton, who was aware of this project and offered numerous good suggestions; and to Tom Harrington, the excellent CBC TV journalist, who suggested the subtitle and assisted in other supportive ways, too.

In my last book about former Ontario premier John Robarts, I offered thanks to someone who actually had nothing to do with the book: Ron Ellis, my favourite hockey player of all time. Ron, in this book I offer my gratitude to you again, and in a book about hockey (in which you're quoted) it makes more sense. From the time I had my picture taken with Ron in the Leafs' dressing room in 1970, he has occupied a special place in my world. He probably has no idea how much joy he brings to me on the occasions when our paths cross, and we exchange a hearty handshake and pleasantries. What an honour to know you, Ron. And I still keep your hockey card in my wallet.

Finally, nothing would be achievable without the support of seven other people. My wife, Francesca, who has now been a literary widow four times, but couldn't object this last time since she, too, wrote a book for Penguin last year. Thank you for absolutely everything, Fra. To my four children, Zachary, Henry, Teddy, and Giulia, none of whom will likely ever play for the Leafs, but all of whom make me incredibly proud whenever they lace up the blades. (Actually, they make me proud all the time.) And to my parents, Marnie and Larry, to whom this book is dedicated. Growing up in Hamilton, I was immensely lucky that they took me to hockey games too numerous to count, sent me to hockey camp despite my having no apparent talent to play the game, and instilled in me a lifelong love of Canada's national sport.

I am fortunate indeed to have these people in my life.

—Steve Paikin

# *INDEX*